Loyola Pastoral Studies

Faith

and

commitment

aim of religious education

Tilmann	Godin
Dheilly	Vergote
Van Caster	Nebreda
Jungmann	Ramsauer
Fortmann	Liégé
Haering	Fichter
Delcuve	Ranwez
Ingen-Housz	Guitton
Arnold	Grasso
Taymans d'Eypernon	Hofinger

Chicago 1964

Loyola University Press

Distributed in Canada by
PALM PUBLISHERS, LTD., *Montreal*

IMPRIMI POTEST John R. Connery, S.J., Provincial of the Chicago Province, March 25, 1964. NIHIL OBSTAT John B. Amberg, S.J., *Censor deputatus*, April 6, 1964. IMPRIMATUR Most Reverend Cletus F. O'Donnell, J.C.D., Vicar General, Archdiocese of Chicago, April 8, 1964. THE NIHIL OBSTAT AND IMPRIMATUR ARE OFFICIAL DECLARATIONS THAT A BOOK OR PAMPHLET IS FREE OF DOCTRINAL OR MORAL ERROR. NO IMPLICATION IS CONTAINED THEREIN THAT THOSE WHO HAVE GRANTED THE NIHIL OBSTAT AND IMPRIMATUR AGREE WITH THE CONTENTS, OPINIONS, OR STATEMENTS EXPRESSED.

Preface

This book has two goals. First it seeks to make available to teachers of religion a profound, synthetic presentation of the modern, biblical-liturgical approach to the teaching of religion. Toward this end it has assembled under one cover twenty-six of the decade's finest catechetical studies carefully selected from *Lumen Vitae* by a team of religious educators.

The second purpose of this book is to provide the teacher of religion with a framework for continuing his study and readings in modern catechetical approaches. Toward this end the book has been carefully laid out and executed according to its present format.

The book is divided into three major divisions: (1) God Meets Man (revelation), (2) Man Meets God (faith), and (3) Transmitting God's Message (catechesis).

Part One considers the fact of the Christian mystery: in His infinite love and goodness God created man and invited him to share in His own divine love and life. Part One systematically explores this mystery of love as it is found: (1) recorded in the Bible, (2) contained and continued in the liturgy, (3) formulated in doctrinal statements, and (4) authenticated by Christian witness. Through these four signs or media God meets man and graciously invites him to a life of intimacy and love.

Part Two of the book considers man's response to God's message of love: living faith. It views faith in its full dimension as: (1) confidence in God as loving Father and source of all truth, (2) an intellectual assent to God's message of love, and (3) a complete gift of self to God. Next, it studies faith according to its growth and development as it normally occurs in the individual believer.

Part Three of the book studies religious education proper: the transmission of God's message to others. It begins by analyzing the aim of religious education: living faith. It then describes in detail the three stages according to which God's message is transmitted to others: (1) pre-evangelization,

iii

which addresses the unbeliever and seeks to dispose him for God's message; (2) evangelization, which proclaims God's message to the unbeliever and seeks to win from him a response of living faith; (3) catechesis, which explains God's message to the believer and seeks to lead him to full Christian maturity.

Next, the mentality and the milieu of the person to whom God's message is addressed is discussed in order to show how these factors influence the way the person receives and thinks about God's Word. The book concludes with a discussion of structures (family, school, parish) and methods (teaching materials and techniques). A suggested program for further reading is then given.

The editor is deeply indebted to the editors of *Lumen Vitae*, the International Review of Religious Education, especially Father Georges Delcuve and Father André Godin, for their helpful suggestions and marvelous cooperation all during the preparation of this volume. He is also indebted to Father Alphonse Nebreda and Father Theodore Stone for invaluable assistance and collaboration in working out the structure and content of the book.

Descent of the Holy Spirit   MARK J. LINK, S. J.
May 17, 1964   *Editor*

Contents

1 God Meets Man

2 Man Meets God

3 Transmitting God's Message

1

God
Meets
Man

Biblical Sign

God makes Himself known to man through four
privileged signs or media. The first of these is the Bible.
It is the primary source and guide of Christian doctrine.
For this reason the teacher of religion must be steeped in
its spirit, versed in its structure, familiar with its language,
and faithful to its content.

The Bible, Source of Christian Doctrine

by Klemens TILMANN

The encyclical of H. H. Pius XII on the Bible contains this pregnant sentence : " In this treasure (the Bible) which came to us from Heaven, the Church sees the most precious source and divine guide of her dogmatic and moral teaching. " The catechism, a summary of dogma and morals, must therefore for many reasons be penetrated by the spirit of the Bible and borrow its language ; it must follow God's method of revelation, be biblical in structure and contents. Only thus will the teaching of catechism and the Bible become a single religious world for the child.

I. THE BIBLE MUST GOVERN THE ARRANGEMENT AND TEXT OF THE CATECHISM

1. *Organic and Historical Structure.*

God did not reveal Himself by means of clearly defined abstract treatises ; these are the work of theological science. God did not reveal Himself by formulae which only have to be explained, as for example, the list of the seven sacraments. The substance of the divine revelation is rather an *organism* in which the particular truths are intimately connected and react on one another. For instance, when we speak of baptism we are bound to speak also of God, Christ, grace, the Church, the theological virtues and Heaven. If we tell of the mercy of God, we shall probably mention Christ's

---

1. Dr. Klemens TILMANN, priest of the Oratory, was born in Berlin on the 31 st December, 1904. He spent his youth in Silesia and Hesse ; he studied at Innsbrück, Tübingen and at the Major Seminary of Meissen. Ordained priest in 1930, he worked for four years in Dresden and for six years in Leipzig. His religious pedagogical writings are well known in Germany, and he also took part in the composition of the new German catechism. Amongst his writings are : *Christusverkündigung an die Jugend der Gegenwart* (1953), *Die Erziehung des Kindeszum beten* (1954), *Um die Arbeitsmethoden in unserer Seelsorge* (1954) and numerous other pamphlets. — Address : Nürnbergerstrasse, St. Laurentius, München 19, GERMANY (Editor's note).

death on the Cross, the sacrament of penance and grace. Christian truths are inter-penetrating for the object of our Faith is an organism.

Moreover, the realities of the Faith are above all an *event*. This event begins with the creation, reaches its central point in the Life, Passion and Triumph of Christ, and attains its close on the day of the Last Judgment, which is at the same time the dawn of Eternal Life. Taking this history of salvation as the leading principle of Christian doctrine, we come to the great classification of the Creed : God, Creator of Heaven and earth ; the action of Christ in three stages : the Incarnation, Passion, Triumph, and the Second Coming ; the Holy Ghost, the Church and the Sacraments (remission of sin) ; the Resurrection of the Dead and Eternal Life, the consummation of the history of salvation.

Therefore, the new German catechism is *derived from the history of salvation*. The Creed, the methodical summary of all Christian doctrine, is its framework and model. The special dogmatic treatises on grace, the Trinity, the Sacraments in general for example, are inserted into this framework as judiciously as possible. At the same time, its method is *organic*. The great subjects (God, Christ, grace, the Church, the Christian Life) are woven into the web of the catechism, though each receives special treatment in the appropriate place.

In this way, the catechism reflects the character of the biblical content and the mode of revelation chosen by God.

2. *Text in Close Contact with the Bible.*

The organic and historical character of the Bible must not only shape the structure but also influence the style. A catechism composed only of brief questions and answers cannot take into account the organic coherence of the Christian truths, or the questions would be too lengthy. Nor can it consider the aspect of ' event, ' which would require a narrative text and long explanations. But if biblical terms are to be adopted to express biblical categories, it must then take the form of exposés.

This is why the new German catechism is composed of exposés, 136 in all. Each begins with an *intuitive passage*, often a short biblical extract, generally narrative, which sets an event before the child, or in the case of a truth with a general bearing, a biblical example. The illustrations direct the child's eyes to the biblical event to which the intuitive passage refers. Then follows the exposé as such : a clear, practical explanation, suited to the child's understanding, and in close contact with the Bible, from which it frequently quotes literally. The next section is composed of *questions without answers* on the salient points of the exposé. Then come *sentences to be learnt by heart* in the form of questions and answers. Here again preference is given as far as possible to biblical expressions, sometimes the very words of the Bible. In the *supplementary passages*, a paragraph consists entirely of quotations from the Bible and is headed " Word of God. " The paragraph " For my life " is also usually based on the Bible. Finally, the *exercises*, which accompany most of the exposés, draw the children within the sphere of Holy Scripture : research, collation of texts, answers to questions on the Bible, prayer with reference to a biblical event. The new German catechism has thus been influenced by the Bible, yet not exclusively.

II. THE CATECHISM IMPREGNATED BY BIBLICAL THOUGHT

Having considered the plan and text of the catechism, let us pass on to the principal Christian truths. Here indeed the Bible can and must become " the most precious source and the divine norm of dogma and morals. "

1. *The End of Man.*

Many catechisms begin by putting the question of man's last end and reply that man is on this earth to love God, serve Him and thus reach Heaven. This definition only partly covers man's aim. Jesus, the best of catechists, presents him with another and begins His preaching by saying : " The appointed time has come, and the kingdom of God is near at hand ; repent, and believe the gospel. " [1] He puts before mankind the final goal in its entirety : the kingdom of God, whose triumphant entry into the world will be marked by the end of time. This covers the salvation, not only of the soul, but of the whole man ; not only of the individual, but the community, of all redeemed humanity ; not only the happiness of creatures but the glory of God.

This universal end of which the Bible speaks is in tune with present-day conditions, for according to the text, all values competing with religious values are subjected thereto. The immensity of the universe, atomic power, the great political powers, the materialistic paradise to come... all that is good in them is found in the Kingdom

---

1. *Mark*, I, 15.

of God ; all the evil in them is vanquished by God, all is purified and renewed. No longer does a wall separate earth from the Hereafter.

2. *God.*

Many catechisms, following the method employed by Deharbe about a hundred years ago, deal first with the conception of God from which they deduce the divine attributes : Being, Intelligence, Will and the moral attributes. This method is foreign to the Bible and to the child. God has not revealed Himself by abstractions but by deeds. By these actions, to which the revealed Word is added, He reveals His Nature and attributes. If we wish to take the Bible as " source and norm " of our teaching on God, our catechism must first speak of His action, and then of His essence. This does not mean that these lessons must be relegated to the end of the catechism ; they have their place at the beginning of dogma, according to the following scheme. For instance : God speaks to us ; thereupon we show His veracity and fidelity. Or else God draws good from evil, and we point out His infinite wisdom and power. God rewards good and punishes evil and we conclude that He is just and holy. Such an exposé not only induces clear notions in the child, but also gives him a living image of God, complete and moving, a reflection of revelation.

3. *Jesus Christ.*

The catechisms of the last hundred years often reduce their teaching on Christ to the following points : Jesus is Son of God and true God, His Incarnation, His death on the cross, His Resurrection Ascension and Second Coming, which last is only just mentioned. Only articles 3-7 of the Creed are explained. The text is almost silent on the public life of Jesus. The proclamation of the Good News, the holy life of the Saviour by which He glorified God and served man, by which also He became both our model and our master. Such a picture of Christ is incomplete and impersonal). It is useless to say that all this is dealt with in the Scripture lessons at school, for these only touch on particular narratives and do not trace a complete image of the Lord. How can children learn to know Christ reigning in Heaven as Doctor, High Priest and Pastor if we omit His activity as Doctor and Pastor during His public life ? How will they understand these same functions in the Church if we do not show them the original Jesus Doctor and Pastor in His earthly life ? Here also the Bible must be the source of the catechism. The children must learn the key ideas for the understanding of the New Testament. As regards Christ, we find in the German catechism :

Jesus messenger of the Kingdom of God ; Jesus lived for the Father ; Jesus took pity on mankind ; Jesus Son of God and true God. Then follow the questions on the hypostatic union, the Incarnation and a first lesson on the Blessed Virgin Mary.

4. *Redemption.*

It is useful to refer to the Bible for the explanation of the doctrine of the Redemption. Too many catechisms pass abruptly from original sin to the following thought : a Saviour was necessary and was promised ; this Saviour is Jesus Christ Who has redeemed us on the cross. Then the question is asked : From what has Christ redeemed us ? Frequently the answer is simply : from original sin. This is only part of the truth. What does the Bible say ? It is remarkable that the Gospels do not use the term ' original sin ' nor a similar concept. Jesus does not say : You must first believe in original sin in order to believe in salvation. He proceeds otherwise. Addressing men present in the flesh before Him, as in the Sermon on the Mount, He tells them what they must be if they want to approach God Who is near them. He places before them the exigencies of salvation, so much so that the disciples, disconcerted, ask " Who then can be saved ? " [1] If we build up the doctrine of salvation on original sin only, sin and redemption have their place prior to the coming of the children into the world, hence are outside their lives. If, on the contrary, we start like Jesus at the actual guilt of men, returning from it to original sin, then the children recognize man's present condition and that they themselves are in need of salvation. This realization of a personal need of salvation is the necessary basis for the acceptance of the doctrine of redemption.

The catechism begins with the lesson : the Son of God has been rejected by the leaders of the chosen people. It proclaims the messenger of God who manifests by signs the Kingdom of God, lives a holy life, full of love for men, but will not be received by them but will be rejected and put to death. This central event of world history throws a clear light on the guilt of man. Here is the second original sin. Here the guilt becomes actual and the need for redemption obvious. Here also appears the evil done to mankind by the first sin. Now it becomes easy to speak of the personal guilt of the children, so that the doctrine of redemption penetrates their lives, and no longer remains something foreign and distant.

When we explain the death of Christ, it is well to insist less on

---

1. *Mark*, X, 25.

the sufferings and death, the physical pain, than on the obedience and love, opposed to the disobedience and lack of love involved in every sin.

5. *The Resurrection of the Dead.*

When we compare the ideas of the faithful about the Resurrection and Ascension with the Bible statements, we again find certain deviations. These come from the catechisms which, for the most part, dwell on the reality and certitude of these events, but hardly mention their redemptive value. The thought expressed in the Easter preface is ignored : " Qui mortem nostram moriendo destruxit et vitam resurgendo reparavit. " [1] Or, as St. Paul says : " He was delivered for our sins and raised again for our justification. " [2] St. Peter's First Epistle also stresses the salutary effect of the Resurrection : God has " begotten us anew, making hope live in us through the resurrection of Jesus Christ from the dead. We are to share an inheritance which is incorruptible, inviolable, unfading. It is stored up for you in heaven. " [3] Yes, God has already " given life to us in Christ, " " raised us up, enthroned us above the heavens, in Christ Jesus. " [4] That is why a Catholic catechism must establish a close connection between the teaching on the Resurrection of Christ and on our resurrection by baptism, according to the pattern of the solemnities of the Easter vigil ; it must also present the Resurrection of the Lord as the beginning and the pledge of our rising at the last day, and in consequence, as the source of all renewal.

6. *Christ, Seated at the Right Hand of the Father.*

The Bible presents us with a glorious vision of Christ and His activities between His Ascension and the Day of Judgment. Christ, entered into the glory of His Father, intervenes actively in this world's events. He continues from Heaven to direct the work He began on earth and to guide it to its goal. He sends down the Holy Ghost, calls Saul, delegates Ananias. Stephen sees Him standing, having therefore left His throne to share the fate of His witness. All the work of salvation has its origin in Him. He calls the apostles and sends them forth. He acts through His servants, gives them

---

1. Easter Preface.
2. *Romans*, IV, 25.
3. *I Peter*, I, 3-4.
4. *Ephes.*, II, 5-6.

7

speech and strength, opens the hearts of their hearers, [1] leads them to conversion, sanctifies them in baptism, walks among them with the seven candelabra, [2] lives in them as His members and feeds them with the Holy Eucharist. He will destroy Antichrist by the breath of His mouth and the glory of His coming, [3] and, finally, will judge the living and the dead and give the Kingdom into His Father's Hands.

Our catechisms give but a feeble picture of this glorified Christ and in consequence His activities are unfamiliar to the faithful. We hear nothing of it in treatises on grace, the Church, the Sacraments. What does baptism do ? is a frequent question. This gives the children the impression that it is a holy thing, but not that it is Christ in person Who acts.

In the apse above the altar the primitive Church represented Christ the Doctor, Highpriest and Pastor, sitting in glory and majesty. The faithful contemplated the " one Mediator between God and men " [4] and believed Him to be present at their services. Our catechisms ought to revive this picture. His presence should dominate the instructions on the Church and the Sacraments as the living centre of the entire work of salvation.

7. The Church.

There is hardly any section of the catechism which can not expect to find more light, clarity, and life from the study of the Bible. If we compare the doctrine on the Church in catechisms influenced by the Counter-Reformation with Holy Scripture, the benefit to be drawn from the Bible becomes obvious. With what warmth and conviction the Church speaks of religion when we look upon her, not only as an institution of shepherds and their flocks, but as the community of the disciples of Jesus ! What depths she reveals as the Mystical Body of Christ ! What a dynamic inspiration she affords us when we consider her as the nucleus of the holy people of God, who will be His people for all eternity in the Kingdom ! What sanctity is manifested by her glorious function, less that of " leading men to eternal happiness " than to glorify God ! What light is shed on the dignity of the laity when they are looked upon no longer as merely the subject of the pastorate but when their part in the family, professions, parishes and public life demonstrates their share in the triple

---

1. See *Acts*, XVI, 14.
2. *Apoc.*, I, 12-13.
3. *II Thess.*, II, 8.
4. *I Tim.*, II, 5.

power of magisterium, priesthood and the government of the Church!

These few indications are sufficient. The matter of our teaching on the Church does not require a great deal of elaboration and an organic presentation has already pretty well covered the subject. It would be impossible, and even unnecessary in a catechism for children, to refer to all the Church's biblical metaphors and explain them.

8. *The Eucharist.*

Some sections of our catechisms reflect not only a kind of dogmatic and scientific speculation, but also the apologetic necessities of their time. This particularly applies to the lessons on the Holy Eucharist. In opposition to the false doctrines of the Reformation, certain points had to be defended. Thus the lessons stress the truths attacked ; the bread is changed in the Eucharistic act ; Christ is present ; the priests have the power to consecrate and exercise it in the Mass. Then, often without any connecting link, the nature of the Sacrifice is dealt with, the liturgy of the Mass, Communion, worship of the Sacrament of the altar. This makes the doctrine on the Eucharist difficult to understand. Why not have a unified, simple and global teaching ? Is there a more simple way, better adapted to the mentality of children ? Yes, we find it in the Bible.

To start with, the story of the Last Supper shows us a holy event, not a holy thing. " *Do* this in remembrance of Me, " said Jesus. This ' doing, ' very simple, consists of three parts : 1) Jesus takes the bread, 2) He says a prayer of thanksgiving and the words : " This is My Body delivered for you, My Blood given, " 3) He distributes the bread and wine.

From this Biblical event, easily grasped by children, the new German catechism develops the doctrine of the Eucharist. If they belong to a Christian family, the family meal has already made them familiar with the picture, for the food is brought to the table, grace is said, and then the meal takes place.

The three principal parts of our celebration of the Eucharist are a clear reflection of the biblical story : 1) the gifts are brought to the altar, 2) the priest recites the great prayer of thanksgiving and sacrifice by the words : This is My Body, this is My Blood, and all answer, Amen, 3) then comes the distribution of the consecrated food. On the basis of this act narrated in the Bible and again in the description of the Eucharistic celebration in the early Christian centuries, the other aspects of the Eucharist are explained : the Presence at the celebration and in the Bread, the doctrine of the consecration, the characteristics of the sacrifice, their connection with the sacrifice of the Cross, communion, the Eucharistic cult and the liturgy of the Mass. The children always have before their eyes the whole of the sacred act.

9. Morals.

At first sight, the catechism seems to borrow its teaching on morality entirely from the Bible. In most cases, the biblical formula is adopted : the First Commandment and the Ten Commandments of God, with the addition of those of the Church. In reality this is where the catechism is most foreign to the spirit of the New Testament. The Old Testament commandments cannot be the primary source of the New Testament attitudes and Christian life.

A. The two essential points of New Testament morality. — Jesus' first demand : Conversion rests on the preaching of the Good News : " The appointed time has come, and the kingdom of God is near at hand ; repent, and believe the Gospel." "[1] Jesus does not derive His appeal from a commandment, but from a reality, which is God's gift : the Kingdom which is near. St. Paul follows the same course in saying : " Because you are risen with Christ, enter into a new life. "[2] " You must befriend one another, as Christ has befriended you. "[3] " Have you never been told that your bodies belong to the body of Christ ? "[4] Here and in many other passages, Christian life appears as the response to the action of God or to a new state of grace founded on Christian baptism. Being and action, the redemptive work of Christ, and life are closely united. The New Testament attitudes and sentiments do not therefore derive from the first Old Testament commandment but from the work of salvation. In the light of salvation also such commandments as " Thou shalt not steal " must be considered in the light of a higher aim towards which we must tend without ever fully reaching it, as we try to fulfil the great commandment to be perfect, [5] and many others put before us by Jesus in the Sermon on the Mount and other teaching. Morality is an integral part of the order of salvation in the New Testament ; to be and to act are closely associated.

---

1. *Mark*, I, 15.
2. See *Rom.*, VI, 4-14.
3. *Rom.*, XV. 7.
4. *I Cor.*, VI, 15.
5. *Matt.*, XII, 48.

There is another aspect of New Testament morality : Jesus does not mention explicitly a number of things such as property, sexual life in marriage, states of life, education of children. He leaves these to natural reason, enlightened by the Holy Ghost. He is silent and leaves to speak for themselves the realities of creation and their laws revealed to us by life. Yet in the parable of the Steward He teaches that we are not the masters and that we are expected to give an account of what has been entrusted to us. We are not servants who must be told all they have to do, but administrators, who must keep their eyes open and act on their own responsibility. This quality of steward in the world extends to the whole of our human and moral life.

B. The essential attitudes required by the New Testament. — The first consequence to be drawn from the above remarks is this : in the catechism also, the New Testament precepts and Christian behaviour must rest on the new order of salvation, as a response to the divine action and a development of the new being which we have received from God. The German catechism has taken this into account.

a) Each lesson on God, Christ, Redemption, Grace, the Church and the Sacraments contains an answer from man, and therefore an application to Christian life. Thus the interior dispositions, virtues and Christian sentiments are constantly upheld and the children learn to act as Christians.

b) The relations between the principal Christian virtues and the principal sacraments, particularly baptism, are fully explained. Before baptism comes conversion, which must precede adult baptism. Afterwards, the catechism passes on to Faith, Hope and Charity towards God and our neighbour, the imitation of Christ and prayer, exteriorization of the life of the baptized person, the practice of the infused virtues and exercise of our new state as children of God. After the Eucharist, the Sacrament of Penance is only dealt with after consideration of certain aspects of Christian life : temptation, sin, the virtue of penitence, a fundamental Christian virtue which already contains contrition and resolution. Then only is the sacrament of penance introduced, when the act of penance, involving the personal return of man to God, is raised to sacramental rank. Thus the teaching of the main Christian virtues is in line with the New Testament.

c) Our attitude towards the natural order of creation. How are

11

we to act in cases which the Lord has not explicitly mentioned ? In matters of natural morality (ethics) which concern our attitude to the realities of this world ? One thing is clear : the Ten Commandments are not the sole criterion on this point. If they were, conscience would be limited to certain realms of action while unable to grasp others ; besides, these realms should be governed by the spirit of the New Testament and not of the Old.

The German catechism treats this aspect of morals after the Sacraments and the fundamental Christian attitudes. This implies that we enter into these spheres of our life in our quality of children of God, men renewed in Christ, living a new life which makes our faith and charity bright and bold. But where can we find the exterior norm for our action ? This is given to us in three stages.

The first is the reality of the created world, the order of creation. We are bound by its laws, compelled by its exigencies. For instance, property, the family, the State, our bodies, the sexes, animal life, etc. We must observe all and perceive the intentions and precepts of God. What we have to do is deduced from what exists. It is the teaching of St. Thomas in his treatise on the virtue of prudence. The steward does not perceive his duties mainly in orders received but in the realities of his charge. " What are the needs of this animal ? This field ? " he asks. " What is my duty towards my wife, my children, the State ? " asks the Christian. These observations form the gist of the first lesson on general morals in the new catechism, headed : The order established by God in creation.

The order of creation however cannot be the sole norm for fallen man, for his knowledge is perverted and his will subject to temptations. Thus certain exigencies of the order of creation are signified to him by God in the Commandments properly so-called, namely, the Ten, the " manner in which the world is to be used, " expressing the will of God to men.

The words and example of Christ are the third source of morality. He is the perfect steward, because He is the Son. He gives us also the universal commandment of love, which must dominate our whole conduct. In the light of these three norms : the order of creation, the commandments and the word and example of Christ, man can by his *conscience* aided by Grace and the Church's teaching, know what is right, what is God's will.

Special aspects of morals also follow three stages in the new German catechism (Lessons 94-126). Earthly realities are first considered from the point of view of children of God. The 4th commandment for instance brings the question : What must the parents be for the children ? The duties which derive from it are confirmed by

12

the commandment of God, which then appears, not as an obstacle, but as a help towards a better reality. Finally, the commandment is enhanced by a thought from the New Testament, the example of Christ or one of His or of the apostles' sayings.

This moral teaching seems to conform to the directives of Pius XII according to which the Bible must be the most precious source and the divine norm of the Church's teaching.

III. ADVANTAGES WHICH THE CATECHISM DERIVES FROM THE BIBLE

Having considered the most important points of Catholic dogma and morals, we have seen what an asset the use of the Bible is to the catechism, how it not only enriches its text, but leads to wonderful improvements of which the chief ones are as follows :

1) The catechism is enriched by the adoption of the plan, ideas and style of the revelation of God, Himself model of catechists.

2) The Bible is the inspired word of God. In adapting itself to this word of God the catechism adapts itself equally to the action of the Holy Ghost Who speaks in the Bible and desires to work in us and in the children through the catechism.

3) Faith and life are closely related in the Bible. Such a relationship, if observed in the catechism, results in a fruitful interaction evoking an ever more living faith and a deep life of faith.

4) What is written in the Bible is written for our salvation. Inspired by this spirit the catechism is no longer an arid instruction on the Catholic religion but tends to the aim appointed by God in His revelation and towards which we must guide the children, their salvation in God.

5) Throughout the Bible there is unity and simplicity : God has created the world and man, has sent His Son, Who calls us to the Kingdom of God, has been given to us as Master and Lord, has redeemed us, preceded us, inhabits us and guides us by His grace, will accomplish what He has begun and remit all to his Father, or more briefly : God has sent us His Son Who leads us to the Kingdom of God which is near. Indeed, in its greatness, it is a very simple story. It contains all the matter of the catechism.

6) The last sense of the Bible rests on the revelation of the glory of God and the entrance of man into this glory. It must be also the last sense of the catechism, aligned on the Bible. The catechism is meant to make known to the children the wonderful revelation of God, to teach them to praise and serve God here on earth and in eternity. If it does this, it fulfils truly its function.

Faith Nourished by the Study of the Bible

by Joseph DHEILLY

Adapted as it is in its application to each soul, the action of God seems also to be governed by invariable principles. Viewed from the angle of supernatural education, we could call them " principles of divine pedagogy. " As they are clearly laid down in the Bible, we will attempt to discover them so as to better understand the way in which God deals with us. And since it is here a question of developing our pupils' faith, it will not be beside the point to show them how God proceeded with regard to our spiritual ancestors. The Old Testament marks out the track for us, hesitant in its details, but clearly traced as a whole. This track led to Christ, Who came to perfect revelation and the believers' faith.

In the course of the present article we will attempt to come to a clear understanding of the two elements in the history of the chosen people which constituted their faith : an intellectual adherence and a realisation in their lives. In our study we will note the respective parts of God and man, and also the features of that activity which consists in " practising the truth. "

It appears to us that we can in this way be drawn to want to delve deeper into the biblical texts in order to nourish our faith still more, and that is the sole aim of the following pages.

---

[1] Born at Dompierre (Somme) on the 28th Dec. 1904, M. l'abbé Joseph DHEILLY has a University of Paris degree and diploma in Higher History Studies, is a Doctor in Theology and holds the diploma of oriental languages (Institut Catholique de Paris). After having taught in the Minor Seminary at Amiens, he was appointed to the Institut Catholique as Director of lectures, conference master and assistant lecturer. — Publications : *A la découverte de la Bible* (1949), *Histoire du peuple de Dieu* (1950), *Le Christ, source de vie* (1953), *Le peuple de l'ancienne Alliance* (1954), Paris, Éditions de l'École. — Address : 23, rue Joubert, Paris IXe, FRANCE (Editor's note).

I. FAITH IMPLIES FIRST OF ALL AN INTELLECTUAL ADHERENCE, ACCORDING TO THE OLD TESTAMENT

This spiritual adherence is required before all else. The object is sometimes an extremely limited one. What did Jahve ask of Abraham, when He called him to have faith ? To believe in one God, almighty and rich in rewards. One might say that it was little to ask. Actually, it was an intellectual revolution in the Patriarch's soul ; this passage from polytheism to monotheism with its orientation towards moral standards, is important enough to be emphasized. It should be added that Abraham's acceptance is at the origin of the monotheism on which Moses will be able to build up the Covenant of Sinai. In the heart of the chosen people and in spite of all vicissitudes, this faith will endure until Christ's coming, and in Him it will reach full growth. It is therefore the starting point for the gradual revelation by God of Himself.

In this intellectual adherence to an object which seems so small to us who have so many truths proposed for our belief, we will not lose sight of the accompanying pedagogic principles ; the acceptance of time, man's slowness, the sociological circumstances in which he acts.

But the importance of the object *increases with time*. The Mosaic period asked more of the members of the community ; the holiness of Jahve was shed upon them and tended to make of them a holy nation and a kingdom of priests.

A new jump forward, or rather an enlargement, with the Prophets. The idea of the Covenant was deepened ; God is He Who loves His people ; He becomes the object of hope, but also the exacting Master Who means to be obeyed.

In the Psalms, the element of knowledge plays a very large part ; everything is referred to God, Who is recognized as the Creator of nature, considered as the director of the history of mankind, and especially of that of Israel, and also looked upon as man's supreme end, beyond death.

Finally, in the books of Wisdom a new development is to be found ; God is so much men's Guide that He is to be their Model in their everyday conduct ; the ideal scribe will be the one who can add to the traditional knowledge personal elements which will enrich the former and allow of a deeper penetration into the secrets of the Lord.

So it is that in the Old Testament faith denotes chiefly an assent of the mind to knowledge conveyed by Revelation. Man does not make his God for himself, to his liking, we might say, to his fancy. Truth is not looked upon in the sacred Book as a subjective activity which man would create according to his needs. Man is content to reflect upon what is proposed to him by a Being Who is his superior. *Truth is objective and imposes itself on the believer's mind.*

If the object of faith is dependent on Revelation, adherence will extend in proportion as the latter progresses. But can we go further along this path and discern the method which God employs to communicate Himself to men ? It seems to us that we can. We should like in this connection to draw attention to two main points :

— God works from within ; we may call it a law of *interior progress*, especially from the Mosaic period to that of Judaism.

— *Man's mind is called upon to collaborate in this work of discovery*, while still remaining closely dependent on the divine Light in the sphere of Revelation.

The progress of which we are aware in the course of the Old Testament is not to be regarded as a kind of evolution or exterior development conditioned by the progress of civilization, without divine intervention. [1]

We may also remark that Moses' original contribution contains in germ many of the elements developed in the Prophets.

The centralization of worship, as we find it in Deuteronomy, is already suggested by the great legislator. If the word LOVE is not pronounced its reality is already included in the monotheistic faith of Sinai. In a general way, the posterior development of the dispositions made by Moses continues in the line traced by him, and the whole will remain Mosaic in its mentality.

When Moses considers holiness, it would seem that it is summed up in the idea of ' separation, ' expressed by the primary meaning of the Hebrew word. Physical separation — " Thou art standing on holy ground " (*Ex.*, III, 5) —, the obligation being transferred to the chosen people itself, called upon to live separately from other nations because of its monotheistic faith ; the term ' holy nation ' (*Ex.*, XIX, 6) —, is to be understood in this way.

But do we not perceive in this the germ of later developments ? If God is separated from His creature, it is because of the absence

---

[1] This does not mean that God cannot make use of this progress ; for instance in the penetration of the idea of survival among the chosen people. But it is all the more characteristic to find that the scribes refused to profit by it as long as they did not judge these ideas to be assimilable by the traditional current of revealed truth.

in Him of defilement ; man will therefore become holy by resembling God in this matter (Is., VI ; Ezechiel, XL-XLVIII). [1]

When Moses, in the Decalogue, declares in the name of Jahve : " Thou shalt not defy me by making other gods thy own, " He is forbidding the practice of polytheism, but not making a direct statement as to the unity of God. Yet, when we read the oracles of the pre-exilian prophets, we feel the conviction that they do not cease to preach the God of the Covenant, and that the ideas conveyed by them are in direct line with the pronouncement of the decalogue ; God is unique. From this basic idea come the complementary ones : God is universal, He is the God of all the earth ; God will reign one day over all nations. Finally, during the post-exilian period, it is once again the light of the Mosaic covenant which is shed on the problem of the coexistence of the Jewish faith with the Greek civilization imposed by Antiochus Epiphanus or favoured by some of the Asmoneans.

If we desire a more exact and detailed consideration of this subject, we must examine the completion of this Revelation in the New Testament ; we can better perceive there this law of interior progress. We shall also better understand how the exterior supports of the vocabulary or even the practical realizations have only a superficial value and are only accepted in the measure in which they can be assimilated. We shall, in fact, realize the transcendent influence of Christ, Who acts with a sovereign liberty, as a Son in the house of His Father. [2]

In spite of this divine influence, in spite of this primacy of God's, we must not consider that man is inactive ; the truth does not come automatically to him, without any effort on his part. Not only is man a free agent, and God treats him as such ; but also his mind is made for Truth, for God Himself. This working of faith will be more than an adherence to a truth which presents itself ; it will be *an active journey of the human mind towards God.*

---

[1] It will remain for the New Testament revelation to show that the holiness of God is essentially positive and that it is formed by the very Being of God, that our christian holiness takes its origin from an act of God which makes us share in His Being, while our collaboration lies in the realization of a total purity, in the absence of sin which is the very contradiction of the divine holiness and the major obstacle to its participation. This was not included in the Mosaic law, yet the Holy Spirit stretched in the first outlines of a revelation which Christ was to complete.

[2] We can link this interior action by God with what St. Paul says of the instruction which the deeds and words of the Old Testament have for us (*Rom.*, XV, 4). With the New, the knowledge of God's design is easier and we can more easily perceive the profound meaning which God inserted in the simple fact or words reported by the Old Testament.

Let us look for an instant at how this faith, which has God as its object, is expressed in the inspired texts. Take Genesis for instance ; read these striking passages in the Jahvist document, with their lively style ; God acts, speaks, feels, like a man, without His holiness being at all affected. Anterior by about two centuries, the Elohist document is much more sober ; God is apart from men, acts invisibly, often even through the intermediary of angels.

These are different and very characteristic ways of considering the same God known by the same Revelation.

Let us, under another aspect, consider the three inspired personalities, the prophet, psalmist and the sage. Each is God's workman, each penetrates the heart of Revelation and shows himself to be an artisan of the work of faith. How different they are, however ! Although the prophet sometimes makes use of the sapiential doctrine (Is., IX, 5), he is above all the preacher of the Covenant and its consequences ; no theorist of the divinity, but a man who penetrates into the intimacy of God and lives by contact with Him. The psalmist is first and foremost the man who exhales his faith in prayer ; nourished by the prophetic teaching, he expresses in his poems the essence of his knowledge, and his poetry becomes the vehicle of Revelation. As to the sage, he follows the rules of his kind, affecting a non-Israelite attitude, but the doctrine which he develops is penetrated by the Jahvist faith borrowed also from the prophets' oracles. If Osee is the prophet of the divine Love, the author of Ps. LXXX brings to us a religious philosophy of the history of Israel, and the Book of Job, the testimony of a conscience revolting against traditional, but unsatisfactory, solutions of the problem of retribution. In these three, we are aware of an intellectual work which is preparing the knowledge of future revelations ; the love of God which calls man to possess Him, salvation brought by Christ to mankind, the redemptive value of human suffering united to that of the Incarnate Word.

We would like to consider this work under one particular aspect, of which we have just spoken : retribution.

The absence of any knowledge of another life and the predominance of the community over the individual have had the effect of both making enquiry more difficult and leading to a kind of fruitful revolt ; man's mind was aware of being in an impasse.

Before Ezechiel, retribution was considered as collective. But the individual could not be satisfied with such a solution. He did not expect, if he was a just man in the midst of an evil group, to be involved in the general chastisement, for if so, what was the use of virtue.

With Ezechiel, therefore, individual and earthly retribution is admitted

(Ez., XVIII, 4). But Jeremias had already been shocked by the good fortune of evildoers (Jer., XII, 1). The book of Job, too, rejects that reply.

Some psalmists, while maintaining individual retribution, seem to have seen it as occurring hereafter (Ps. XLIX, 16 ; LXXIII, 23-28).

Finally, the book of Wisdom is to affirm the immortality of the soul, while the contemporary apocrypha repeat Daniel's statements (XII, 2) and those of the 2nd book of Macchabees (XII, 44) on the resurrection of the body.

It can thus be seen how man's mind, enlightened and directed by the Holy Spirit, collaborates in the discovery of Truth.

Pedagogical consequences.

— The growth of our faith is achieved in us by virtue of the germ placed in our souls on the day of our baptism. We should therefore do well to emphasize the baptismal vocation and the nature of the germ.

— The knowledge of God, although first of all a divine work, cannot be arrived at without an intellectual activity on our part ; Truth must be sought and study is necessary, not in order to answer objections but to obtain positive contact with God Who is Light.

II. INTELLECTUAL ADHERENCE IS ACCOMPANIED BY A LIVING REALIZATION

This adherence of the mind does not appear as the essential element in the Old Testament. Chronologically the first, it is overtaken by the other : the living realization. Truth is not merely accepted, it is lived.

This is revealed by the study of the chief biblical characters.

For Abraham, to believe in Jahve, the One God, means leaving country and family, to live the adventure of faith. On the point of arriving at the peak of his religious life, he considers offering to God what he holds most dear, his son Isaac.

Moses loses himself in his vocation. Because he believes in Him Who is calling him, he no longer belongs to himself. Up to the last moment he will be the leader of this people, entirely alone and vowed to his hard office of mediator. Moses' faith is inconceivable outside the frame of the Covenant and the long desert marches.

Elias has an extraordinary faith in this God Whom he serves. He demands a miracle in order to prove that Baals do not exist, that Jahve is the One God and that he, Elias, is his authentic emissary. His faith is active.

Isaias draws political consequences even from his faith in Jahve ; God is enough, the alliances with pagan peoples are harmful and quite useless.

Jeremias, in spite of the numerous revolts, sometimes violent ones, of his sensibility, accepts terrible sufferings for Him Who has called him to the prophetic ministry. And if he sometimes asks : " Did it cheat me like some empty water-course, my hope in Thee ? " (XV, 18), he is always conscious of a devouring fire burning in him : " I was worn out with it, and could bear no more " (XX, 9). He firmly believes that Jahve is with him and remains faithful to his vocation.

Under the Seleucid domination, faith meant a heroic testimony : that of blood. Having the choice between death and denial, many Jews will give their lives to remain faithful to their ideal.

If we turn to the doctrinal aspect, the impression we get is the same.

There is no separation between theory and practice. The abstract knowledge of God is unknown to the prophets ; it is always a matter of a living intimacy. We speak of " moral monotheism " to indicate the relation between the dogma of the divine unity and the moral activity which resulted. The possession of the Temple, the Law, the Holy City, although elements of truth, were not enough to arrest the corresponding divine chastisements. For religion is formalist and no longer based on sentiments of faith (Jer., VII, 9-10). Faith, indeed, finds expression above all in the interior life (Osee, VI, 6), and the sacrifice of the altar presupposes contrition and humility of heart (Ps. LI, 19).

The composition of the Book of Chronicles was caused by the wish to view the whole history of the nation from the angle of faith. But above all the post-exilian restoration is the manifestation of this faith in life ; the Jewish people had partly failed in their vocation ; it was not made to be one nation among others, but a religious community, a theocratic State, waiting in trials and tribulations for the ancient promises to be realized. It is in this light that we must understand the history of the five last centuries preceding Christ, the revolts of the Asmonean period and even the Essenian schism.

Speculations will be the privilege of the scribes, those ' sages ' who flourished in the period of Judaism. There again we shall see the practical nature of this ' Wisdom ' on which there is so much meditation during the Persian or Greek domination. First of all it is a matter of the practical conduct of life, in which experience plays its part, and still more the imitation of God contemplated in His rule over the world, especially over the chosen people. Sometimes God's plan is not discerned (Job) ; there is nothing then for man but to adore God's holiness and this renunciation is a magnificent act of concrete faith.

This aspect of life stamps the faith of the men of the Old Testament with certain characters, of which we will consider a few. It appears primarily as a growing plant ; *Faith is progressive.*

In Abraham, this progress is particularly obvious. The faith of this ancestor of Christ manifests itself as an ascending path ending at the summit. At the point of departure, the effort asked of him consists in believing in the unity and the omnipotence of this God Who calls him, at the same time in realizing a social unity — his clan — in which this faith will find its expression in an appropriate worship. The second stage appears when this old man has a son by his servant Agar and may believe that the divine promise is at last fulfilled ; a new effort is then required of him, he has to realize that the servant's son will not inherit the promise. Finally, when Isaac has been born and is a young man, and the Patriarch foresees that descendance more numerous than the stars in heaven and the sand on the seashore, then the divine voice makes itself heard in his heart : " Take thy son, thine only son, Isaac whom thou lovest, and offer him to me as a holocaust... " (*Gen.,* XXII, 2). A drama of faith, which still moves us nearly 40 centuries away. Abraham's acceptance is not only the realization in his life of an extraordinary faith which makes him the " Father of all believers, " but it is also the peak of his faith. [1]

The broad lines of Abraham's development can be followed, while its details escape us. The history of the chosen people leads us to perceive that the route is not uniformly an ascending one ; there are many backward twists, which are both falls and infidelities. *The route of faith is represented by a broken line.*

The cunning Jacob does not always seem to have kept, especially during his stay at Haran, to the purity of his grandfather's worship (*Gen.,* XXXV, 2). In the same way, the Egyptian education which Moses received surely introduced some pagan elements into his religious life. But research is more interesting and profitable after the Covenant of Sinai. The proposition which Moses transmitted was clear, the acceptance of the Hebrews was unqualified : " Everything that Jahve tells us, we will do " (*Ex.,* XIX, 8). From that time until Christ, how does the faith of this people appear to us, before it shines forth ? This faith appears often deficient, with numerous eclipses.

In Moses' absence, we have the incident of the golden calf. It was certainly meant to represent Jahve, but it was a disobedience, a weakness of faith. The murmurings which will be so frequent during the journeying in the desert indicate that the adherence to faith remains in theory, but that it has not passed sufficiently into life and that in practice it is refused when it becomes a burden or requires too great an effort.

---

[1] For the details of this progress in Abraham's faith and its characteristics, we may refer to our work : " Le peuple de l'ancienne Alliance, " 108-117.

The period of the Judges is one of diminished faith ; there is a general lack of intransigeance, a refusal to envisage the absolute. Jahve is not abandoned, but the Hebrews return instinctively to polytheism (the Chanaanians are of the same extraction) or perhaps prudence is their guide (Jahve may be only the God of Sinai).

There is a parenthesis in David's time ; the realization of the theocratic kingdom is accompanied by the transport of the ark to Jerusalem, the beginning of a settled liturgy and a certain enthusiasm for the religious life. Faith is penetrating life.

The period which follows the schism is marked by a great lowering of the standard of faith. Until the destruction of Jerusalem in 586 there are few moments when the kingdom is able to recover itself ; Elias' attempt is made with the vague consent of Achab, but the violent opposition of Jezabel ; Josias' reform does not reach the people's hearts and ends in a fiasco with the king's death at Megiddo (609). On the contrary, a king like Manasse will encourage the introduction of paganism into the Holy Land and it is the kings, too, who originated the idolatry at Samaria.

After the Babylonian exile (586-538) the crisis of faith reaches its height ; the triumph of Babylon, the splendid liturgies of the conqueror, the discouragement of the deportees leads to a split among them, the mass evolving towards formalism or religious indifference, only an élite understanding and accepting suffering.

The return to the Holy Land (537) is, on the contrary, a move of faith. It is God Who is recalling His people, Who destroys the obstacles in their path, Who renews before them the miracles of the Exodus (second part of Isaias). God is the first to be served ; the altar of the holocausts is restored first. The effort is made to set God in the centre of the community which is thus reconstituted. It is because of the lively faith of the repatriated that the help of the Samaritans is refused in the erection of the new walls and marriage with foreigners is proscribed. If the later Prophets speak of negligence in worship, if the social activities still comprise faults, sometimes grave ones, newcomers, especially such as Nehemias and Esdras, renew the Jewish faith and orientate it towards the Kingdom of Jahve. The martyrs of the years 167 and following are witnesses of the strength of a faith which has at last entered into life.

It seems, therefore, that we have in the history of the chosen people long periods in which faith is low, especially between the schism and the return of the captives, and that the five last centuries which follow are a period of profound faith. But an objection then arises : how are we to explain this Judaic faith if the seven preceding centuries have not prepared it ? How did this revolution occur ?

There are two considerations to be made.

If the Jahvist faith appeared incontestably too heavy a burden during the period of the kingdom, if slackening and even apostasy sometimes threatened to destroy the ancestral faith, we must add that during the darkest hours there was an élite to keep the deposit of faith. Elias always found friends to hide him and help to escape Achab's messengers. Isaias entrusted his oracles to a group of disciples (VIII, 16). Jeremias, morally so isolated, still had Baruch with him and partisans even among the high functionaries of the king. There is therefore a persistent current, whose subterranean waters are ready to spring up at a favourable time. This faith kept by a minority seems to possess an extraordinary amount of force, capable of astonishing efficiency.

The Babylonian exile can be understood in the same light. The chosen people followed a way which was not its own. Living by secular ambition, it was lost. Babylon is the instrument of a providential chastisement as both Jeremias and Ezechiel pointed out. Erased from the map of nations, Israel regains consciousness of its proper vocation and of the worth of its faith. It is doubtless thanks to this suffering in exile that neither one nor the other was lost.

Faith appears as an *adventure*.

Abraham obeyed God's call, but without knowing where he was going (*Heb.*, XI, 8-9). God's promises refer to a future which is, humanly speaking, uncertain.

The exodus from Egypt of those Hebrew tribes more or less in rebellion against Pharaoh is also an adventure. An adventure, too, that Covenant with a God Who showed Himself as exclusive, jealous, exacting, stern in repression. An adventure, those forty years wanderings in the desert, where life is at the mercy of a hidden spring or an unforeseen flight of quails. The conquest of a country whose inhabitants were of an advanced civilization while the conquerors were simple nomads was also an adventure.

What shall we say of that position of a buffer-state between the two great empires of Mesopotamia and Egypt, awaiting the conquest of Alexander and the coming of the Roman legionaries ? It is adventure all along the line of this history, in which God always carries His people on the wings of an eagle and in which Israel's trust is maintained by the sole faith in the God of the Covenant : " You will be My people and I will be your God. " [1]

It is in the sphere of faith that one sees what God did with this hard-headed and stiff-necked people ! In spite of their falls, in spite of their sometimes lamentable history (see St. Stephen's speech in *Acts*, VII), they believe in their mission. Their thinkers were not conscious of having to learn from anyone ; they were great and called to do great things.

This adventure, beginning in a dim light, becomes clearer gradually.

---

[1] It is especially in this that the hope of Israel is laid.

Abraham may see a motive of prudence in the command to leave his family ; for a change of religion of such importance, a new clan must be formed. But how can the promised posterity be acquired ? What will be the illustrious child who is promised ? Abraham does not know yet. Isaac will be a light on his way. A day will come when the Patriarch will see " Christ's day " and when this light will fill him with joy, giving him the reason for his faith.

Moses understands what he has to do : deliver the Hebrews from their Egyptian slavery. But where will this beginning of adventure lead him ? He knows from God that he will return to Sinai, but the future is hidden. The signs which Jahve gives him do not go beyond the banks of the Nile. At Sinai, though, the adventure becomes clearer ; if the Hebrews have left Egypt, it is because God wishes to make them His people, through Moses' mediation. If their leader has received a princely education, it is because he must become the Hebrews' lawgiver ; Cades follows Sinai. And Moses slowly begins to understand the inner meaning of this march towards the Promised Land, this long march which begins, is interrupted, begins again, and wearies the most courageous. The conquest of Chanaan is not to be achieved by the generation which has known slavery, clothed in wellbeing, in the land of Gessen ; it has to be carried out by men brought up in the freedom of the desert, hardened to the great heat, the hunger and thirst, which temper souls and bodies.

Above all, the leader realizes more and more that it is not his work, but God's which he is accomplishing, and he acquiesces in being the workman who is useful, but not necessary ; he himself will not lead the Hebrews into the Promised Land.

When Jeremias hears the prophetic call, everything is dark. He tries to escape the Word : " I cannot speak... I am a child... " His fears are soon realized ; he has to cry out, announce violence and devastation ; he will only encounter opposition and ill will. Chastisement becomes a certainty. From the top to the bottom of the social scale, all is sin ; high and low, priests and prophets, all, not excepting the kings, refuse to keep the Covenant and to do penance. Here he is denounced, there he is reproached for predicting misfortune ; a priest strikes him, a prophet contradicts him ; the king tears up the parchment on which Baruch has written his master's oracles. This time the adventure does not clear up and Jeremias will die in the greatest apparent inefficiency.

But if we look closely, we shall discover here and there some less sombre moments ; there is the great tenderness towards God which springs up in Jeremias' heart (XIV, 17-21). From this aspect the horizon lightens, in the midst of inner suffering. The prophet progressively discovers intimacy with God. His faith is purified ; denuded of exterior help — the frequenting of the Temple and participation in the liturgical worship — it rises. The religious life of the seer of Anatoth becomes more interior, he better understands the intimate requirements of God and is directed towards His paternity.

He has come to believe in the invisible efficiency, in spite of the failure which pursued him to his last day, and the prophet must have seen, beyond his death, how he had orientated the religious life of his people. Afterwards the adventure is luminous ; a man had to discover through his suffering the true nature of the Mosaic Covenant and announce in advance how the chosen people would see their faith expand in the New Covenant (Jer., XXXI).

Finally, this faith leaves man *in his own period*.

When God calls Abraham to the faith, He does not stop the course of natural laws, nor human evolution ; He takes the Patriarch such as he is, in his pagan civilization. The divine action will lead this man to become, in the Chanaanian environment of the XIXth century before our era, a holder and witness of the monotheistic faith. Abraham will be the head of a clan like others, doing justice and defending those who belong to his tribal group, offering God the traditional sacrifices. His faith does not elevate him out of his epoch nor his environment.

It also leaves him to struggle with personal difficulties. In the warfare between Sara and Agar, he appears weak, submitting to the inconveniences of a polygamy which God has not yet forbidden.

Moses, in spite of his magnificent faith, belongs to his time in many ways. The legislation of which he is the promoter has borrowed largely from the different codes of the period. It is monotheism which gives its own mentality to these dispositions, which in themselves are the same as others.

Elias concludes the scene on Carmel, where he revived for a moment the faith of the Israelites, by an order which we think cruel, but which is in accordance with the customs of the times : " Seize the prophets of Baal and let not one of them escape ! " (*I Kings*, XVIII, 40).

What are we to say of the curses and calls for vengeance which we find in a prophet like Jeremias and in numerous Psalms ? It will not be difficult, if we rapidly study the milieu, to find the explanation of similar expressions which shock our christian mentality, but which then seemed perfectly normal.

These are the imperfections which accompany man in his daily life. But there are also in the most outstanding of the biblical characters an influence of their faith which is exercised sometimes in one period, sometimes on the entire history of the chosen people.

Abraham will always remain the great ancestor, he who will receive in his bosom those of his children who have a faith like his own. Moses was the pedagogue who gave the chosen people the necessary education, he with whom Jesus will converse on the day of His Transfiguration as with the premier representative of the Old Covenant. Ahias of Silo will play a political role after the death of Salomon. Elias, Amos, most of the prophets, will consider that their religious duty is to influence the social life of the nation.

Faith does not take man out of his milieu ; there is, on the contrary, a reciprocal influence of the one on the other, man remains so greatly a part of it.

Pedagogical consequences:

— The value of our faith will depend not only on the religious knowledge which we possess, but also on the efficacity which it has in our life. Faith is not separated from generosity, that is to say, from Love. In this light we must appreciate the value of our faith ; is it a " received faith " (hereditary), or «conquered» (conviction) ?

— It will be a good thing to guard against discouragement ; our path will not be a straight line, any more than was that of the Hebrews. The essential thing is that it shall mount up. Our march can be more or less slow ; what matters is that we accept the stages as they present themselves.

— We must also insist on the character of adventure which marks the life of faith ; risk appeals to youth. It will be good to show them that God gives Himself to us insofar as we surrender ourselves to Him ; faith is not a matter of mathematical evidence, nor of the calculation of probabilities ; it is the gift of oneself.

CONCLUSION : CHRIST AND FAITH

In the path of faith, Christ continues an important stage. After an attentive study of the Old Testament, it seems that Christ will be the achievement of all that has been foretold, the midday after the dawn, the reality after the image. Abraham's faith seems now to have attained its object : Christ has come. The community of Israel finds its fulfilment in the Church. The Mosaic law ripens into the christian law. Holiness is a participation in God. The Pharisaic perfection is replaced by the perfection of the Heavenly Father. Above all, the very object of faith — God — is made present by the Incarnation, and salvation is already accomplished by the Redemption. Henceforward the true temple in which God dwells is the soul of the baptized, who participates in the qualities of child and priest which Jesus possesses fully.

And yet, our journey is not at an end. Christ is Himself an object of faith, being both God and Man. If we read again chapter VI of the Fourth Gospel we see Jesus giving Himself as our food, not only by the Eucharist, but by faith in Him. Eternal life consists

26

in the knowledge of the Father, but also of Him Whom He has sent (John, XVII). And when Christ requires an essential disposition for a miracle perhaps, it is faith which He mentions. He is also not an end in Himself, He leads to the Father ; He is the Truth and Life, but also the Way. What He tells us of the kingdom, the intimate life of God and the requirements which he asks of His disciples, all is the object of faith.

We thus go along our way, helped by Christ already before us, assured of final victory, because Christ has already won. The faith is for us a march in the light, towards the total Light. Christ, object of knowledge and love, came both to fulfill the revelation of the Old Covenant and to incite us to make part of our lives the Truth which He brings us and which He is eternally. There is only one answer : " I believe, Lord. Lord, help my unbelief. "

The Substance of the Christian Message : the Mystery of Salvation

by Marcel VAN CASTER, S. J.

The improvement in the methods of religious instruction is largely due to the influence of the active school and to applied psychology. There are, however, still too many teachers who consider these factors, which have been borrowed from secular pedagogy, as the chief elements in catechetical progress, whereas the truth is that it is only the first phase in the contemporary movement of revival. It is continuing, because it is still far from its conclusion. Since the appearance of Fr. Jungmann's important work on the essential nature of the " message of salvation, " [2] however, catechists have recognized that the principal element in the catechetical revival consists in a better understanding of the substance of our teaching. [3]

If this substance is only known through the abstract formulae of a certain form of speculative theology, of which many catechisms were, so to speak, only a summary, a very inadequate notion of the Christian religion is reached. The required understanding is obtained through close contact with the sources of revelation.

What our catechesis needs above all is to place again the Christian message in the full light of its living sources. The articles contained in the two preceding numbers of this periodical [4] were aimed directly

---

[1] Address : 184, rue Washington, Brussels.

[2] *Die Frohbotschaft und unsere Glaubensverkündigung*, Regensburg, 1936.

[3] Resolutions of the Catechetical Congress at Salsburg (1949), ' *Verbum,* ' XVI, p. 182 ; articles by Prof. SOLZBACHER. *Vérité et Vie,* no. 57, by Fr. COUDREAU, *Catéchistes*, no. 10, and by Fr. J. JUNGMANN, *Lumen Vitae*, pp. 271-276 ; the recent book by the last mentioned author, *Katechetik*, Freiburg, 1953 ; French translation, Brussels, 1955.

[4] *Lumen Vitae*, X (1955), nos. 1 and 2-3.

at this mark : the Bible, history of salvation, is still the living Word of God; the liturgy is the principal element in the life of the Church.

We propose this time, by dealing especially with the ' doctrine, ' to demonstrate more systematically how the fundamental substance of these sources is the mystery of salvation. We shall study it from three points of view : dogmatic (the divine revelation), psychological (man's attitude) and didactic (instructions).

I. DIVINE REVELATION

1. *The Substance of the Christian Message.*

SS. Peter, Paul and John expressed authentically and succinctly the essential elements of the message which the Church has to announce. Their message is the echo of the Good News which Christ Himself brings to us by His actions and words.

At Pentecost St. Peter, inspired by the Holy Ghost, proclaims " *Jesus of Nazareth, Whom you have put to death, God has raised up again* " (*Acts*, II, 22-24). Later on St. Paul establishes this same event as the foundation of all his teaching : " The word of salvation which is sent to you, *verbum salutis: repromissionem Deus adimplevit ressuscitans Jesum.* God has redeemed his promise by raising Jesus to life. " (*Acts*, XIII, 26-33).

Summing up in a few pregnant words the apostle's message and function, St. Paul writes : " I entered the service of the Church, I received a commission from God for the benefit of you Gentiles, to complete the preaching of his word among you, *ut impleam verbum Dei, mysterium:* the mystery which is Christ among you, your hope of glory. " (*Col.*, I, 25-27).

God conceived a great plan from all eternity, which He accomplished and revealed in time, a complete plan of which Christ is the centre. That is why Christ is " the first-born of all creation " (*Col.*, I, 15). But through their sin men have refused their original calling. God's plan then became a ' plan of salvation ' and Christ's mission one of reparation. " The hidden purpose of His will. It was His loving design, centred in Christ, to give history its fulfilment by resuming everything *in him, all that is in heaven, all that is on earth, summed up in him.* " (*Eph.*, I, 9-10).

The central theme of the Johannine epistles is this same substantial manna of the divine revelation, expressed in terms which underline the truth that this design of God is a design of love, making us live in the divine charity : " What has revealed the love of

God, where we are concerned, is that he has sent his only-begotten Son into the world, *so that we might have life through him.* " (*I John*, IV, 9-10).

Here the apostles are repeating what is perhaps the most important phrase in the Gospel, in which Jesus Himself summed up in a prayer to His heavenly Father the supreme aim and complete meaning of His whole work and therefore His message : " *So that all may be one, as you, Father, are in me and I in you, so that they also may be one in us* " (*John*, XVII, 21).

What, then, have we to teach ? Jesus Christ, in Whom the whole mystery of salvation is contained.

Salvation has both a negative and a positive aspect. The first is secondary, the condition which follows on sin : liberation through forgiveness and healing. The positive aspect is primary : it is the living communion with the God of all holiness, the union of love, benediction, eternal bliss. Christ is our Saviour by Whom we attain to union with God in a life of charity.

Salvation is supernatural, because it is a gift of God which surpasses all the forces and exigencies of nature, but it is not separate from natural values. These are assumed by the supernatural life insofar as they are good.

The substance of the Christian message is a ' mystery ' in four ways : 1. a hidden reality ; 2. a truth which, even after having been revealed, is beyond our understanding ; 3. an event in our history ; 4. an institution of visible signs having a supernatural efficacy. These four ways are linked organically with one another. We shall here dwell chiefly on the third. The mystery of salvation is something which is taking place, an event, a reality in action, an encounter between living persons. [1]

---

[1] Fr. A. HAMMAN's study of the *Mystère du salut* (Paris, Plon, 1954 ; first edition 1949 : *La Rédemption et l'histoire du monde*) is chiefly a biblical theology of the dogma of the redemption. The Protestant book by Mme S. DE DIETRICH : *Le dessein de Dieu* (Neuchâtel, Delachaux, 1948) gives a luminous picture of the development of revelation before Christ and the attitude of faith which God expects of men. With certain modifications, this book will also be very useful for Catholic teachers. We have not, however, found in it the exact pronouncement of the Design of God in the sense in which we have summarized it.

The subject is presented with applications for the pastorate by the Rev. H. OSTER, summing up an article by Fr. FERET in *Vérité et Vie* (Strasburg), no. 180, and also by the Rev. HASSEVELDT, who has made it the point of departure for his book : *Le Mystère de l'Église* (Paris, Éd. de l'École, 1953).

2. *Characteristics of the Mystery of Salvation.*

A. *Rhythm of action: God's initiative, man's response, the achievement by God.*

The mystery of salvation is a supernatural action, an event which takes place because God takes the initiative of raising man to Himself. He calls us to supernatural charity and gives us the ability to live by it.

A false trail is therefore followed when the Christian doctrine is taught in an anthropocentric manner : man seeks happiness ; what are the truths which man should admit ? What should man do ? What means should he employ ? — the substance of religious teaching is *theocentric* in its fundamental dynamism : God works at His plan of salvation ; what does God do to reveal to us the truth regarding His design ? What collaboration with His grace does God expect of man ? How does our response of faith, acting in divine charity, turn towards the complete acceptance of what God does to achieve His design ?

B. *A coherent whole, with successive developments.*

a) An organic unity with complementary aspects.

The mystery of salvation is an organic unity because it is found complete in the *Mystery of Christ*, of which it is the development.

The substance of catechesis does not therefore consist in a series of truths and practices, following one another. Its subdivisions are more like the spokes of a wheel of which Christ is the centre. The Christian message is *christocentric* as regards the means by which God achieves His mystery of salvation.

This stands out clearly from the place which Christ occupies in the rhythm of the mystery of salvation. He is first *the Son* of God, sent by the initiative of the Father to bring God's invitations to men (that is to say, to make them known completely and to achieve them). Christ is next in His humanity the *Servant of Yahweh*, Who gives the response which God expects to His invitations of charity in His own name and in ours ; through the reparation which He thus makes, He delivers us from sin. — He is finally the glorified *Lord*, Who has risen to the beatific union which the Father bestows upon Him and Who makes us sharers 'in Him' in the achievement of God's plan.

The organic unity of the mystery of salvation derives then primarily from its unification in Christ ; it consists also in the

31

fact that its different aspects — historical, dogmatic, sacramental, moral, and even apologetic — mutually complement one another.

We must therefore avoid a system of parallel courses in Sacred History, Liturgy and Catechetics ; we should rather present the substance of the Christian message as a unity under its complementary aspects. We shall return to this question later.

b) A successive development.

The four fundamental phases of the mystery of salvation are :

1) *Preparation in the Old Testament.* The mystery of salvation is not merely announced in advance, but already enters into action ; it moves towards Christ, and in its inchoate form, is a beginning of realization.

2) *Realization in Christ.* Not only ' by ' His merits, but ' in ' His Person and His acts (see above : Christ the centre of the mystery).

3) *Continuation in the Church.* The mystery of salvation issues from Christ and penetrates all the members of His Mystical Body and by their action is spread throughout the entire world.

4) *Achievement in Heaven.* The mystery of salvation then becomes definitive and for all : eternal life in the Christian community of love with God.

The Kingdom of God *transcends time* and is thus in a certain sense always present ; but it develops successively in time until its achievement. The Kingdom of God has already come, it is continually arriving, and in the end will come in a complete and definitive manner. We already know it entirely without knowing it perfectly ; we have already the charity of God in us without being yet definitely confirmed in the perfection of that love.

We have considered two characteristics of the manner in which this mystery of salvation becomes active ; a third defines the way of its revelation.

C. *Revelation through facts and words.*

If we consider the substance of religious instruction as being chiefly theoretical, we shall be inclined to look for the principal form of divine revelation in ' words, ' preferably in written words. But the mystery of salvation, which constitutes the substance of the Christian message, is primarily, as we have just seen, a reality in action, a progressive event. God reveals His plan of salvation chiefly by realizing it : He speaks mostly in deeds. His words clarify the meaning of the facts of salvation.

The most important ' signs ' in which revelation is given, are therefore to be found in the facts of salvation themselves, which contain their own significance.

The capital fact is that of the Passover : God acts to deliver His people and lead them into the country of His benediction. This event was the preparation for Christ's Passover : His death on the cross and His glorification. The same fact is continued in the Christians' Passover until its achievement in Heaven.

The other great events of salvation are linked with this central fact. The vocation of Abraham, the return from captivity, Jesus' miracles, the celebration of the Eucharist, etc. are above all facts of salvation, of which some elements, e. g. the passage through the Red Sea, the eating of manna, etc., are to be found again with their significance in the symbolic actions of worship. These facts and actions form " themes of action " in which the significance of salvation must be explained.

The ' words ' used by God in His revelation serve to make this significance clearer. We also find in them expressions which continually reappear and whose significance becomes increasingly full. Note among these ' word themes, ' the elect, the son, the head of the nation, the prophet, the people, the earth, the temple, the kingdom, the vine, the bridegroom and bride, the covenant, the day, the hour, the harvest, the ' agape ' (at the same time love, community and meal).

In the most remarkable way all these themes meet together in the Person of Christ.

These biblical ' themes ' of action and word also constitute the chief means of expression in the liturgy. Finally they form the tissue of Christian life. [1]

The substance of religious instruction is therefore a *living revelation* in its entirety. The message of salvation is not a dead theory, but very practically a doctrine of life. A doctrine with a view to life, but also one drawn from life, developing under the action of God. The sources are living ones, not only because the living God speaks through the writing of a bygone day, but because He speaks through the very life of those in whom He is acting, principally in the historical life of Christ, and His life continued in the Church.

---

[1] See L. Bouyer, *La Bible et l'Évangile*, Paris, Éd. du Cerf, 1951, e. g. pp. 103-119 ; Dom C. Charlier, *La lecture chrétienne de la Bible*, Maredsous, 1950, pp. 179-227 ; J. Guillet, *Thèmes bibliques*, Paris, Aubier, 1951. A scheme of several themes in their progressive unity : A. Becker, in *Lumen Vitae*, VIII (1953), p. 449. In particular the paschal theme : R. Poelman, in *Lumen Vitae*, VII (1952), pp. 285-295.

This message should be proclaimed to men, who should welcome it and commit themselves to the mystery of salvation. What favourable and unfavourable factors can we distinguish in the attitude of these men with regard to revelation ? That is the basis of adaptation.

II. MAN'S ATTITUDE

1. *Adaptation to the Reality of the Mystery of Salvation.*

God gives His grace ; He has created man so that he can receive it. Grace itself renders men capable of collaborating in the fulfilment of the mystery of salvation. But since original sin and because of our own failings we are also under influences which set a screen between us and the light of revelation and tend to counteract the supernatural influence of God. In the fundamental attitude of each man there is thus a battle between his radical orientation towards God and his anthropocentrism.

That is why it is not possible to subdivide the factors which influence his behaviour into two clearly marked categories, stepping-stones or obstacles. For example, material want, national oppression, changes in the social and political structure, technical progress, the sense of human beauty, etc., all have an ambiguous value for the message of salvation. Christ brings with Him deliverance from our wretchedness and the finest development of a harmonious humanism, but His solution to our problems is situated on a higher plane than the simply human. His message is the reply to men's highest aspirations, but it surpasses them and does not exactly fulfil human expectations. His gift is better, but it is other. Thus, in order to receive the Christian message and live by it, each man must " *be converted.* "

The fundamental principle of adaptation is in " conversion to the highest. " We cannot amputate the divine message of salvation and only keep what our audience likes to hear ; we have to proclaim it in its integral and authentic value.

We may mention as *unfavourable factors* in human attitudes : the earthly orientation of modern man, which confines his horizons to worldly success ; the selfsufficiency of the scientist or technician impervious to other ways of knowledge and efficiency ; the pelagian tendency of youth, which thinks that the whole of moral life consists in the exercise and control of its own strength ; religious practice marked by egoism, which seeks to put God to the service of material wellbeing, social or national.

34

Fortunately, there also exist *favourable factors,* such as : the revival of a sense of mystery ; interest in everything which gives life a ' higher ' meaning and incites to a generous love. Especially the moral problems of the young and their exuberant vitality are valuable starting points for a better commitment to the Paschal mystery. [1] In many ways the man of the 20th century is thus nearer than his predecessor of the 19th century to what is called " biblical man, " that is, the man who is open to God.

2. *Adaptation to the Form of Revelation.*

A) *In principle* the message of salvation can make use of all the forms of expression of the different human civilizations. We should, however, be on our guard against a false adaptation, which is not orientated to the highest but to the lowest. For instance, modern man thinks by means of images taken from technology and his forms of civilization are to a great extent less personal. A comparison between grace and a lamp or an electric motor is doubtless easily understood by him, but it is not a good way of expressing the eminently personal nature of grace. The use of technical terms in religion is a deplorable adaptation in the direction of the lower. On the other hand, the progress of everything that is truly human continually presents new possibilities for expressing the inexhaustible riches of the mystery of salvation.

B) *In fact* God has revealed His mystery of salvation in ' signs ' which are to be found in the Bible and continued in the liturgy, in the declarations of ecclesiastical authority and in all authentically Christian life. These forms of expression can never be neglected.

Amongst these forms the Bible takes a preponderant place. The advantages of the biblical forms are eminent :

1. They are *for the most part universally human.* They are concrete and personal, communal as well as individual. If the Semitic way of thought is less rationalist than the Western thought of the last centuries, it is no less human, on the contrary: among many peoples we find this same disposition to a contemplative view of the whole, and it is to be noted that scholastic philosophy of today fulfils itself in the same sense. The unified, progressive and dynamic presentation given by the Bible is not only always striking, but

---

[1] P. POELMANN, R. WAELKENS, Th. MAERTENS, *Le Seigneur passe dans son peuple,* Brussels, Ed. Lumen Vitae, 1952. — A. LIÉGÉ, O. P., *De la liberté de l'adolescent à la liberté pascale,* in *Supplément de la vie spirituelle,* Paris, no. 30 (1954), pp. 243-254.

also allows us to understand that the imperfections of a former stage of the mystery of salvation must be overcome in a later one.

2. The biblical forms are above all specially *adapted to the substance of the mystery of salvation.* We have just stated that these forms are concrete, personal and dynamic in their unity. These are the characteristics of the mystery itself. We may now remark that in its ensemble the biblical form is fundamentally ' Christian, ' because the Person, life and doctrine of Jesus Christ are the centre of orientation and the living summary. — The whole Bible is the inspired word of God : this characteristic is of capital importance : it follows that the message of salvation is the word spoken to us by God and requiring our reply. This inspired word is proclaimed and interpreted by the Church. This form of expression therefore perfectly brings out our share in the revelation and the mystery of salvation itself through and in the Church of Christ.

C) In comparing therefore what has just been said of the form of revelation in principle and in fact, we come to the following conclusion : we can and we must ' *translate* ' the message of salvation in a way that is suited to every nation and every man. We shall present it in their language in the means of expression of their civilization. But every translation requires a perfect understanding of the original form in its true sense. It is therefore necessary that we help our contemporaries to understand by a sufficiently vital assimilation the testimony of the Bible and of the Church which continues it.

III. DIDACTIC PRINCIPLES

1. *The Basis of Catechesis.*

God Himself has chosen the most didactic manner of communicating His message of salvation to us. He has expressed the mystery of salvation in living facts and in words. They are his ' signs, ' which carry their own meaning. Christ is the perfect sign containing the whole meaning of the design of God. He has entrusted to the Church the task of proclaiming His message and explaining its meaning.

The basic procedure of our religious teaching therefore consists in *placing God's signs in the full light of Christ and explaining their meaning under the Church's guidance.*

This was the original procedure of catechesis. Other ways of teaching which later became only too frequent have falsified the relations between living facts and theory. The present catechetical movement is going back to the earlier and exact relationships. That is the Copernic revolution which is taking place in catechesis : we are not dealing with an abstract theory which must be more or less ' illustrated ' or ' applied ; ' but with the mystery of salvation, which is essentially concrete, revealed by living facts and by symbols, and which is explained in a coherent doctrine. [1]

In this basic procedure we can distinguish various nuances. Previous issues of this periodical have studied the Bible chiefly as being the history of salvation, and the liturgy as its ' representation ' ; in this number we are mainly considering the catechism doctrine as the message of salvation. But these practical subdivisions are not mutually exclusive ; we must on the contrary be aware of the fact that they continually interlock. The history of salvation is itself the message; the liturgy is a period in this history which is continuous ; in the other forms of the Christian life, for instance, in an act of charity of daily life, the mystery of salvation is also " present in action ; " as for the doctrine, it is only the explanation of the testimony of the Bible, the liturgy and the whole of the Church's life.

While admitting that there must be appropriate ways of procedure for each section, we must insist that the nature of the ' proclamation ' of the mystery of salvation in action ' must be the same for the whole of catechesis taken in its broadest sense.

After an eventual introduction, with a psychological trend, the catechesis which always starts from the signs by which God reveals His mystery of salvation in course of realization, is called kerygmatic. The word may be avoided, if it is thought too learned, as long as we keep to what it implies.

2. *Structure of the Course in Doctrine.*

For the reasons indicated we avoid a radical division between three kinds of lessons : 1) biblical ' stories ' which one tries to make edifying by means of rather arbitrary moral applications ; 2) descriptions, either up to date or archaeological, of the liturgy in the manner of a guide to a museum ; 3) philosophical expositions of dogma and morals. It is obvious indeed that Sacred History, the liturgy and ' doctrine ' form together an organic whole.

Various possibilities present themselves to safeguard this unity. We can adopt a course of doctrine following the *chronological*

---

[1] See J. COLOMB, *in* ' Catéchistes, ' no. 7 (1951), p. 3.

order of the history of salvation : the doctrine then emanates successively from the progressive revelation.

For instance, the doctrine on the Old Testament as the preparation of salvation through Christ. The ' preparation ' goes hand in hand with the ' prefigurations ; ' but these latter remain subordinate to the former. It is not chiefly because the Old Testament contains prefigurations of the New that it is a preparation, but inversely because the Old is a real preparation (by facts), an outline of the mystery which will be realized in the Christ which it prefigures (in an imperfect reality and by symbols), and which will appear later in its perfect form. We do not therefore have to look for exterior coincidences in order to accumulate more or less exact ressemblances and to fix on to them a doctrine which was not then revealed completely. We have to discover how the true significance of the facts is progressively completed. Take the following schema :

1. Abraham = election by God and response in faith.

2. Moses = the first liberation (the Passover) the solemn Covenant (and Law).

3. The kings (David) and prophets (before and during the Exile) = blessing and infidelity ; chastisement and a new hope.

4. The return from exile=the second liberation, but not yet a complete blessing ; hence a more definite expectation of the Messiah.

5. Christ's Passover and the liturgical Pasch continued in the life of the Christian.

The signs of the mystery of salvation are thus presented in striking personages and fundamental facts. The doctrinal significance, simple and reduced to the essential, is understandable even to the youngest.

A second possibility consists in following the *liturgical order of initiation into the sacraments.* The Bible and the rites will be closely linked. To explain the doctrine some teachers like to start from the rites that the pupils can see and experience, in union with the actual Christian assembly ; they then return to the Bible which is at their origin. We prefer the method which starts from the Bible with its real and symbolic signs, to rediscover them in the liturgy, insisting on the fact that the mystery of salvation finds there its realization. For instance, the Eucharistic doctrine. The schema usually employed, which seems to us to be deficient, comprises : an abstract definition of sacrifice ; illustrations taken from daily life and non-Christian religions ; an often debatable

38

application of this definition to the Cross and the consecration ; practical conclusions with regard to the commandment relating to Sunday Mass.

According to the basic procedure described above, we suggest the following schema :

I. The signs of God. — A. Preparation: a) the facts as lived : the Paschal event in the Old Testament ; b) the symbolical signs : the bread, wine, blood, lamb, meal. — B. Realization : the efficacious signs of the Last Supper.

II. The doctrinal significance. First, the significance of each sign ; then the synthesis : the interior and exterior sacrifice, rising to God and meeting with Him. Realization by Christ and by us with Him. Detail of the ceremonies. Active participation.

Then there is the third possibility : to follow the *systematic order of the doctrinal handbook* (the official catechism or a more elaborate exposition). In many cases such a handbook is necessary. Note first of all that for several of its sections, we can follow closely the chronological or liturgical order mentioned above. Thus for the chapters on Our Lord and the redemption, or to explain the sacraments. We can take another classic example of a point of dogma : doctrine on the Church.

A conceptual catechesis is constructed on the basis of definitions applied to the Church : " perfect society, " head, members, aim, means, rights, etc. A kerygmatic catechesis does not talk of the juridical " structure of the Church " until it has sufficiently dealt with its ' mystery. ' We cannot indeed grasp the true meaning of the Church as an institution except in the light of the Church as mystery in action. The signs of this mystery are to be found in the Bible, the liturgy and the whole of the life of the Church as it is now. To present these signs in an ascending order, here is a schema which seems to us to be suitable for older pupils :

First part : The Church at work. I. Civilizing influence. II. Sanctification of men and glorification of God.

Second part : The Mystical Body of Christ. I. The mystery of the Church : 1. The people of God in the Old Testament ; 2. The Church in Christ and by Him ; 3. The new people of God on their journey (perfect and imperfect) ; 4. The complete structure of the total Christ. II. The structure of the Church.

A course thus based on the unity of the Bible, the liturgy and the whole of Christian life and doctrine, really presents this doctrine as the message of the mystery of salvation. The task of the teachers and pupils is directed to the same end. We will end by a few remarks on this subject.

3. *The Task of Teacher and Pupil.*

Both teacher and pupil often have an erroneous idea of what is meant by *the concrete*, so necessary in religion. We must avoid reducing it to what is perceived by the senses or by the imagination. The mystery is a concrete reality, a meeting of persons. On the supernatural plane it is at the concrete that we must aim. Pictures, films, handiwork, can be very useful in catechesis ; but we must take care not to ' petrify ' the living substance of the spiritual message. [1]

The principal road to the sense of the supernatural mystery is that of the *sense of the wonderful*. [2] Compared with our familiar environment God is the " all other. " He reveals Himself and His mystery of salvation by wonderful signs. Not ' strange, ' nor above all ' sensational, ' but ' suggestive ' of a higher reality than that which has become banal for us. The wonderful is that by which God appeals to our faith. The mystery suggested by the wonderful sign is not a wall before which we ought to stop and capitulate, but on the contrary, a road which God opens to us, the end of which is still hidden, and on which we have to set out with Him. The art of religious instruction is especially the aptitude to bring out what is wonderful. [3]

Religious teaching must not be too cold, nor too materialistic nor too rationalistic nor too pragmatic : neither can it ever be unreal, as though it was fabulous. Its task is to bring out the true *mirabilia Dei* so forcibly that these call for that complete faith which is the acceptance of the truth of salvation in supernatural light and the commitment of the whole person to the most perfect realization of the mystery of salvation.

---

[1] H. AGEL, *L'Écriture Sainte à l'écran*, in *Bible et Vie chrétienne*, No. 5, pp. 109-111.

[2] This word has several meanings, between which distinctions must be made. It can be taken in the special sense of a form given by our imagination to a truth, and the miraculous, which latter is definitely a fact. We are taking the word ' wonderful ' according to the etymology of the Latin word — ' mirabile, admirari ' — in the sense of something arousing wonder ; we lay aside the more or less pictured form in which it presents itself, but we include the miraculous in it ; we in fact insist on its value of reality and of sign contained. We also wish to define in what way the wonderful is a means by which man rises beyond himself and becomes open to the revelation of God.

[3] Fr. WEBER, *Das Christusgeheimnis in der Katechese*, Freiburg, Colmar, s. d.

It is therefore equally certain that all the pupils' activities, particulaily those which are called " directed exercises, " should be orientated towards the activity of faith, acting in charity.

CONCLUSION

The substance of the Christian message is : the mystery of salvation. This mystery revealed by God contains in itself the foundation of catechetic methodology : the setting of God's signs in full light and the explanation of their significance.

The basic procedure applies to every religious course. It will be used without difficulty when we deal specifically with the history of salvation and the liturgy. But it can also be applied quite normally when explaining " Christian doctrine. " It is greatly to be wished that the catechism handbook should be biblical and liturgical as well as systematic. It is essential that the catechism course should be so.

Doctrine should be summed up in words and phrases, controlled by the ecclesiastical authority. The ' letter, ' specially that of the official catechism, is indispensable. But the principal question of religious instruction is not to know how to give a lesson so that this letter be understood, retained and applied. The fundamental question is to try to bring the pupils to see the signs of God in the best light, and to understand them, and live in faith their living significance.

To know one's religion is not merely to have by heart the stereotyped replies to foreseen questions ; it is to have assimilated in a vital manner the love of God communicated in Jesus Christ ; to realize in faith what is passing on the plane of the divine action, when Abraham left his country, when Jesus died and rose again, when a child is baptized, when the priest celebrates the Mass in the midst of the faithful, when a sister of charity watches by the sick, when a believing workman does his work conscientiously or when a man deceives his neighbour, and above all, when a Christian dies.

God realizes and reveals in Christ His great design of love. The presentation of Christian doctrine, proclamation ceaselessly renewed and made fuller of the Christian message, the living and authorized message of the Church, should be orientated so that the whole substance of the religious course stands in the perspective of the mystery of salvation, which we find and live ' in Christ. '

Liturgical Sign

Salvation history presented through the Bible leads
inexorably to the liturgy. The liturgy is not "only a grateful
looking back to that time when salvation was
achieved. Such a conception," says Father Jungmann,
"is too narrow, not to be called inexact." The liturgy is the
privileged continuation into space and time of
God's self-revelation and self-communication to man.

Liturgy and the History of Salvation

by Joseph-André JUNGMANN, S. J.,

As a result of the catechetical movement of recent years it is now generally admitted that catechesis, when dealing with the truths of the Faith, should transmit to the children not merely a considerable number of formulae to be retained, but should rather provide an attractive picture of the history of salvation, a living image of the figure of Christ, Who has come into this world in the fulness of time, has proclaimed the word of God to men, achieved our redemption on the cross and collected around Him a new people of God.

We now also understand how the liturgy of the Church can be of great assistance in the accomplishment of this task, for all the great turning points in the history of salvation are celebrated by a liturgical feast or even by a festive season : Christ's coming by Advent and Christmas time, the Saviour's Passion by Passiontide, His glorification by Eastertide, the feasts of the Resurrection, the Ascension and the Descent of the Holy Ghost ; the actual fruit of the redemption is set before us by Corpus Christi and in the feasts of the saints, distributed throughout the year. The catechist has only to adapt his teaching programme to the course of the liturgical year and, in his explanations, to attract attention to the coming feast. Its celebration will then contribute efficaciously to the imprint upon the child's soul of the corresponding mystery of the Faith.

Various articles in this number of *Lumen Vitae* will deal in detail with this catechetical value of the liturgy and thus bring out this most important aspect of the part which it can play in religious formation, although not the only one. This opening article must look further and penetrate more deeply into the mystery of the liturgy. Holy Mass is the centre of every liturgical feast. If we are

---

[1] See the biographical notice in *Lumen Vitae*, X, 1955, 1, p. 117. — Address : Sillgasse, 8, Innsbruck, AUSTRIA (Editor's Note).

only considering the instructive side of a feast we can stop, so to speak, at the Mass of the Catechumens, for the trend of this preliminary part of the Mass is instruction : the lessons bring to our minds the event of salvation which is being celebrated. But the main liturgical action comes later : the sacrifice. God has spoken to us in the Epistle and Gospel ; now we, the assembled Church, have to speak to God, reply to Him in praise and thanksgiving and especially by the Holy Sacrifice, which we are authorized to offer to God with Our Lord Jesus Christ. The ' euangelion, ' the Good News, sent from above precedes the ' eu-charistia, ' the thanksgiving overflowing with joy, for the ' charis, ' the grace, which has been given to us.

The most recent catechesis has well understood this law, already applied in many catechisms which aim at making the children not only understand a doctrine and perhaps store it in their memories but respond with their hearts to God's call which is contained in the doctrine. This response is made certainly in prayer, but also in sharing in the Church's liturgy : when united in public worship we thank God for His love, through this or that prayer of the Church, in this or that of her feasts.

But this is not all. This glorification of God in the liturgy involves more than what we are now doing in common in God's House, or are trying to do individually elsewhere. By directing children to the liturgy, we are leading them to the stage on which the history of our salvation is being continued. The great event which took place in the fulness of time, is the establishing of a new order, the beginning of a new period for mankind. It was then that the grain of wheat was cast into the earth which was to bear " much fruit. " Since Pentecost this seed has grown up all over the world ; its flowering and growth have never ceased either in bad weather and storms or under the rays of a benevolent sun. The good earth which bears this multiple vegetation is sacramental life, the domain of liturgy. In the liturgy the sacraments are carried out, by which the Body of Christ is ceaselessly built up. In the liturgy the sacrifice is celebrated which Christ gave to His Church and that with her He offers to God. The liturgy forms the section of the Church's life in which the history of salvation continues with the greatest intensity.

Perhaps we have grown up with the idea that the history of salvation ended with the Ascension of the Saviour and the descent of the Holy Ghost on the day of Pentecost ; what followed was only the distribution of the treasures, merited for us by Christ and entrusted to His Church, only a grateful looking back to that time when salvation was achieved. Such a conception is too narrow, not to call it inexact. [1] It is akin to that other idea, dating from the Enlightened Century and forming part of the deistic theories, that is to say : God created the world at the beginning, but afterwards retired from the scene and now leaves the direction in men's hands until He Himself again takes over the government at the end of the world. In the same way, Our Lord Jesus Christ in the fulness of time brought salvation through His cross and passion, and acquired a treasure of merit ; He entrusted this salvation and these merits to the fostering care of the Church ; He Himself would take no more part in what was to happen later.

This way of looking at things is incomplete, full of gaps. It is true that Divine Revelation came to an end with the death of the last of the Apostles, but the course of the history of salvation is only now coming to its full growth. Certainly, Our Lord deprived His own of His visible presence on the fortieth day after His resurrection, but the Saviour ascended into Heaven still remains through the Holy Ghost as near to them as before : " Behold I am with you all the days until the end of the world " (Matt., XXVIII, 20). He said, not referring only to His presence in the sacrament, but to His will to be with His apostles and their successors, while they govern the Church and preach His doctrine. He willed to be in Peter's boat, navigating it over the stormy sea of the world's history. His saving action had to be spread over the whole earth and throughout the centuries in which the sacramental life has been carried on ; for the thousands and thousands of priests, the two thousand bishops, in the Catholic world, can only act as His emissaries. He is the High Priest who, by their ministry, baptises, confirms, forgives sins and above all renews His own sacrifice on our altars ; they are only the mouthpiece by which He speaks and the hands with which He blesses. The history of salvation which, in the days of old, Pontius Pilate being procurator of Judea, attained its culminating point on Calvary, is not finished for all that but continues until the end of time.

We may here remark again upon the faculty which the liturgy has of transcending time and space. While the Church is continually entering upon new periods, we do not get further away from our starting point, but are always close to it. We are not launching out into unknown seas, but are describing new circles around a sun which is radiating light and warmth.

---

[1] See F. X. ARNOLD, *Grundsätzliches und Geschichtliches zur Theologie der Seelsorge*, Friburg, 1949, pp. 123-130.

This sun is Christ and His work. He is still active amongst us in the sacraments and the celebration of the Eucharist , especially in the latter, which is by design sacrifice and memorial. It is a sacrifice and every time a new sacrifice: the religious sacrifice of the Church at work here and now ; it is the sacrifice of former times : that which Christ offered on the cross and by which He achieved the salvation of the world. It is just as much the living memorial of the work of redemption among us : the memorial " of the blessed passion of Christ, of His resurrection from the dead, His ascension into Heaven. " Yes, of the Resurrection and Ascension, the glorification of the Lord ! We do not only commemorate the Lord's death, when, under the separate species, the immolated Body, as though marked with the five Wounds, is to be seen on the altar, but also His glorification. Is it not the glorified Saviour Who puts Himself into our hands like the immolated lamb ? Is it not the glorified Saviour who, as High Priest, acts on the altar through His representatives ? At that moment the central element of the whole work of redemption enters into each of our days and, from that fact, the life and work of the Lord comes within our grasp. What the Gospel tells of Him is no longer in the distant past, but is actually perceived by us who gather round His altar, just as the men of His time thronged round Him hoping for help and salvation.

This nearness full of mystery is particularly brought out by the Eucharist in the celebration of the Christian feasts. During the course of the year we celebrate the great events in the history of salvation, from the birth of the Lord up to the diffusion of the Holy Ghost on the budding Church ; and there is not one of these feasts which does not culminate in the sacrifice of the New Testament ! Because the Eucharist constitutes the culminating point, each time, the event of salvation, the subject of the feast, becomes mysteriously near to us. That is why the Church dares to sing at Christmas : *Hodie Christus natus est* and, in the night of Easter, the deacon does not weary of proclaiming that " this night " is blessed which is as much the night of the Paschal feasts as that one in which breaking the chains of death " Christ rises conquering from the dismal regions. "

Theologians argue much about the exact nature of this actuality. The controversy was started thirty years ago by a thesis by Fr. Odo Casel, a monk of Maria Laach († 1948), stating that the essence of the liturgy consists in the celebration of mystery, that is to say, that the event of salvation becomes present in the liturgical act ; by participation in it, the celebrating community obtains salvation. [1] The difficult point in this thesis called the " thesis of the mysteries " lies in admitting that a past event can truly enter the present time. Casel and his friends tried to circumvent this difficulty : certainly, the event of salvation cannot enter again into the present in a physical sense, neither can the historical circumstances become actual once more ; but it is possible to conceive a ' becoming present ' which would be produced in mysterio in a sacramental manner. Other authors, having recourse to platonic theories, prefer to say that it is not the event of salvation in itself but its image which becomes present in the participants, each time they receive the sacraments (G. Söhngen). When a person is baptized, the death and resurrection of Christ are accomplished in him and he is thus justified ; when we take part in the Eucharist, the immolation of the Lord is again imprinted on our soul and we grow more and more in resemblance to Christ. Still other authors think of the inner act of oblation which Christ accomplished on the cross and which is perpetuated in Heaven as the supra-temporal act, in the marks of the wounds, in the acceptance of the Father, in the intervention for us and becoming present in every Mass (L. Monden, E. Masure).

But we can leave aside this theoretical question and keep to the traditional Catholic doctrine, even if some elements in it have passed into the background of the religious consciousness of the last centuries. It should be enough for us to know that the events of the history of salvation enter *in some way* into our present, in a mysterious manner, a manner which does not occur in any other historical event. The centenary of a great historical occasion is commemorated by speeches, represented in pictures, made obvious by its effects, but the event itself remains distant, as the heroes of it remain the heroes of a time which has long passed away with them. Our case is different. Even if the events of the history of salvation remain in the past, for an act can only take place once, their hero, Christ Our Lord, is in the midst of us and in several ways.

When we think of Christ's presence amongst us, we usually think primarily and perhaps exclusively of His presence in the Sacrament, the closest presence and the most intense, because He is present there " truly, really and substantially. " But His presence does not exhaust itself there : to the Body of Christ in the Sacra-

---

[1] We find a summary of the developments of this discussion in Th. FILTHAUT, *Die Kontroverse über die Mysterienlehre*, Warendorf, 1947. For more recent years, see B. NEUNHEUSER, O. S. B., *Mysteriengegenwart*, in *Archiv f. Liturgiewissenschaft*, III (1953), pp. 104-122.

47

ment corresponds the Body of Christ which is His Church. The Church becomes visible in the liturgical assembly which gathers every Sunday around the Eucharistic Body of the Lord. In it His life continues. As the organism begins by a primary cell to which new ones are continually being added, so the Lord, as the first-born of those who have risen from the dead (see *Col.*, I, 18), continually draws new persons towards Him by faith and baptism ; so the Church has become " the fulness of Christ " (*Ephes.*, I, 23), it is as St. Augustine says, *Christus totus*. The Church is the living Christ.

But we have to distinguish yet a third presence. Christ is not simply identical with His Church. He is its divine Spouse, its Head. Where the Church is, there are not only all those who belong to the Saviour by faith and grace but the Saviour Himself as ' Head, ' vivifying the members. This is especially true in the liturgy. Pius XII's encyclical on the liturgy expresses this clearly : " In every liturgical act, the divine Founder is present as well as His Church : Christ is present in the holy sacrifice of the altar, either in the person of His minister, or especially under the Eucharistic species ; He is present in the sacraments by the virtue which He infuses into them so that they may be efficient instruments of holiness ; He is present, finally, in the praises and prayers addressed to God, according to Christ's words : There where two or three are gathered together in My name, there am I in the midst of them. " [1]

And — do not let us forget — it is the risen Christ Who is among us in this way and acts with regard to us. We ought certainly to look always at the earthly life of Jesus, for we are still pilgrims on this earth and are struggling in the dust of the road. He became like us in everything except sin so that we could find in Him an example and a model, a model in our relations with men, a model for perseverance in the known good, a model of devotion to the will of the Heavenly Father. That is why it is so important, not only to read the Gospel accounts of the life of Jesus with the children, but with them to meditate upon these texts, so that we may model our lives continually upon them and learn from them how to carry out our duties. But it would be a mistake to limit ourselves to the earthly life of Jesus. He is no longer the infant in the crib, He is no longer the traveller on the stony roads of Palestine ; He is no longer the man of sorrows. He is risen ; He is " in the glory of God the Father, " as we sing at the end of the *Gloria*.

Besides the events of former days and the work of our salvation,

---

[1] *Acta Ap. Sed.*, XXXIX (1947), p. 528.

do not let us neglect what is happening today and always, in which the whole of the past work of the Lord is summed up and enclosed. Beyond the earthly ways of Christ do not let us forget the Christ of the final achievement. For it is with the total Christ, glorified, that we are to be united for ever.

And we must not lose sight of our own consummation. We are already grafted into the vine which is Christ. We are already assumed in His resurrection. St. Paul says more boldly : We are already " risen with Him " (*Coloss.*, III, 1) ; God has already caused us to " relive " with Christ and has already raised us with Him and transported us to Heaven (*Ephes.*, II, 5-6). All is not, however, at an end : " it is in hope that we have been saved " (*Romans*, VIII, 24) ; we have still to hold on. But we have already received " the firstfruits of the Spirit " (*Romans*, VIII, 23) ; we have already received in us in grace the life of the resurrection, we are the risen people.

It is good and praiseworthy to describe to children in catechesis the splendours of divine grace and to exhort them to keep the garment of grace spotless ; but let us also show them the original which grace will make them resemble. Let us reveal, especially to the older ones, the great perspectives which are discovered by meditation on the life of grace of Christ at Easter, the Christ of the liturgy. Here the new creation has commenced ; here the spiritual temple is being built of living stones ; here the priestly people is assembled, from all nations and all centuries, able to offer the worthy sacrifice to God, because Christ the high priest is at its head. [1]

If we proceed in this way, youth will more easily understand that we have not only the duty of saving our souls, to save them perhaps at the last drowning hour of a spoilt life, but that we are called to glorify God in this world. We have to work at the building up of the kingdom of God, collaborate in the realization of the words of the prophet Malachy, seeing God in the centuries to come and crying out with divine joy : " Thy name shall be great among all nations. " We must glorify God by a holy life, by a service ceaselessly renewed thanks to the pure and holy sacrifice which is offered to God " from the rising of the sun to its setting ! "

One of the chief tasks of our catechesis is to initiate children into the history of salvation and familiarize them with the meaning of the events of redemption. This initiation must not be simply a narrative of things which have happened ; it should lead them to the knowledge of what happens now in the Church's life, of what we have

---

[1] See the *First Epistle of St. Peter*, II, 5.

ourselves received and continue to receive as Christians, of what we are and are called to be.

In ancient Christian times the mystagogical catechesis existed. It was intended for those who had been baptized, had already participated in the celebration of the Eucharist and who should now be " initiated " further into the knowledge of the " mysteries " (μυστ-αγωγία). Our catecheses are fundamentally always or nearly always " mystagogic. " We are dealing with baptized children and we must make them understand what they already are as children of God : they are in the light of Easter morning. We have also to show them the grandeur of the vocation which has resulted from it for them : proclaim by a holy life the acts of Him Who has called them from the darkness to His admirable light (*First Epistle of S. Peter*, II, 9). They must enter joyfully into the circle of those true adorers, who adore the Father in spirit and in truth (*John*, IV, 23).

Towards a Development of Faith by Means of Liturgical Life

by H. M. M. FORTMANN

In the Apostolical Constitution " Divini cultus," Pius XI recalled the close connection between the liturgy and faith.

" The liturgy, " he wrote, " is most certainly a holy thing. By it in fact,
we are raised and united to God, *we bear witness to our faith* and we acquit
ourselves of a sacred duty with regard as much to benefits received as to
calling unceasingly for help. Hence, dogma and liturgy are intimately united
as are also Christian worship and the sanctification of the people. Celestine I
considered that the rule of faith is found expressed in the venerable formulae
of the liturgy ; and said, Legem credendi lex statuat supplicandi. " [2]

Every teacher who is anxious to develop faith among adolescents
(as also among children and adults) will naturally ask himself if
our young people do actually find in the liturgy, not only the occasion of giving expression to their faith, but also and chiefly the help

---

Born on the 15th June 1912. After having been ordained, H. M. M. FORTMANN
studied classics and experimental psychology. His thesis for the doctorate was enti-
tled *Aandachtig bidden, een psychologische studie*. The Abbé FORTMANN was engaged
in the parochial ministry in the north of the country for four years (1943-1947).
In 1947 he was appointed as chaplain to the general Council for Dutch Catholic
Youth and became editor of ' Dux. ' He has published numerous important articles, especially in that review.

[2] AAS, 21 (1929), 33. Quoted by Karl FEDERER, *Liturgie und Glaube. Eine theolo-*
giegeschichtliche Untersuchung, Paulusverlag, 1950, p. 128.

K. FEDERER's book is a penetrating study of the meaning of the formula ' Legem
credendi lex statuat supplicandi ' and the relations between the liturgy and faith.
From his conclusions we take the phrase following which applies to our point of
view : " Die Liturgie ist aber nicht bloss Bekenntnis des unfehlbaren Glaubens der
Gesamtkirche ; sie ist auch mit und neben dem Lehramt — also dem sichtbaren,
aktiven Faktor im Glauben der Kirche — Trägerin und Zeugin der Tradition, "
pp. 125-126.

which they need. If his question receives a mainly negative reply, he will try to find an explanation in order to improve the situation.

When we observe the reactions of youth in the course of liturgical manifestations, we receive the impression that the liturgical movement — which has certainly arrived at splendid results — meets a certain resistance on their part. This cannot only be attributed to lack of understanding of difficult texts, or ignorance of Latin, or again to an insufficient theoretical knowledge of the structure or meaning of the Mass or the cycles of the liturgical year, nor even to the negligence or haste which sometimes characterize the celebrations. All these things may have a certain influence and play a capital part in practice. But more than that is involved. This state of things can be put down to other causes, which may provisionally be defined as follows : young people who are practising their faith live in another world. *Between the world of the liturgy, between the attitude of the faith which finds its expression in the liturgy and the attitude of youth there is a yawning chasm* which present day methods of liturgical training do not span.

Let us look back on the path followed by the liturgical movement down to our days ; many useful ideas have been disseminated among young believers. The missal has been widely brought into use ; liturgy is taught in all the Catholic primary and middle schools. The meaning of Mass and the sacraments is taught with patience and perseverance. Priests have a thorough knowledge of the historical evolution of the liturgy, and the specialized reviews display an impressive amount of learning.

The moment has perhaps arrived for pushing our investigations further and asking ourselves to what we must attribute the mediocre success which has been obtained after so much effort. For the fact is there, indisputably ; there is a hitch somewhere.

I. WHY DOES NOT THE LITURGY NOURISH THE FAITH OF YOUNG PEOPLE TO A GREATER DEGREE ?

1. *Young people no longer appreciate the symbolism of things.*

Must we attribute this state of things to their age ? To a certain extent, yes. But it seems to us that the crux of the problem lies in the fact that the creators of the Roman liturgy — among whom we count the sacred authors of the Old and New Testaments —

thought in symbols, which we no longer do. In his daily life, man will always spontaneously make use of symbols and signs. He will always express admiration and love by means of kisses and flowers ; his ideals and dignities by decorations and honorary distinctions ; his emotions by poetical images. But what we have in a large measure lost is the faculty of creating and experiencing a *religious* symbolism. Now, in the liturgy we are constantly coming across this principle : things, objects, stories in the Old and New Testament, the gestures, attitudes, even the people themselves, have a symbolic meaning. They are not there for themselves, they are not only themselves, but they raise the contemplative mind to higher spheres. They are symbols, signs, images, allegories.

What, then, is a symbol ? It is the exterior, visible veil, behind which lies hidden another reality. This reality is partially revealed by the symbol, but is also partly concealed by it. The vase contains, ' envelops ' the balm, we only perceive the perfume. The man who sees a symbol in a person or an object discovers a profounder, greater reality than the ' material envelope ' which is obvious to his senses. The material thing possesses its own tangible reality, accessible to all, but it also contains a deeper one to which it alludes and which one has to ' read ' in it. Two worlds, two realities meet in a symbol. The Greek word ' sum-ballein ' (throw together) which is the etymological origin of ' symbol, ' makes this clear.

That is why knowledge through symbols is a dynamic knowledge, which does not stop at the material object, but which tends to penetrate its hidden meaning. That is also why knowledge by means of symbols is sometimes, for our limited intelligence, so much more fecund and living than knowledge based on definitions ; it incites man's mind to sense the presence of a mystery, to look for ' the other meaning. ' A knowledge such as this, imperfect though it may be, is none the less full of great affective potentiality. It evokes worlds which, without being entirely revealed, are suggested.

Our minds need clearcut ideas, and this clarity is productive of the highest joys. But the clear idea and the direct word do not always possess the impulsive strength which emanates from the symbol. It is precisely by this mixture of shadows and concrete tangibility that the symbol sets the living forces of the soul in movement. Flowers speak louder than words ; comparisons are more attractive than theories. That is why the symbol is especially indispensable to youth. To try to explain everything causes weariness, satiety, boredom and risks the destruction of the taste for mystery. This is all the more true when the reality is so transcendent that it is not susceptible of being explained except by symbols. Our conceptual knowledge is a true one and worthy of trust, but is incomplete, and for that reason cannot do without those things to which it refers.

The symbolism of an object depends primarily on the dispositions of him who contemplates it, on the mind which does not consider facts such as they are, but sees in them the expression of something unknown as well. Thus, what is a symbol for one, is not necessarily so for another. That is why symbolism is par excellence the poet's domain, for he sees in them another world beyond cold reality.

Symbolism plays a very important part in *religion*, which, by definition, has relations with the ineffable. We will not linger over natural religions. It is not an exaggeration to say that in virtue of the Christian doctrine on the *creation*, according to which the Father created in and by the Son, all things have become signs, transparencies, allegories.

They depend on their fundamental origin, not only as the effect depends on its efficient cause, but also as the artistic work depends on the model and the conception of the artist. They find their exemplary cause in the Son. All is made in His image and is His imprint and likeness. The Son is " the first-born of all creation. All is created by Him, in Him, for Him. " (*Colossians*, I, 15-17). " Everything that is, is more than it is, " Guardini says in *The End of the New Times*. Each event signifies more than a simple accomplishment. Everything connotes a relationship with what is above or behind. It is there that each thing finds its achievement. To deny this principle is to precipitate realities into the void, to take away their meaning; they can no longer convince us.

Everything evokes the memory of the Son. The liturgy does not hinder us from looking at all things in Him. Far from it. We shall never penetrate the spirit of the liturgy if we lose sight of the fact that everything borrows from Him not only its existence, but also its essence. Already the sole fact of divine creation is a justification of the manner in which the liturgy makes use of material things and the attitude which it adopts in consequence, when it protests against unilateral spirituality, tending to reduce religious life to a pure matter of spirit.

Moreover, there is the *Incarnation*, by which the Son was made man and by which the entire world was ' consecrated ' (Roman Martyrology for Christmas Eve).

Even admitting that matter has ever been unworthy of God, it is no longer so. On the contrary, it has become a sign and symbol in an absolutely new manner. God envelops Himself in matter, becomes visible in it, hides Himself in it. He who believes in Him says : " You are the Son of the living God, " and he who does not believe in Him : " Is not this the son of Joseph the carpenter ? " So Christ is Himself the first sacrament. One might even say : the symbol of God, if one does not mean something unreal by that. Christ is a sacred Sign, which reveals and hides the reality at the same time. God has entered the world. He accomplishes His works in it, and they are always signs and symbols of His Kingdom. These signs are not to be taken in a purely subjective way ; quite the contrary, they are full of reality and are dispensers of grace.

" His works had a meaning ; as sacramental actions, they ' signified ' something while bestowing it ; or again, they dispensed a gift while signifying something else. While they bestowed something visible, they suggested something which was invisible ; they were symbols and facts at the same time, and even sometimes silent parables, such as the figtree which was rendered sterile by a curse. Christ Himself attached the healing of the body to the conversion of the heart by a single phrase. The paralytic picks up his bed and walks, thereby proving that the rigour of sin has disappeared. The blind man given back his sight will sin no more. The miraculous draught of fishes tells us of the divine Fisher of Men and the nets holding fast their captives, of divine grace. The meal in the desert reminds us of the manna of old and prefigures the new faith, by which we nourish our eternal life. This meal took place on the eve of the great discourse in the synagogue in Capharnaum, by which the bread from heaven is promised us. " [1]

In this way His visible actions became active signs and symbols.

Is it not in the logical order of the divine plan — which willed the Incarnation — to link the continuation of the Kingdom to tangible realities, which contain and signify a deeper reality : the Church and the sacraments ?

That which the poets have always known ; the symbolic function of things, which the human mind spontaneously produces when its faculties of knowledge and expression fail, becomes, in an almost normal way, but not without divine intervention, an active force. The symbol is henceforth more than a sign ; it contains and dispenses grace, gives a divine force. The sign has become a sacrament.

This principle is only enlarged and applied by the *liturgy*. In truth, it cannot raise to the dignity of sacrament more symbols than the Saviour permitted. But it can enrich and amplify the suggestive power of the symbol.

It can transfigure, thanks to the splendour of the faith, the thousand and one things which man uses in his daily life : the stable, the kneading trough, the school, the earth, water and fire, the fireplug, the aeroplane — and in this way bring out the deep meaning of these realities. It applies this maxim : " There is more in you than meets the eye. " The elements speak an eloquent language for those who can hear with recollection and faith. *Lapides clamabunt.*

The liturgy can take other objects from their secular use : the candle, the incense, ashes, and especially water and fire, to put them to the exclusive service of the contemplative and believing soul. The candles are not lighted on the altar because we could not see without them, but because they help us to realize what it means to burn, to be inwardly illuminated. The succes-

---

[1] F. VAN DER MEER, *Catechismus,* Het Spectrum, p. 183.

sion of the seasons, the rhythm of day and night, the sun, darkness, life and death are more than natural phenomena ; in them there is a more intense light, the reminder of more profound darkness. Christ is the Life, the Sun of the world and he who turns away from Him is plunged in a more opaque darkness than the man who walks in the night. That is why the liturgy respects natural phenomena. It celebrates the birth of the Light of the world on the day on which the sun begins its annual course. The resurrection takes place after the first new moon of spring, on the threshold of summer. Every morning, it salutes the rising sun as the *Oriens ex alto* and on Saturday evening the setting with *Jam sol recedit igneus*. It asks Him, the *Lux perennis*, to shed His light in our hearts. A " theology of earthly things " has been spoken of. The liturgy is precisely ' the living theology ' of these same things, the theology which is real, the symbolic representation of what is taught.

We have said that the liturgy ' enlarges ' the principle of symbolism. We could as well and even better have said that *Holy Scripture* itself has done so. The Bible sees in everything symbols, signs, made active by divine institution or by the intention of him who uses them and communal prayer, thus becoming the vehicle of ineffable realities.

With a group of young people search might be made for the meaning given to water in the Testaments, both Old and New. Water is the source of fecundity, rather than for purification and the quenching of thirst. This would be a far more efficacious introduction to the intentions of the liturgy than that which the handbooks of the beginning of the century, still in frequent use, imparted to us. We may note that reference is always made to the natural and original meaning of things. The Bible incites us to see a profound parallelism between the natural order and the supernatural. That is why it is easy, in one way, to introduce young people to the spirit of the liturgy (with some exceptions which we will deal with later on), because the meaning of things, such as the liturgy proposes to us, strikes them as soon as they have been taught to open their eyes. Violence is not done to nature, and the great symbols, the oldest ones, directly taken from the Bible, are clear and do not need the slightest ' explanation. ' Their meaning should not be taught, it ought to be discovered.

When one reads the Bible with the intention of discovering what it says about human things — marriage, sickness, war, commerce and taxation, but also the rock, the seed, fishing net and wild flowers — one is struck by its immense wealth, one feels it to be so close to human life, one realizes that it does not hesitate to mention the most familiar things. It deals with children's games as with household problems where every farthing has its value, with the late and inopportune visit of a tiresome neighbour, with the glass of cold water offered in the summer's heat. There is here no question of literary researches nor of anaemic allegories which could easily be replaced by a less flowery language. All this suggests a world of contacts between God and men.

Jesus speaks in parables, not for the sake of clarity, for all were not meant to receive the explanation, but because events and human facts have their mission of sharpening the wits of the faithful and of leading them to their source.

Things have therefore their deep meaning. They are symbols. Why do not the young (and also their elders) realize this symbolism ? Why do they remain impervious to this conception of the world ? Is it because the Bible is very ancient, because the liturgical symbols have their roots in an outworn civilization ? In some cases it might be so. Certain symbols which date from the Middle Ages (the term allegory seems more adequate) no longer strike our imagination. Think for instance of the meaning given to the priestly vestments. Oil also, can give rise to some difficulties. It played a different part in former ages than in our day. It no longer suggests to our minds the idea of unction, of curative virtues, of wealth, but makes us think of machines, fats and chemical products of all kinds. It would be interesting to make a detailed comparison between the use to which oil and unguents are put in Bible times and in our own. However, we think that most of the chief symbols have a general human significance and the lack of receptivity shown by modern youth must not be attributed to the cause of which we have just been speaking.

It seems to us to be preferable to find the cause in the fact that youth of today has simply not learnt to ' think ' in a Christian way of these human things. In the last century theology perhaps attached too little importance to earthly things and did not sufficiently cast upon them the light which is shed by the Incarnation. And when young people had learnt something of the liturgical symbolism, this had been achieved in an unfortunate way, by answering such questions as, " What do the pillars of the church mean ? " They had to learn stereotyped answers by heart and no one attempted to teach them by means of their eyes and their experience what a column really is.

This comprehension was equally lacking to the previous generation. An excessive spirituality has for a considerable time impoverished religious life. We must also not lose sight of the fact that, on the other hand, modern life leaves no place for a religious conception of nature. Our period is realistic ; it appreciates things according to their utility, their economic value, or their scientific composition. The schoolboy learns that water is H_2O and contains an infinite quantity of microbes. This is in no way contrary to the symbolism of the preface for the benediction of baptismal fonts, which sees fecundity and purification in water. On the contrary, our greater knowledge of nature opens up vaster horizons for us in the sphere of religious instruction. But so few efforts have been made in this direction, at least in schools. Nature has partly delivered up her secrets to us and young people are accustomed to see in her a force which can be mastered thanks to scientific formulae, rather than a mysterious world (which she still is), closely linked up with our own life and the divine plan for our salvation. If I am not mistaken, the greatest liturgists of our day, Guardini and Doncoeur, are pleading for a return, not to romanticism, but to our efforts to perceive mystery and mystique in nature.

2. *Youth no longer perceives the symbolism of the history of salvation.*

We are also aware of symbolism in the manner in which the liturgy and the New Testament interpret the historical facts of the Redemption. In *Les questions paroissiales et liturgiques,* [1] Dom Capelle complains that the faith and the catholicism of youth is different from the catholicism of the liturgy : " Our schoolboys' religion seems to me to exist in a different atmosphere. " Is this so astonishing ? Is not the spiritual life of us who are older carried on in a different rhythm from that of the liturgy ?

The liturgy does not make use of bizarre metaphors but rejoices in the fulfilment of symbols. The Old Testament is accomplished in the New. He who does not understand the Old cannot comprehend the New.

The Old Testament, that chaos of enigmas, becomes simple when read in the light of Christ. [2] The Paschal liturgy is not only full of allusions to the Old Testament, but it is founded on the principle that everything which preceded Christ is a prefiguration of the fulness of time. It must be so, because the Lord Himself announced His coming. He is, indeed, the fulfilment of the prophecies and the key to the Old Testament. " He Himself quoted the prophecies, sometimes attributing to them the meaning generally admitted, sometimes giving them a higher interpretation, and revealed by Him for the first time. He makes His own the grand story of the book of Jonas and shows it as a prefiguration of His Resurrection, a prefiguration which later became one of the splendours of Christian funerary art in the first centuries. The inscrutable dialogues between Jahweh and his King in the psalms and

---

[1] May/June 1951, p. 108.
[2] F. VAN DER MEER, *Catechismus,* p. 184.

the prophets become in His mouth conversations between the Father and the Son. He demonstrated without words how in His Person the antitheses were resumed which opposed the earthly king of the psalmist and the prophets to the man of sorrows of Isaias. All the old misunderstandings, all the narrow interpretations, are revealed as fugitive lights on this paradoxical divine silhouette." [1]

Christ's own miracles play a similarly symbolical part in the liturgy. The ancient Church always took the miracles as signs in a double sense ; on the one hand, as works of the Almighty and signs of divinity, and on the other as symbols or at least as allusions to the mysteries of the Kingdom. They could not see the widow of Nain without thinking of holy Church our mother, rejoicing in the resurrection of her Son. At the bedside of the daughter of Jairus and by Lazarus' tomb, they thought less of the person raised from the dead than of the Resurrection at the Last Day and Christ's words : " I am the Resurrection and the Life. " When He gave sight to the blind they evoked the enlightenment of Baptism and when the paralytic got up and began to walk, they had before their eyes the deliverance by absolution and the second pardon of sins. The wine of Cana, the multiplication of bread and the meal on the shores of the lake after the resurrection reminded them of the Eucharist. The pool of Bethsaida, the Jordan, the lake of the miraculous draught of fishes, recalled Baptism.

In order to realize to what extent the liturgy lives by this symbolism, how it searched the Scriptures and made generous use of all the events, not only in the manner of a teacher calling upon allegories to explain difficult things and illustrate abstract truths, but like the poet who raises the veil to reveal the inner meaning, it is enough to open the Roman Ritual.

The language of the Bible is spoken in it as always. It draws from that source the images which are necessary, sometimes with a profound seriousness, sometimes with a light touch. But these images are always moving, and a subject of wonder to those who do not know any but the modern prayerbook, so full of subjectivism. It says : ' In the same way as... ' and knows that it thus introduces the events and needs of mankind into the sphere of the Kingdom of God, which since Abraham has formed the leaven in everything.

At the bedside of the dying, it supplicates God to liberate his soul as He delivered Enoch and Elias from this earth, saved Noe from the flood and Abraham from Ur, the city of the Chaldees. What have we in common with Enoch and Noe ? That we are ourselves, as they were, in the hand of God, and that what was prefigured in them is being fulfilled in us with a greater plenitude.

---

[1] *Ibid.*, p. 184.

How is it that so many young people are uninterested in the liturgy ? We said " Because they have not learnt to penetrate the meaning of what is visible. Because they have not been taught the symbolism of everything. " We might add, particularly of the things in the Old and New Testaments. The young do not know their Bible and do not see that the New Testament prolongs the Old and that it is the fulfilment of it. For the dogmatic teaching of religious education being detached from the economy of salvation has greatly hindered, not only its capacity for suggestion, but also, and chiefly, its theological depth. The Kingdom of God as revealed to us is above all things historical, that is to say, it is a series of events, of which Abraham is the starting point and the Last Judgment the end. If this past and future are lost to view, only mutilated fragments remain, with no perspective.

Now, if this historical sense does not animate religious teaching, how can the liturgy still interest our youth ? We agree with Dom Capelle when he says : " His religious teachers speak (to youth) two languages. Why should we be surprised that one of them — that of the Mass (the language of the liturgy) — is incomprehensible to them ? They have not been prepared for it. " [1]

3. *Young people no longer sufficiently appreciate the expressive rôle of gestures.*

We must also draw attention to another aspect of unilateral spirituality and this unfortunate incapacity to notice symbols ; religion is considered as being exclusively an affair of the soul in which the body does not share.

It is not easy to define the sources of this false spiritualism, against which a reaction has started in the course of the last few years. We may mention, on the one hand, theological tendencies towards the ancient Manichaeism, condemned by the Church, and on the other, the general cultural impoverishment of the West which no longer has the faculty of finding expressive forms which exteriorise the interior life and thus liberate it. Our teaching, which depreciates manual labour, imagination and creative work for the sake of memorized knowledge, is a characteristic symptom of this state of affairs. We may also mention the realism of our period ; in reaction against the formalism of the past, and in its hunger for truth, it has not kept enough sense of style and form. Our contemporaries have an aversion to everything which is stamped with solemnity,

---

[1] *Loc. cit.*, p. 110.

formal beauty, to all manifestations which bring about the question :
" What is the good of all this elaboration ? " We have the impression of being distracted in our prayer when worship in common asks us to rise, kneel down or to sit. This impression is due to the conviction that all etiquette is misplaced in God's presence, and that one can, and even that one should, pray without one's body.

In introducing the liturgy we must therefore attempt to give gestures and movements their true meaning, not by learning it by heart, but by conveying their significance with regard to daily life. It is only by restoring to the body its expressive function that the liturgy can revive. It is not uniquely a question of religious reorientation, but much more a complete rehabilitation of the body (or a return to the respect which ancient times showed to it). The soul is indeed the body's form (Aristotle-Thomas). The body is the symbol of the soul, its translation (Pinsk).

What philosophers have rediscovered at the price of many battles, must also be rediscovered in practical life. The cult of forms of expression, to which fortunately more and more attention is being given (theatre, dancing, music), makes access to the liturgy easier. The symbol must come to life again. But we are a wretched generation ; while the preceding centuries ratified events and important conventions by symbolic actions, we have recourse to reams of paper and innumerable formularies.

4. *The symbolism of the liturgy is impoverished.*

It would be surprising if the change in the manner of envisaging matter and the impoverishment at the same time of symbolic thought had been without repercussions in the official liturgy. A complex collection of factors has contributed to reduce the importance attached to material signs to the strict minimum.

Can one expect youth, which has a natural aversion to formalism and whose interior life is constantly threatened by it, to be still sensitive to symbols which have become unrecognizable and devoid of meaning ? Can one hope that the liturgy of the dead should strike the young, that the respect for them shown by the Church should be clear, if we are content to incense an empty catafalque, as has lately been done ? Can we reasonably believe that the solemn dismissal of the " Ite Missa est " can still have a meaning for the secular flock when the parish priest is at the same time making every effort to keep them in his church during the Last Gospel and the Prayers for Russia ? We could complete our list by other examples. But the restoration of the Paschal vigil gives cause for hope that the future will bring forth great happenings.

II. PRINCIPLES FOR A LITURGICAL EDUCATION
TO NOURISH FAITH.

What we are about to write by way of conclusion will be very incomplete. Several aspects of liturgical teaching, as, for example, the communal sense, the problem of the vernacular, will not be touched upon. We are only dealing with directions and general principles, to the application of which much reflection is required.

1) In the framework of actual possibilities, the best possible liturgical education consists in a dignified, respectful execution of the sacred rites. Everything which goes on in the church and everything to be found in it, should ' speak ' and fulfil its symbolic function. This cannot be too much emphasized. This is the essential condition for bringing youth back to the liturgy, and amongst this youth, we must not only count those who understand Latin but also the unlearned. Those who are in contact with Catholic youth know that they need church services which will move their hearts. Some popular paraliturgies — after missions, sacramental weeks, etc. — have more influence on sentiment than the official liturgy which is so full of restraint and sobriety. But in no case can one underestimate the moving and attractive strength of a beautiful worship.

2) Besides this, an education which attempts to make young people share in the liturgy exacts knowledge of the Bible as a necessary condition. All religious education which puts youth in contact with the word of God equally favours its liturgical ' capacity. '

3) Exposition of the doctrine of the Faith must especially be done in the *spirit of the liturgy*. Doctrine cannot be detached from all that the Church does and says in its daily liturgical life. He who tries to discourse on baptism without paying the slightest attention to the baptismal rite and the paschal night, nor to the biblical symbols of the baptismal grace, not only makes a didactic error, but, which is worse, he parts realities which have been united by God and the Church. For instance, death should not be spoken of without associating it with the liturgy of the dead (one of the most beautiful rituals which we possess). It follows that the whole of religious instruction ought to be inspired by the Bible and the liturgy. Christian doctrine postulates this as much as the liturgy.

4) In a more general way it might be said that knowledge by

means of symbols remains indispensable, in addition to knowledge by means of definitions and concepts, of which the Church gives us an example in its dogma and theology. And by this we mean above all, the symbols, parables and stories in the Bible. On every occasion we ought to take up the words of the Saviour : " The Kingdom of Heaven is like... " It is knowledge like this which stimulates young minds and at the same time makes them sensitive to mystery. It may be wearying to talk constantly of mystery, especially when the audience is inclined to rationalism, but the presentation of a fine symbol, action, story, or game, introduces us without difficulty into the realm of mysteries.

5) With regard to liturgical teaching properly so-called, after a certain amount of technical instruction (missals, the liturgical year, etc.) in the course of the first years in the middle school, we may begin to penetrate into the mind of the liturgy. We think that historical details relative to its development should be reduced to the minimum (the Mass cannot, however, be dealt with without regard to its history). The present is the most important and should be the starting point. Symbols can be found in daily life, whether actions or objects, and their meaning sought. Also the Bible can be searched to see what things and images signify in it and then connect them with daily life and the liturgy. I think that we may say, generally speaking, that everything is summed up in these three points : the Bible, the Liturgy, and daily life. Certain dogmatic facts can also be pointed out in the missal, as for instance, the action of the Holy Spirit, the Eucharist, the union of Christians in Christ, the kingship of Christ in the liturgy of Holy Week. Such studies do not require great power of memorizing, because a great deal can be found out for oneself.

6) All education which develops the creative faculty of personal expression, is a preparation for the liturgy. When the taste for form and style is given its right place in daily life and exterior things are looked upon as the mirror and image of the soul, the formal beauty of the liturgy will not seem so strange. Liturgical teaching will explicitly demonstrate that the attitudes and liturgical movements are a stylisation of relationships current in daily life and that the liturgy is setting out a definite ideal for humanity. In this order of ideas, it is enough to recall what Maria Montessori and her pupils have done for little children.

Technical Attitude and Approach to the Liturgical World

by Bernard Haering, C. S. S. R.

The liturgical revival has now reached a point where it is no longer only a question of injecting new life into church ceremonies; as in the days of the early Church, the celebration of the Holy Mysteries is seen more and more as the centre of the whole unity of life. We must, however, fully realize that our progress must be orderly, i. e. as long as the celebration of worship is not intelligible, living and joyful, its rays will not penetrate the whole of our life. Efforts to bring fresh life to the liturgy will come up against the traditional difficulties; but, above all, we must watch the psychological reactions of modern man, insofar as they are influenced by the technical way of life.

Positivist Law and Technical Observance
of Rites.

The liturgical education of the clergy at the time of the Carlovingian theological renaissance showed an ardent love of symbolism, compared to the preparation of future ordinands to the altar during the last century. Each act of the priest during the celebration of the Holy Mysteries was interpreted as the sign of a truth or mysterious reality. On the other hand, in the spirit of XIXth century positivist law, teaching primarily, if not exclusively, consisted in asking : " What does the law lay down ? " Earnest priests, imbued with the spirit of their day through no fault of their own, endeavoured to be interiorly pious and recollected during the celebration of the Holy Mysteries and, at the same time, faithfully to observe all the rubrics. Obedience is unquestionably a value ; but the value of the

---

1. See biographical note in *Lumen Vitae*, XIII (1958), 3, p. 416. — New address : Academia Alfonsiana, via Merulana 31, Rome, ITALY.

Christian virtue of obedience was reduced to outward observance. The characteristic Christian element was lacking : living obedience, the effort to understand the true meaning of the rites prescribed. This purely external application of the law and obedience estranged the priest further from the meaning of liturgical symbolism.

This mainly " rubricist " formation of the clergy could hardly lead us to expect great efforts on the part of priests in initiating the faithful in the meaning of symbols and liturgical gestures. " Prayers to say during Mass, " quite independent of the liturgy according to the rubrics, were taught far more than understanding of the hidden mystery of our salvation. A custom still observed in many Roman parishes shows how completely these held sway : on Sundays and feast days there is a sermon lasting from the Offertory to the Consecration, and even quite often to the Communion, to keep the faithful's minds busy while they are " making their Sunday duty. "

This is right where the present liturgical movement comes in : the idea is to *bring the rites to life again,* together with the texts as eloquent signs, *as intelligible symbols of the mysterious reality being celebrated.* A book illustrating this is Romano Guardini's " Von Heiligen Zeichen " (The Sacred Signs). The classical expression of the object to be attained is found, among others, in the postcommunion of the feast of the Beheading of St. John the Baptist : " *Magnifica significata veneremur* et in nobis potius edita gaudeamus. " [1]

Difficulty in Restoring the Meaning of Liturgical Symbolism.

There are innumerable difficulties, which are further increased by the technical mentality of modern man, in replacing the Sacrifice of the Mass and the sacraments in the centre of Christian life, by rendering the symbols articulate and immediately intelligible. The purely legal observance of the outward prescriptions in the liturgy was already a way of " technicalising " actions which originally tried to express the feelings of those participating and, in this particular case, be the expression in worship of the community at prayer. The legalistic attitude towards the original symbols of religious reality was a deviation towards technique, further aggravated by a large number of prescriptions whose meaning could no longer be understood. Often people were satisfied with an outward " technical " performance.

---

1. Grace both to venerate what is signified by the glorious sacraments which we have received, and to rejoice at what they have wrought within us.

The too technical man considers *output and results* instead of paying attention to the immediate *sense* or reality expressed. He is more interested in the *practical result of action* than in understanding a truth which brings joy and finding rest therein. The visible sign is no longer a source of meditation. He considers it more important to *master the reality* than to understand its message about God. Technical mentality seeks more to possess, to seize an object, rather than that which is beautiful, good and true. The increase of artificial products has made modern man partially lose the direct relationship between the gifts of nature and their symbolic language. In the first place, the city-dweller is no longer as close to nature's symbols as the countryman. Even the agricultural worker, technically equipped, bound to capitalist farming whose sole concerns are investment returns and increasing output, shows a psychological tendency to see only *matter to be used* in the gifts of the earth.

Let us now examine these difficulties which, heightened by technical mentality, hamper access to the liturgy.

Output and Efficiency.

The Book of Genesis does not say that God " manufactured " a world. There is nothing in the bible story of the creation of the world which evokes the picture of a technician, who calculates the utility of his action. All is expressed in function of the person. God spoke a creative word full of power and love. " It was through Him that all things came into being, and without Him came nothing that has come to be " (John I, 3). Man created in the image of God can try to penetrate the *meaning* of the creative word and thence give things their name (Gen. II, 19). Man's resemblance to God is expressed by his power to rule the earth by moulding it (Gen. I, 27 et seq.). However, man adores only when he participates, through worship, in God's rest on the sabbath, is faithful to his mission in creation and keeps his resemblance to God (see Gen. II, 3). Hence reverent silence, attention to the meaning of things, to what they tell us about God, are the preliminary condition for a " technique " worthy of man, for a production in the divine image in creation. If man does not labour in a spirit of worship here on earth, he increasingly loses the sense of direct worship. When work becomes an end in itself, it is inconsistent with worship, with adoration of the sovereign domain of God.

The man of today who, in the face of the works of creation, behaves more as *homo faber* than homo sapiens, finds it more difficult to understand his inner nature of *homo orans*. The process by which the

" homo faber " engulfs the lower social classes is shown by his special propensities when he wishes to be religious, when he first approaches sacred things : he sees them above all in terms of technique, useful work and success.

Modern man's predominantly technical mentality explains, to a certain extent, why sacramental doctrine in moral and pastoral theology is preferably given in terms of *results* and *duty*; similarly, in dogmatic theology and preaching, this same sacramental doctrine is considered from the point of view of efficacy, of *effectus*. Certainly the sacraments must be effective ; the point is to know, when they are spoken about, from which aspect and in which category. It is a very different thing to speak of *signa* efficacia, stating that the sacraments bear fruit inasmuch as they are *eloquent signs of God's love*, and to dwell almost exclusively on the problem of the moral or " physical " efficacy of the sacraments. There is a great difference between the following two attitudes : in the sacraments, always see the Lord speaking to us through signs of His love, try to understand what He is telling us through His gifts and what He is asking of us by giving and acting — or else talk of the effects of the sacraments as though everything did not depend on God acting personally and on the words he speaks to us in His love, words to which man must render himself accessible by listening to them and receiving them in all humility.

Technical man's basic theme of " output and efficacy " veils the categories of person and worship proper to the word, symbol, encounter in love and gift of self. He thus loses sight of the " efficacy" proper to the sacraments, or, to put it in a better way : their fecundity.

Utility instead of Gift and Offering in Return.

Fallen man is tempted to seek and see in all things primarily *their utility for his personal ends*. The man of worship, on the other hand, sees in everything the manifestation of God's love, the gift of divine love. Hence the great problem of his life is this : " The Lord's mercies have never failed me ; what return shall I make to Him ? " (Ps. CXV). In worship, man offers the gifts received from God, saying to Him through symbols : " I have received everything through Thy love and I belong to Thee ; accept from me these gifts Thou hast given me ; accept me myself. " That is the profound meaning of the sacrifice and desire. Through this attitude, he who is faithful to worship and the liturgy can grasp the true language of things. Offering them in worship, for him they are gifts of God's love, symbols of His designs of eternal love and means of love.

A man turned entirely towards technique has difficulty in understanding the highest expression of the liturgy and the interior attitude of a man of worship. When technical mentality dominates, it strengthens the tendency of fallen man to consider everything solely from the point of view of its use in serving his own ends.

Yet it would be wrong to seek all the obstacles in the way of the liturgical education of man solely in the craze for technique. The influence of the *century of light*, which tried to overcome the incomprehensible formalism of the liturgy, but closed true access to worship by considering the liturgy almost exclusively as a means for man's moral progress, is still with us. The first aim, adoration and thanksgiving, had to give way to moral progress. This objective, highly moral in itself, was thus put in the wrong category. When worship has the first place, our life ordered according to faith and orientated towards adoration means : consecration to God. God sanctifies us in worship ; He makes to shine upon us rays of His wonderful love. And this brings the tender command : " Be holy, walk in sanctity ! " God has placed us in the light of His sanctity, by His saving action in the sacraments. And this is its effect on our life : " It is yours to proclaim the exploits of God who has called you out of darkness into his marvellous light " (I Peter II, 9). The Christian's moral effort thus participates in the fulness and sublimity of worship. Moralism, on the other hand, means that moral life severs itself from the sphere of worship, theocentricism, and the history of salvation.

That moralism of the century of light has been able to settle down and hold its own in catechesis, and even in teaching on the sacraments, is due, at least in part, to today's predominantly technical style of life.

There is no doubt but that the liturgical efforts of the century of light strongly resembled in detail the present liturgical movement ; then too, criticism of the use of Latin, which the people did not understand, arose out of the desire to make the liturgy intelligible. The motives and ultimate aims were, however, different. The century of light lacked a respectful understanding of the Mysteries ; they wanted to put everything into purely rational categories. Thus the fight against the predominance of Latin in the liturgy was then linked to antipathy for the symbol, insofar as it reminds us of an unfathomable, mysterious reality, which surpasses reason and the moral idea of perfecting the world. Today, on the other hand, the fight is more against the " mystery " of sounds unintelligible to their hearers and bygone formalism, so as to open the way to a respectful understanding of the true mystery.

Attempts by Magic and Technique to
Dominate the World.

As the attempts made in the century of light to reduce the liturgy to the purely rational plane were related to technical mentality, some people may perhaps be tempted to consider this entirely misunderstood liturgical " mysterious " symbolism as an antidote to technical mentality and a means of preventing it from filtering into worship. But this would be wrong ! When the symbol no longer conveys a meaning and consequently is no more indistinguishable from words we understand, there is a danger of either being satisfied with a purely external, legal performance, or, worse still, fostering ideas and hopes of a magic type, more in line with a " technicalising " attitude than with religion.

As history of religions and phenomenology of religion show, magic is man's primitive attempt to run the world and its hidden forces, by mysterious " forces " and foul means. That is why the category of results and utility to man predominate in this naive attempt to dominate the world just as in love of technique. Both have in common the absence of personal encounter between " me " and " you. "

Many discreet surveys have proved that quite a number of Catholics attribute a special " virtue " to Latin in worship, precisely because they do not understand it. This is above all noticeable with some formalist Christians, who are still ignorant of the fact that all the liturgical rites proclaim and mean something in conjunction with a liturgical language understandable in itself. These people have more confidence in the priest's blessing (especially in exorcism) given in Latin — incomprehensible — than that given in their mother tongue. A classical reply is that given by an otherwise intelligent lay brother : the first time a Clothing and Profession was celebrated in his Order in the vernacular, he said how delighted he was that everything was so beautiful and understandable, but added pensively : " Does it still work ?" Several nuns in an Order who had to say three rosaries in Latin every day, when asked why they were not allowed to say the rosary in their mother tongue replied : " They say that a rosary said in Latin has more effect, even if we don't understand a thing ! " It is a long way from this attitude, and the " technicalising " attitude, to listening respectfully to what is proclaimed about a mystery by an intelligible symbol and the words accompanying it ; it is a long way from this attitude to adoring God in spirit and in truth, where body and soul must both be expressed in the symbol and word.

Man of the technical age, principally the city dweller, no longer understands many parables of the Bible and liturgical symbols so spontaneously and directly as men in days gone by.For example,when a factory worker, or even a highly cultured man living in a city, hears the parable of the Good Shepherd and his flock, he has scarcely any idea of the nearness and trust which united the shepherd of olden days to his flock, how much he loved each animal and how attached each animal was to him. Modern man used to electric light does not perceive so directly, in the liturgical symbol of light, the warmth of living light which in burning itself out brings light to all in the house. The bread, wine and oil symbolize higher realities far better to the man close to nature, used to receiving directly from the hands of God the fruits of the earth, than to inhabitants of large cities who, amongst the many artificially prepared foods, buy these gifts of nature ready for consumption. To quote another example, how could the family meal eaten together still be a warm and striking symbol of the community partaking in the sacramental feast, the mensa coelestis, coena vitae aeternae, when working in shifts and other motives rarely permit the family to enjoy a meal quietly in common ?

These are certainly serious difficulties in the way of a revival of liturgical piety. Should we not, therefore, seek new symbols, immediately accessible to modern man ? To a certain degree, liturgical symbols will have to be adapted to the various mentalities of modern peoples and men. But even if we find appropriate symbols in the technical field, we must not lose sight of their inherent dangers : technical man is apparently inclined to consider these things first of all according to categories of utility and use. In addition, the central symbols of the liturgy are determined by divine institution. They are original symbols to which men of all times and places are, at least subconsciously, intimately bound. It is a matter of bringing them to realize this. As access to symbols is no longer as direct and spontaneous for modern man, the accompanying words obviously take on a much greater importance than in former times. Specialists in depth psychology, in particular C. G. Jung, have shown that man still has, in the deep layers of the subconscious a very powerful and primitive connection with original symbols. Deep down, ultra-civilized man longs for these treasures to break through to the threshold of consciousness.

Listing the difficulties which hamper technical man's access to the liturgy should not be considered as resentment or enmity. Technique, as such, and a technical profession are not obstacles to worship and orientation towards a life of worship. The danger lies principally in an attitude of considering technique as the be-all and end-all of everything. Many people say that today we have reached a turning-point. Through their progress, natural science and technique are discovering the bounds which touch on mystery. The age of unfeeling technical utilitarianism would appear to be over. The engineer and naturalist find ever more pleasure in using their knowledge in the service of that which is beautiful, true and good. The Brussels World Fair offered much evidence of this.

Just as a narrow " technicalising " view makes man unapt from the liturgical point of view, so technique can and must serve the liturgy. The greater the possibilities of technique, the more it can be guided in its structure by the spirit and interior finalities of the liturgy. The latter must do everything, too, to attract men imbued with modern technique.

United Efforts.

In face of the multiple difficulties which hamper technical man's access to the liturgy, efforts towards liturgical revival must be universal. For example, it is not enough to organize and outwardly regulate community worship. Here too, we must beware, in a certain sense, of technical man with regard to the celebrants and the community. If the community Mass is to create the spirit of community and make the congregation feel this fellowship through the sacred signs, at the same time we must perseveringly explain the deep meaning of the Holy Mysteries as a sign of community, as a source of the unity of God's people and see that these explanations bring life to each gathering of the community. The preaching of the Word and the form of worship must help each other ; similarly, the most expressive symbol possible (the symbolic act) must become one with the Word which enlightens and is intelligible. The symbol, i. e. the symbolic act, and the Word go together like body and soul.

To quote a very simple example, when, today, many bishops prescribe that priests must say the words " Dominus vobiscum " audibly and intelligibly and exhort the congregation to reply thereto in unison, we must not just consider this as a new law, but convincingly explain the meaning of this greeting and answer. Even this will not be enough if the priest's own action, while saying these words, does not constitute an invitation to reply, or if the priest, turning round, moves hurriedly towards the missal before the congregation has time to answer. The faithful must be able to perceive the seriousness of these acts in the priest's manner of greeting them and welcoming their response.

The place of worship itself is very important. The church must neither simply conform to principles of utility, nor look like a utilitarian, cold factory hut, but be the expression of the sacred realities which are celebrated there. The church must itself be adoration, sursum corda, an invitation to gather round the altar.

The greatest disadvantage of modern technical man is the " absence of a centre, " splitting up his life into a series of ill-assorted aims. Many textbooks have the same inconvenience in their conception of the liturgy. Thus, for example, most XIXth century textbooks on moral theology presented the sacraments and the Mass as a complementary " collection of duties " alongside purely moral commandments. Preachers — this is a particularly well-known example — based their teaching about the duties of marriage on numerous special applications and always ended by saying : " If it is difficult, married people have the grace of the sacrament in order to do their duty." Married people must, of course, be led to the sources of salvation so as to overcome their difficulties ; but that will only be done practically and efficiently by presenting their entire state as a road to salvation, starting with the sacramental meaning of marriage and not dissociating from it the grace which helps the total sense of the sacrament. The actual duties imposed by marriage and family only acquire all their Christian greatness if they are presented as a form of sacramental sanctification, as a task bringing grace and honour. The liturgy must neither remain apart from life, nor be added as a simple means of grace on more or less secular lines.

The Eucharist, together with the sacraments, must be the centrum fides through the manner in which they are celebrated and, hence, by their extension into the whole of life. *Not only piety and sacerdotal life, but all Christian piety and life too, must find their unity in the liturgy of the Church.* The celebration of the Holy Mysteries must allow every Christian to experience, in the community of salvation of the redeemed, the personal meeting with God and in God's gifts reap knowledge of his duty in the conduct of his life.

Doctrinal Sign

Divine revelation as found in the Bible is expressed in human terms. It bears all the marks of a specific culture and a specific age. Doctrinal formulation of divine revelation aims at stripping away the cultural expression of the truth and laying bare its eternal meaning. It makes it possible to study the truth more deeply and to reformulate it in terms of present-day language and relevancy. Remaining faithful to the magisterium of the Church, the religion teacher must strive to present the eternal truth in a way that is positive, compelling, and joyful.

73

The Growth of Faith
and the Study of Doctrine

*An attempt to introduce adolescents
to the mystery of the Holy Trinity.*

by George DELCUVE, S. J.

For some years the biblical and liturgical movements have been helping us to discover God's plan of salvation in His word, and to approach His mysteries in the worship which celebrates and perpetuates them. The reading of the Bible and liturgical life ought normally to stimulate the believer's meditation and promote Christian life. A frequent recourse to the inspired text, a doctrinal study based on the declarations of the teaching authority of the Church, an increasingly thorough study of the liturgy, these are three methods, none of which ought to be left out, and which gain by being employed together. We would like to demonstrate this quite simply by tracing the broadlin of the presentaion of a mystery to young adolescents. [2] We have purposely chosen that of the Holy Trinity; on the one hand, it is thought difficult and there is a temptation to treat it too briefly; on the other hand, it is of ' vital ' importance, and the ignorance of many is regrettable, their ignorance being to a certain extent the responsibility of catechists, religious teachers and preachers.

" For many Christians, the Divine Persons are unknown, as for the so-called Christians of Ephesus, whom St. Paul asked, ' Have you received the Holy Spirit ? ' and they replied, ' The Holy Spirit ? We do not even know of His existence. ' (*Acts*, XIX, 2)

" There is no more unfortunate misconception ; if Christ came to reveal to us that the true God is Father, Son and Spirit, if that is the

---

[1] Address : 27, rue de Spa, Brussels, BELGIUM.

[2] We worked with pupils in the sixth Latin form (12-13 years old).

primary truth, the substance of dogma and the basis of our charity which is the essence of christianity, how can we pretend to be Christians when we look upon the mystery as an abstract theorem, a statement of no importance, a facultative corollary to the chapter on ' God, ' something extra in Christian life ?

" In reality, this Christian life is one of intimacy with the Divine Persons. " [1]

Normally speaking, this intimacy should increase with the years. [2] This spiritual growth should not be precipitated, nor should our human labour be substituted for the work of God's grace. In any case, there is no reason for dwelling on these exaggerations, nor are we inclined to do so. Especially in this matter, we more often sin by default ; we sometimes need to remind ourselves that our pupils " are, in terms of life, growth and grace, what has to be explained to them in terms of speculation, progressive explanations and dogmas. What they are through Christ bears witness to what is said to them in His Name. " [3]

The introduction to the mystery of the Holy Trinity will be an active one ; but it will be an activity which is both natural and *supernatural*, the latter being the result of the docile collaboration of the young believer with the divine Persons Who dwell in him.

The teacher will define the stages in the road which is to be followed in a few words. The pupils will immediately begin to *search* the Gospels and at the end they will have collected together the basic texts. During the *doctrinal lesson*, the teacher, continuing to call upon his pupils' collaboration, will classify the texts so as to form an exposition of the mystery; [4] he will then develop his exposition by means of analogies ; finally, the light of his teaching will illuminate prayer and action. The activity which has been aroused and stimulated in class will be prolonged in *personal work* and will continue to be exercised in private and liturgical prayer and in their whole behaviour.

---

[1] G. SALET, *Richesses du dogme chrétien*, Le Puy, Mappus, 1946, p. 166.

[2] From the didactic point of view, the first presentation of the mystery of the Holy Trinity will come at the end of an instruction which will have helped the child to clear up his successive relations with Father, Son and Spirit. This will not have to be repeated in the secondary schools. There are even advantages in presenting the mystery of the Blessed Trinity very early.

[3] É. MERSCH, S. J. *Le professeur de religion. Sa vie intérieure et son enseignement*, in *Compte rendu du IIIe Congrès international de l'enseignement secondaire catholique*, Brussels, Van Muysewinkel, pp. 130-144.

[4] The teacher could also combine the doctrinal development with the classification of the Gospel texts, in order to condense and simplify the instruction.

I. RESEARCHES IN THE GOSPELS

There will be three series of enquiries ; the first to show the Father's love for His Son , the second, the devotion and intimacy characterizing the relations of the Son with the Father, the third, the relations of the Holy Spirit with the other Persons.

A word as to method. Under the heading RESEARCHES, the pupil writes in his exercise book for the first series : " Scenes from the Gospel in which the Father expresses His Love for His Son ; " then he writes the reference, Mark I, 9-13, [1] this followed by the heading which he will find at this place in the Gospel. The pupils read the passage in silence, looking for the verse or verses which are characteristic. After this, the teacher interrogates them, controlling (and if necessary, setting right), and bringing out the value of the teaching contained in the characteristic phrase, which is then written down. In this way, the pupils have in their exercise books the heading which reminds them of the actual episode and the text which illuminates an aspect of the Trinitarian life.

To help the reader, we reproduce the passages examined ; the phrases written in the exercise books being in italics.

1. **Scenes in the Gospels where the Fathers' love for the Son is expressed**. — *a*) MARK, I, 9-13 : BAPTISM AND TEMPTATION OF JESUS. — At this time, Jesus came from Nazareth, and was baptized by John in the Jordan. And even as he came up out of the water he saw the heavens opened, and the Spirit, like a dove, coming down and resting upon him. There was a voice, too, out of heaven, *Thou art my beloved Son ; in thee I am well pleased.* Thereupon the Spirit sent him out into the desert : and in the desert he spent forty days and forty nights, tempted by the devil ; there he lodged with the beasts and there the angels ministered to him.

b) MATTHEW, XVII, 1-9: THE TRANSFIGURATION. — Six days afterwards Jesus took Peter and James and his brother John with him, and led them up on to a high mountain where they were alone. And he was transfigured in their presence, his face shining like the sun, and his garments becoming white as snow ; and all at once they had sight of Moses and Elias conversing with him. Then Peter said aloud to Jesus, Lord, it is well that we should be

---

[1] The teacher will avoid pointing out only one verse, or there would be no ' research. ' He will indicate a passage which is not too long (the boy would get lost and the search take too long), nor too short (as a rule, ten to twenty verses are sufficient). So as not to make this article too lengthy, we have reduced the quotations and have not inserted the numbers of the verses.

here ; if it please thee, let us make three arbours in this place, one for thee, one for Moses and one for Elias. Even before he had finished speaking, a shining cloud overshadowed them. And now, there was a voice which said to them out of the cloud, This is my beloved Son, in whom I am well pleased ; to him, then, listen. The disciples, when they heard it, fell on their faces, overcome with fear ; but Jesus came near and roused them with his touch ; Arise, he said, do not be afraid. And they lifted up their eyes, and saw no man there but Jesus only.

And as they were coming down from the mountain, Jesus warned them, Do not tell anybody of what you have seen, until the Son of Man has risen from the dead.

c) JOHN, V, 1-21, 26 : THE HEALING OF THE PARALYTIC AT THE POOL OF BETHSAIDA ON THE SABBATH-DAY. [1] — After this came a Jewish feast, for which Jesus went up to Jerusalem. There is a pool in Jerusalem at the Sheep Gate, called in Hebrew Bethsaida, with five porches, under which a multitude of diseased folk used to lie, the blind, the lame, the disabled, waiting for a disturbance of the water. From time to time, an angel of the Lord came down upon the pool, and the water was stirred up ; and the first man who stepped into the pool after the stirring of the water, recovered from whatever infirmity it was that oppressed him. There was one man there who had been disabled for thirty-eight years. Jesus saw him lying there, and knew that he had waited a long time ; Hast thou a mind, he asked, to recover thy strength ? Sir, said the cripple, I have no one to let me down into the pool when the water is stirred ; and while I am on my way, somebody else steps down before me. Jesus said to him, Rise up, take up thy bed, and walk. And all at once the man recovered his strength, and took up his bed, and walked. That day, it was the sabbath : and the Jews said to the man who had been cured, It is the sabbath ; it is not lawful for thee to carry thy bed. He answered them, The man who gave me back my strength told me himself, Take up thy bed, and walk. So they asked him, Who is this man who told thee, Take up thy bed, and walk ? The cripple who had been healed did not know who it was ; Jesus had drawn aside from so crowded a place. But afterwards when Jesus found him in the temple, and said to him, Behold, thou hast recovered thy strength ; do not sin any more, for fear that worse should befall thee, the man went back and told the Jews that it was Jesus who had restored his strength.

The Jews took occasion to rouse ill-will against Jesus for doing such things on the sabbath. And Jesus answered them, *My Father has never ceased work-*

---

[1] Contrary to our misgivings, a large part of St. John's Gospel is understood by sixth-form pupils. When indicating the passage for research, the master will eventually forestall a difficulty by a word of explanation or will omit some verses which do not bear on the chief subject for exposition. — This passage not only illustrates the Father's love for the Son, but also the intimate relations between Father and Son ; so as not to return to it in the second series, we also underline the phrases which refer to this second theme.

ing, and I too must be at work. This made the Jews more determined than ever to make away with him, that he not only broke the sabbath, but spoke of God as his own Father, thereby treating himself as equal to God. And Jesus answered them thus : *Believe me when I tell you this, The Son cannot do anything at his own pleasure, he can only do what he sees his Father doing ; what the Father does is what the Son does in his turn. The Father loves the Son, and discloses to him all that he himself does. And he has greater doings yet to disclose to him, for your astonishment ; just as the Father bids the dead rise up and gives them life, so the Son gives life to whomsoever he will... As the Father has within him the gift of life, so he has granted to the Son that he too should have within him the gift of life.* [1]

2. **Gospel scenes in which Jesus shows His love for the Father and His intimacy with Him.** The three first passages deal with the devotion of Jesus, the two last with the unique intimacy.

a) LUKE, IV, 1-13 : FAST AND TEMPTATION IN THE WILDERNESS. [2] — Jesus returned from the Jordan full of the Holy Spirit, and by the Spirit he was led on to the wilderness, where he remained forty days, tempted by the devil. During those days he ate nothing, and when they were over, he was hungry. Then the devil said to him, If thou art the Son of God, bid this stone turn into a loaf of bread. Jesus answered him, It is written, Man cannot live by bread only ; there is life for him in all the words that come from God. And the devil led him up on to a high mountain, and shewed him all the kingdoms of the world in a moment of time ; I will give thee command, the devil said to him, over all these, and the glory that belongs to them ; they have been made over to me, and I may give them to whomsoever I please ; come then, all shall be thine, if thou wilt fall down before me and worship. *Jesus answered him, It is written : Thou shalt worship the Lord thy God, to him only shalt thou do service.* And he led him to Jerusalem, and there set him down on the pinnacle of the temple ; If thou art the Son of God, he said to him, cast thyself down from this to the earth ; for it is written : He shall give his angels charge concerning thee, to keep thee safe, and they

---

[1] In the dialogue which follows, the master will point out the phrase which brings out most clearly the love of the Father for the Son. It is verse 20 : " *The Father loves the Son.* " By means of questions he will make the pupils explain the proofs of this love. The verse quoted ends with these words : " *(The Father) discloses to him all that he himself does.* " All the miraculous *works* of Christ are therefore explained by a gift of the Father's love. Is that all ? No ; the Son receives His *life* itself from the Father ; " *He has granted to the Son that he too should have within him the gift of life* " (verse 26). Hence Jesus calls God His own Father.

[2] The whole passage witnesses to the devotion of the Son to His Father. Jesus prefers poverty, humility and obedience to material goods, sensational exploits and temporal power. He is the perfect Servant of God, foretold by the prophets. The master will point out this instruction which is contained in the story of the temptation before emphasizing the most expressive phrases.

78

will hold thee up with their hands, lest thou shouldst chance to trip on a stone. *And Jesus answered him, We are told, Thou shalt not put the Lord thy God to the proof.* So the devil, when he had finished tempting every way, left him in peace until the time should come.

b) JOHN, IV, 27-34 : JESUS' CONVERSATION WITH HIS DISCIPLES AFTER THE DEPARTURE OF THE WOMAN OF SAMARIA. — (Before the pupils read the text, the master will help them to recall the conversation between the Saviour and the woman of Samaria). With that, his disciples came up, and were surprised to find him talking to the woman ; but none of them asked, What meanest thou ? or Why art thou talking to her ? And so the woman put down her water-pot, and went back to the city, to tell the folk there, Come and have sight of a man who has told me all the story of my life ; can this be the Christ? So they left the city, and came out to find him. Meanwhile, his disciples were urging him, Master, take some food. But he told them, I have food to eat of which you know nothing. Whereupon his disciples said to one another, Can somebody have brought him food ? But Jesus said to them, *My meat is to do the will of him who sent me, and to accomplish the task he gave me.*

c) JOHN, VIII, 48-58 : DISCUSSION BETWEEN JESUS AND THE JEWS. — Hereupon the Jews answered him, We are right, surely, in saying that thou art a Samaritan, and art possessed ? I am not possessed, Jesus answered ; it is because *I reverence my Father* that you have no reverence for me. *Not that I am looking to my own reputation;* there is another who will look to it, and be the judge.

Believe me when I tell you this ; if a man is true to my word, to all eternity he will never see death. And the Jews said to him, Now we are certain that thou art possessed. What of Abraham and the prophets ? They are dead ; and thou sayest that a man will never taste death to all eternity, if he is true to thy word. Art thou greater than our father Abraham ? He is dead, and the prophets are dead. What dost thou claim to be ? If I should speak in my own honour, Jesus answered, such honour goes for nothing. *Honour must come to me from my Father, from him whom you claim as your God : although you cannot recognize him. But I have knowledge of him ;* if I should say I have not, I should be what you are, a liar. *Yes, I have knowledge of him, and I am true to his word.* As for your father Abraham, his heart was proud to see the day of my coming ; he saw, and rejoiced to see it. Then the Jews asked him, Hast thou seen Abraham, thou, who art not yet fifty years old ? And Jesus said to them, Believe me, before ever Abraham came to be, I am. Whereupon they took up stones to throw at him ; but Jesus hid himself, and went out of the temple.

d) MATTHEW, XI, 25-27 : PRAISE OF THE FATHER. — At that time Jesus said openly, Father, who art Lord of heaven and earth, I give thee praise that thou hast hidden all this from the wise and the prudent, and revealed it to little children. Be it so, Father, since this finds favour in thy sight. *My Father has entrusted everything into my hands; none knows the Son truly except the Father, and none knows the Father truly except the Son, and those to whom it is the Son's good pleasure to reveal him.*

e) JOHN, X, 22-33 : SOLEMN DECLARATION AT THE FEAST OF THE DEDICA-
TION. — And now the Dedication feast was taking place at Jerusalem, and
it was winter ; and Jesus was walking about in the temple, in Solomon's
porch. So the Jews gathered round him, and said to him, How long wilt thou
go on keeping us in suspense ? If thou art the Christ, tell us openly. Jesus
answered them I have told you, but you will not believe me. All that I do in
my Father's name bears me testimony, and still you will not believe me ;
that is because you are no sheep of mine. My sheep listen to my voice, and
I know them, and they follow me. And I give them everlasting life, so that
to all eternity no one can tear them away from my hand. This trust which my
Father has committed to me is more precious than all else ; no one can tear
them away from the hand of my Father. *My Father and I are one.*

At this, the Jews once again took up stones, to stone him with. Jesus answered them, My Father has enabled me to do many deeds of mercy in your
presence ; for which of these are you stoning me ? *It is not for any deed of
mercy we are stoning thee,* answered the Jews ; *it is for blasphemy ; it is because
thou, who art a man, dost pretend to be God.*

3. **Passages from the Gospels which refer to the Holy Spirit.** — *a)*
LUKE, III, 21-22 ; BAPTISM OF JESUS. — *It was while all the people were being
baptized that Jesus was baptized too, and stood there praying. Suddenly heaven
was opened, and the Holy Spirit came down upon him in bodily form, like a dove,*
and a voice came from heaven, which said, Thou art my beloved Son, in
thee I am well pleased.

b) LUKE, IV, 1, 14-21 : THE RETREAT IN THE WILDERNESS ; THE PREACHING
AT NAZARETH. — *Jesus returned from the Jordan full of the Holy Spirit,
and by the Spirit he was led on into the wilderness... And Jesus came back to
Galilee with the power of the Spirit upon him ;* word of him went round through
all the neighbouring country, and he began to preach in their synagogues, so
that his praise was on all men's lips.

Then he came to Nazareth, where he had been brought up ; and he went
into the synagogue there, as his custom was, on the sabbath day, and stood
up to read. *The book given to him was the book of the prophet Isaias ; so he
opened it, and found the place where the words ran ; The Spirit of the Lord is
upon me ; he has anointed me, and sent me out to preach the gospel to the poor, to
restore the broken-hearted ; to bid the prisoners go free, and the blind have sight ;
to set the oppressed at liberty to proclaim a year when men may find acceptance
with the Lord, a day of retribution.* Then he shut the book, and gave it back
to the attendant, and sat down. All those who were in the synagogue fixed
their eyes on him, and thus he began speaking to them, *This scripture which
I have read in your hearing is to-day fulfilled.*

c) JOHN, XIV, 15-26 : JESUS TWICE ANNOUNCES THE COMING OF THE HOLY
SPIRIT. — *If you have any love for me, you must keep the commandments which
I give you ; and then I will ask the Father, and he will give you another to be-
friend you, one who is to dwell continually with you for ever. It is the truth-giving*

80

Spirit, for whom the world can find no room, because it cannot see him, cannot recognize him. But you are to recognize him; he will be continually at your side, nay, he will be in you.

I will not leave you friendless ; I am coming to you. It is only a little while now, before the world is to see me no more ; but you can see me, because I live on, and you too will have life. When that day comes, you will learn for yourselves that I am in my Father, and you are in me, and I am in you. The man who loves me is the man who keeps the commandments he has from me ; and he who loves will win my Father's love, and I too will love him, and will reveal myself to him. Here Judas, not the Iscariot, said to him, Lord, how comes it that thou wilt only reveal thyself to us, and not to the world ? Jesus answered him, If a man has any love for me, he will be true to my word ; and then he will win my Father's love, and we will both come to him, and make our continual abode with him ; whereas the man who has no love for me, lets my sayings pass him by. And this word, which you have been hearing from me, comes not from me, but from my Father who sent me.

So much converse I have held with you, still at your side. *He who is to befriend you, the Holy Spirit, whom the Father will send on my account, will is his turn make everything plain, and recall to your minds everything I have said to you.*

d) JOHN XVI, 5-7, 12-15 : JESUS ANNOUNCES THE COMING OF THE HOLY SPIRIT FOR THE THIRD TIME. — Now, I am going back to him who sent me. None of you is asking me, Where is it thou art going ? So full are your hearts with sorrow at my telling you this. And yet I can say truly that *it is better for you I should go away; he who is to befriend you will not come to you unless I do go, but if only I make my way there, I will send him to you...*

I have still much to say to you, but it is beyond your reach as yet. *It will be for him, the truth-giving Spirit, when he comes, to guide you into all truth. He will not utter a message of his own; he will utter the message that has been given to him; and he will make plain to you what is still to come. And he will bring honour to me, because it is from me that he will derive what he makes plain to you. I say that he will derive from me what he makes plain to you, because all that belongs to the Father belongs to me.*

II. THE CLASSIFICATION OF THE TEXTS

The materials are to hand. The moment has come to set them in order. A good way to proceed would be to write on the blackboard, as the lesson proceeds, the headings of the principal points. That done, the master asks the pupils (who may use their exercise books) to look up the facts which have been noted and the phrases transcribed bearing on the theme. When one or several points have been elaborated in this way, a pupil reads the instruction on them out of the manual.

As it is impossible to reproduce the conversation between master and pupils, we will confine ourselves to pointing out the chief stages. The reader will understand that *after the references have been found*, the lesson becomes animated and relatively easy.

1. OUR LORD TEACHES THAT THERE IS ONLY ONE GOD. — In order not to add to the number, we have not suggested a research on this subject. When asked, the pupils will no doubt remember Our Lord repeating Moses' words : The Lord is one. Thou wilt love the Lord thy God with thy whole heart. If necessary, they will be asked to open the gospel of St. Mark at chapter XII.

2. AT THE BAPTISM OF OUR LORD, THE FATHER AND THE HOLY SPIRIT MAKE THEMSELVES KNOWN. — The unity of God having been recalled to mind, we pass on to the manifestations of the Holy Trinity during Jesus' life. The pupils will mention the baptism. Details will be asked for.

3. JESUS IS GOD LIKE HIS FATHER. Jesus passed for an ordinary man at Nazareth ; He manifests gradually to His disciples that He is God. How ? Spontaneously, the pupils will go from the exterior to the interior, from the actions to the nature from which they arise.

a) *Jesus does what only God can do.* — Remember the Saviour's miracles ; in such circumstances, He does not hesitate to put Himself on a level with the Father : " My Father has never ceased working, and I too must be at work. " (John, V, 17).

There is, however, more than this. A child's privilege is to know his parents in a way that no stranger can, and it is this privilege that Jesus claims :

b) *Jesus knows what God alone knows.* — None knows the Son truly except the Father, and none knows the Father truly except the Son, and those to whom it is the Son's good pleasure to reveal him (Matt., XI, 27).

Finally, how are we to explain the miraculous works and the privileged knowledge of Christ ?

c) *Jesus and His Father are one.* — All that I do in my Father's name bears me testimony... My Father and I are one (John, X, 25, 30).

4. JESUS RECEIVES EVERYTHING FROM HIS FATHER. — Jesus and His Father are one. Must we then say that Jesus is the Father ? If not, why not ? Do the texts which we have read enlighten us on this point ? Yes. The Son can only do what he sees his Father doing ; what the Father does is what the Son does in his turn. *The Father loves the Son, and discloses to him all that he himself does* (John, V, 19, 20).

And to sum up : As the Father has within him the gift of life, so *he has granted to the Son* that he too should have within him the gift of life (John, V, 26). In short, the Son receives everything from the infinitely loving Father.

5. THE HOLY SPIRIT IS GOD. — Again, the role attributed to the Holy Spirit by the evangelists instructs us as to His nature. Let us re-read the passages. Our Lord calls the Holy Spirit : " He who is to befriend you, " " the truth-giving Spirit "; He speaks of Him as being *another Himself* who will remind them of the Master's teaching and make them understand it.

6. THE HOLY SPIRIT RECEIVES ALL THAT HE IS FROM THE FATHER AND THE SON. — Jesus does not speak of Himself ; He gets His message from the Father. Neither does the Holy Spirit speak of Himself : " He will derive from me, " says Jesus, " what he makes plain to you "; He will also derive it from the Father, for if Christ declares that the Holy Spirit will derive his message from Him, it is because all that the Father has is His. In short, the Holy Spirit obtains all that He is from the Father and the Son; He thus unites them in an intimate way.

III. FURTHER DOCTRINAL
AND CATECHETICAL DEVELOPMENT

It is possible to stop at this inventory and classification of Gospel texts. For the growth of faith and, still more, for the development of charity, it is desirable and possible to go further, even with young adolescents. How far ? It is for the master to judge, taking actual circumstances into account.

This doctrinal development will begin by a *succinct summary of the Gospel facts* which refer to the matter in hand, will continue by *an appeal to the experience of human relationships*, and end by a more *intimate knowledge of the Divine Persons*, which will bring the *formulae of the catechism* to life.

In this article, we have to adopt the form of a continuous exposition, but in class, master and pupils will converse all the time : " Does the Father receive His life from anyone ? What does He give the Son ? What have our parents given us ? Only the life of the body ? What do they give us besides ? etc. "

1. THERE ARE THREE PERSONS. — a) *The Father and the Son.* —
The Father " has within him the gift of life ; " He does not receive
it from anyone else. He gives it entirely to the Son, much more
than a father or mother gives him or herself to their child.

Our parents have given us the life of the body and we resemble them in
our features. As we grow, they teach us what they know, they tell us who
they love and make us love them: the family, friends, God, Our Lady.
Because of that, we also resemble our parents in our thoughts, sentiments,
piety. This resemblance may constantly increase, but it is always imperfect.

God the Father, perfect Spirit, has not given a body to His Son,
since He has not got one. But from all eternity He has spoken and
expressed His thought, secrets and perfections. He has thus had,
from all eternity, a Son perfectly resembling Him, having the same
perfections as Himself (the Divine nature) : Deum de Deo, Lumen
de Lumine, Deum verum de Deo vero. [1]

b) *The Father, Son and Holy Spirit.* — The Father " is well
pleased " with His Son Who has all the Divine perfections ; He
loves the Son much more than parents can love their child. On his
side, the Son only seeks His Father's glory, from Whom He has received everything ; He loves the Father much more than a child
can love his parents.

Our parents love us very much. We also love them very much. The love
of parents and children is a very strong bond which unites the whole family.
Yet, this love remains   always imperfect, because we are only human.

God the Father puts all that He is into His love for His Son,
that is to say, all His infinite riches, all His perfection. In the same
way, the Son puts into His love for His Father, all that He is, all
the infinite riches that He derives from Him. Thus, the fruit of the
love of the Father and the Son is as perfect as the Father and the
Son : it is God ; it is the third person of the Holy Trinity : the Holy
Spirit is the perfect bond which unites Father and Son. [2] *Credo in
Spiritum Sanctum qui de Patre Filioque procedit.*

---

[1] If it is thought desirable, a note may be added which will help the pupil to
understand the beginning of the Gospel of St. John, so often read at the end of Mass.
Like men express their thoughts in words, the Son of God is called by St. John,
the Word, that is to say, the Word of the Father Who has expressed all that He
knows, all His wisdom. " At the beginning was the Word... and the Word was God. "
" Hear Him, " the Father says to us, and you will know Me.

[2] We could add here a note which would help the pupils better to understand
the ending of the prayers which he hears so often. It is why, we could say, we finish

2. THESE THREE PERSONS ARE ONE GOD. — The Father has perfect life in Himself and He has given this perfect life to the Son in Himself. In His turn, the Holy Spirit, love of the Father and the Son, derives all that They are from Father and Son. Since these three Persons possess one and the same Divine life, one and the same Divine ' nature, ' They are one and the same God. [1]

3. HOW DOES THE ONE GOD IN THREE PERSONS APPEAR TO US ? — The doctrinal development ought to contribute to the increase of a faith penetrated by charity. It is suitable, to point out the infinite goodness of the Blessed Trinity. Our pupils' small human experience will help them to recognize the *love, beauty, happiness,* of the Blessed Trinity and also to realize how these perfections surpass all that we have experience of.

Love. — What makes a man give generously of his money, time, life ? Love. But what man gives himself as generously as the Father ? — Why do a son and daughter devote themselves to their sick or old parents ? Because they love them. God the Son has only one thing in mind : the good pleasure, the glory, of His Father. — What is it which unites friends, parents and children ? Again, love. The Holy Spirit is the fruit of the love of the Father Who gives Himself utterly to the Son, and of the Son Who gives Himself wholly to the Father. Truly, God is love.

Beauty. — Here again, we start from the pupils' knowledge. What moved us and what did we find to admire in the film ' Monsieur Vincent ? ' When we read the lives of Père Damien, Don Bosco, St. Francis Xavier ? When we think of all that our parents have done and do for us ? — Generosity, devotion, love. — But these human devotions are only very imperfect images of the love of the Divine Persons.

Happiness. — Among men, happiness comes from the intimate

---

the prayers at Mass by this formula : " We ask You this through Our Lord Jesus Christ, Your Son, Who lives and reigns with You, *in the unity of the Holy Spirit,* for ever and ever. "

[1] To elaborate this, the following might be made use of : Among men, each person has a distinctive nature. For example, Peter is a person, a being who thinks, wills and acts by himself ; he has his own nature ; he has a sickly body, a very bright mind, an energetic will ; in short, he has excellent but limited talents. James also has his own nature ; he is strong, very intelligent, but with a weak will. John has also his own nature. Among men, therefore, there are as many natures as persons. There is no doubt but that all have the same kind of nature, human nature ; they are not angels, nor animals, but they have not one and the same nature. In God, on the contrary, one and the same nature exists in Three Persons.

union of several persons who know and love each other. God is not solitary. He is three Persons Who love each other perfectly.

These last considerations make a good transition from the more intellectual study of the matter to the ' spiritual ' applications.

IV. APPLICATIONS TO THE LIFE
OF PRAYER AND ACTION

The lesson ends with prayer. Nothing forced and no constraint. We shall help our pupils to understand better the prayers which they say so frequently in honour of the Holy Trinity, or even to compose others with very simple phrases based on a firm and rich doctrine. We will write them on the blackboard as the thoughts and sentiments of the pupils, guided by their master, give rise to them. Three themes will be the points for crystallisation : *praise, union, imitation.*

I. ADMIRATION AND PRAISE. — After the above mentioned transition, it will not be hard to strengthen these dispositions in our young baptized. They must be helped to express them.

They will be asked to quote prayers in honour of the Blessed Trinity. They will suggest several, among which will be the *Gloria Patri.* Let us consider this as an example, this formula which is usually recited mechanically.

" *Glory be to the Father...* " What are we admiring in the Father ? — His infinite generosity. — Say to Him then : " Glory to You, Father, Who art so... ? " — " Generous. "

" *...to the Son...* " What do we admire in the Son ? — His gratitude and devotion. — Say to Him then : " Glory to You, Lord, Who art so... ? " — " Grateful, devoted. "

" *...and to the Holy Spirit.* " Who is the Holy Spirit ? What do we admire in Him ? — The love of the Father and the Son. — Say to Him then : " Glory to You, Holy Spirit, Who art... ? " — " The love (strong and discreet) of the Father and the Son. "

In this way our lesson will have put new life into a formula which, from time to time, can be explained in the following manner :

" *Glory be to You, Father, Who art so generous!*
Glory be to You, Lord, Who art so grateful!
Glory be to You, Holy Spirit, Who art the strong and discreet love of the Father and the Son! "

Or again, taking the *Pater*, [1] we can guide the pupils to say it as follows :

> *Father, may Your Name be glorified !*
> *Lord, may Your kingdom come !*
> *Holy Spirit, may Your love be spread over all the earth !*

The search for Trinitarian invocations in the *ordinary of the Mass* has been made the subject of team work after the lessons. Whether it takes place in class or outside, the study of the chief texts of the liturgy of the Mass is necessary. We shall thus help our children to unite themselves during the holy sacrifice to the Humanity of the Saviour Who offers Himself so generously to the Holy Trinity.

2. UNION. — Our Lord has not only revealed to us the intimate life of God. He has come to communicate it to us. The Holy Trinity has become our soul's guest when we have been baptized in " the name of the Father and the Son and the Holy Spirit. "

With what feelings do we return home after class or at the end of the week ? — Joy, happiness at finding ourselves among those who love us and whom we love especially. — Let us express to the Father, the Son and the Holy Spirit our joy at living with them.

What shall we say to the Father ? " Father, I am happy to be... ? " — " Your child. "

What shall we say to the Son ? " Lord, I am happy to be... ? " — " Your brother. " — Has He given us a proof of His love ? — " He died to save us. " — Say to Him then : " Lord, I am happy to be Your brother saved by Your blood. " [2]

What shall we say to the Holy Spirit ? " Holy Spirit, I am happy to be... " What did Our Lord call the Holy Spirit ? — The Spirit of truth. — Say to him then : " Holy Spirit, I am happy to be your disciple (or your confidant, your pupil). "

This intimacy with the Divine Persons — which began at baptism — should increase continually and reestablish itself quickly if it has been broken by grave sin. We use again the preceding prayer with slight changes :

> " *Father, make me become Your child more and more !*
> *Lord, make me become Your brother more and more !*
> *Holy Spirit, make me become Your disciple more and more !* "

---

[1] Some think that they see in each of the two parts of the *Pater* a ternary division which is not without a connection with the mystery of the Holy Trinity. Even if one does not agree with this view, our suggestion remains plausible.

[2] If we are addressing girls, the necessary changes are made : " Lord, I am happy to be Your sister, saved by Your blood. "

Or else, recalling the Gospel texts which tell us about the roles of the Father, Son and Holy Spirit, we will compose (with the active help of our pupils) a prayer like the following :

" Father, keep me closer to Your beloved Son.
Lord, give me to Your Father more and more.
Father, Lord, send me your Spirit.
Holy Spirit, lead me ever nearer to the Son and the Father. "

Our piety will never be narrowminded. The Father makes the sun shine on all men ; He is " our Father. " What shall we say to him then ? And prayer takes on a universal appeal :

" Father, make all men Your children!
Lord, make all men Your brothers, saved by Your blood!
Holy Spirit, set all men on fire with Your love! "

3. IMITATION. — The life of the Holy Trinity is the model and source of our Christian life. Now, the life of the Divine Persons is *love, peace* and *happiness*.

We try in a practical way with our pupils to imitate the Holy Trinity in the *family, school* and in all our *contacts*. This investigation will be completed by individual or team work.

But we will suggest to them that they should invoke the Holy Trinity in order to make progress in this imitation and guide them by a prayer, such as :

" Blessed Trinity, dwelling in me,
Help me to work with You
To make Your charity, peace and happiness rule. "

V. INDIVIDUAL OR TEAM WORK

It is a good thing if the course is followed by some work carried on in class or, by preference after school hours (for the horarium ought to suffice for the study of all the subject matter in the programme). The kind of work may vary with the subject. In the present case, the following is indicated :

Individual exercise book. — Each pupil should write a short commentary in his exercise book on the illustrations in the manual representing the baptism of Jesus, the miraculous draught of fishes (a manifestation of the Saviour's divinity), and Jesus stating that His disciples are His mother and His brethren. The contemplation of suggestive pictures is a way of getting to understand the mysteries. [1]

Each pupil has also been asked to answer in his own way the following question : " What will you do so that charity may have more sway in your family, form, team ? "

The team exercise book. — We want the instruction to help the pupils to take a more active and more conscious part in the celebration of the Holy Sacrifice. The ordinary of the Mass has been divided into nine parts : in the four teams (made up of nine members) each pupil analyzes one section and wiites down on a page (bearing his name) prayers addressed to the Holy Trinity. The pages are then inserted in the common exercise book of the team.

" It depends upon us whether God is near or far from us, " said St. Augustine. And Bossuet declares : " Let us form the Holy Trinity in ourselves, united to God, knowing God, loving God. " [2] This essay has had no other aim than to help our pupils to progress in this way.

---

[1] This idea has been developped in *Lumen Vitae*, II (1947), pp. 489-510. — See also André WANKENNE, S. J., *Art and Religious Education*, in *Lumen Vitae*, VII (1952), pp. 549-561.

2. Texts quoted by G. SALET, *op. cit.*, pp. 168-169.

Witness Sign

Today people want concrete evidence that Christ is alive.
This can best be communicated to them through an encounter
or dialogue with a person who is completely motivated by
the implications of the Christian message. The religion teacher
must be a living sign, permeated by and authenticating
the message he presents.

Bearing Witness, Fundamental Task of the Teacher of Religion

by Arnold INGEN-HOUSZ, S. J.

For a long time people failed to grasp the profound difference between the teaching of religion and the teaching of profane subjects. Now, however, there is a growing realisation that religious teaching does indeed belong to an entirely different order, the order of the supernatural. It is not simply a matter of instructing our pupils in a certain number of truths, some of which are beyond the natural powers of reason. This would certainly be an enrichment of the mind, since the mysteries of faith throw a special light on the most fundamental realities. But there is more to it than that. These supernatural truths concern an attitude to life ; they fix that attitude. ' Our first care, then, should be that the possessor of the truth is thoroughly affected by it, whether as individual or as member of society. ' [2]

Such a view of religious teaching will obviously have important consequences for the teacher. With pupils his position is not that of a man who ' knows his stuff ' and instructs the ignorant ; he is a believer in the company of other believers whose faith he is to enlighten. What he teaches is not completely alien to his pupils, for through Baptism and the inner working of the Holy Spirit they are supernaturally inclined towards this teaching. The teacher has

---

Born at Breda (Netherland), in 1914, Father Arnold INGEN-HOUSZ entered the Society of Jesus in 1934. After 10 years of study and mission work in Java (1936-1946) Father INGEN-HOUSZ came back to Holland. While studying theology, he contributed to the catechetical review *Verbum*. Father INGEN-HOUSZ is now teacher of religion at the Preparatory Seminary in Djakarta. — Address : St. Peter Canisius Preparatory Seminary, Djalan Tjodé, Djakarta, JAVA, INDONESIA (Editor's note).

[2] Léon DE CONINCK, S. J., *Kerygmatic Theology, Lumen Vitae*, III (1948), p. 107.

to meet the requirements of this supernatural propensity so that the pupils' faith become more precise and stable. The teacher must, therefore, be a witness. But what does this mean ?

I. BEARING WITNESS

The term requires some understanding, for it originally had its most common meaning as is found in Scripture ; then it assumed a wider sense especially in the era of persecutions when the Christian martyrs bore witness with their lives. [3]

1. *Witness in Scripture.*

First, let us consider Scripture. When Christ said to his disciples at the Ascension : " You will be witnesses of me " (*Acts* I, 22), He was not thinking only of the testimony of ocular witnesses in the juridical sense. The same is to be said of Peter in his speech when a successor to Judas was to be chosen, and again in his first sermon at Pentecost (*Acts* I, 22 ; II, 32). " The apostles understood quite well that the Master was not simply saying that they had seen and heard and that therefore they could give testimony. He was giving them a mission and they considered themselves charged with a mandate. " [4]

Their witness is a mission received from the Divine Master who will continue in and through them the mission He himself received from the Father.

Now Christ was sent by the Father to give the Good News, to preach the joyful message of the Kingdom of God (*Luke* IV, 43). To carry out this mission and thus give testimony of the Father was His food (*John*. IV, 43); it was the way in which He glorified the Father (*John*. XVII, 4-8). His teaching is none other than what His Father wished Him to declare to men : " For I have not spoken of myself, but my Father who sent me, He gave commandment what I should say and what I should speak. The things therefore that I speak, even as the Father said unto me, so do I speak " (*John*. XII, 49, 50). The witness of Christ consisted in making men share in the truth which He contemplated in the bosom of the Father.

This is the testimony which was to be continued by the disciples: as Jesus delivers to them what he has seen and heard of the

---

[3] Hippolyte DELEHAYE, S. J., *Sanctus*, p. 74 ss.
[4] H. DELEHAYE, S. J., *loc. cit.*, p. 76-77.

Father, they in their turn are to make known what they have seen and heard of Jesus. " As thou hast sent me into the world, I also have sent them into the world " (*John.* XVII, 18). And after the resurrection, He says to the apostles : " As my Father has sent me, so send I you" (*John.* XX, 21). And to give a divine guarantee to their testimony, He invests them with his own authority : " He that heareth you, heareth me " (*Luke* X, 16).

Such is the origin of the apostles' preaching and of the transmission of the Gospel truth that has gone on in the Church throughout the centuries. When the teacher of religion gives his lesson today, he is one with this long tradition and he is only retelling what Christ told his apostles and what he had received from the Father. By his teaching he bears witness : an external testimony drawing out and developing faith, and harmonizing with the interior working of the Holy Spirit in the souls of the pupils ; and interior testimony preparing the soul to receive the lesson, understand it, and be convinced of it.

2. *Witness of teachers.*

But the witness borne by the teacher must go further than the mere transmission of the word. This brings us to the wider meaning of the term. The truth brought by Christ is a life, or, to use the more profound expression of St. John, " in Him was life and the life was the light of men " (I, 4). The Word is life, and because life, the Word is light. The power of Jesus' preaching comes less from His words than from His person and conduct. Christ reveals Himself and calls men to the faith by showing them what He is and what He does. And the witness He bears to the Father draws its strength from the giving of Himself entirely, the supreme sacrifice of His life.

Since Christ transmitted the truth by a life-witness, His disciples must communicate it in a like manner. They propagate it by their utter devotion to the Master, a devotion which dominates their whole life and, if need be, accepts martyrdom. It is this complete testimony which is decisive. Do we not often read in accounts of conversions that the laxity of Catholics has been the greatest obstacle to unbelievers ? It is commonplace to say that the Catholic faith is generally judged by the behaviour of those who profess to live by it. This habit is also that of the pupils with regard to their teacher of religion. Without being explicitly aware of the fact, they expect from him more than just a lesson, but the witness of his conviction and way of life. And since he is commissioned to continue the work of Christ and his apostles the teacher is bound to give this witness. With him, also, truth must spring spontaneously from life ; before being a man of learning, he must be a man of faith. He has to give his pupils what is deep down in his heart, what governs his own thoughts and feelings. He has the fearsome yet fundamental task of teaching religion by what he is, even more than by what he says.

II. COOPERATING WITH GRACE

From the nature of religious teaching we conclude that the teacher must be a witness. We are also led to the conclusion that he must cooperate with grace. If we consider this point we shall better understand the significance of his testimony.

The aim of religious teaching is to bring the believer to the possession of a more lively and enlightened faith. Its object is God-made-man, whom we reach through faith. Those being taught are believers in whom grace is at work. Such teaching can, then, succeed only if it is a collaboration with grace and the teacher appeals to that grace of faith. This is essential. The teacher does not appeal ultimately to reason, because faith is not the conclusion of a syllogism ; nor does he appeal to his own authority as a teacher, since such authority is not enough to justify the assent of faith. The sole authority to which he may refer is that of Christ who came to reveal God and who guarantees that revelation. Now, by basing himself on the authority of Christ, the teacher collaborates with the " interior testimony " of the Holy Spirit, who seeks to unite souls to the Person of Jesus and make him the foundation of their thinking and their living. By the grace of Baptism the Holy Spirit is operating invisibly in souls. " He giveth testimony to our spirit that we are the sons of God " (*Rom*. VIII, 16) and " Himself asketh for us with unspeakable groanings " (*Rom*. VIII, 26). Through this Spirit the Father exercises His power of attraction, without which no one can come to Jesus (*John*. VI, 44). There is, therefore, in the human soul a predisposition for religious instruction eagerly receptive of any true preaching of Christ.

As witness of Christ, then, the teacher of religion finds a response in the minds of his pupils. It is not he who is to speak but God through him, according to Paul's words : " Therefore we also give thanks to God without ceasing, because that when you had received of us the word of the hearing of God, you received it not as the word of men, but (as it is indeed) the word of God, who worketh in you that have believed " (*I Thess*. II, 13). The teacher is the

94

witness to the word of God, to the Gospel which is the " power of God for the salvation of all who believe " (*Rom.* I, 16).

" In the Christian religion it is through the Word of God that life is transmitted. But this word does not primarily express abstract ideas and theses but rather the mystery of a Being who is the eternal Word made flesh, who has given Himself by expressing Himself, and who has made fidelity to *His* words the means of making present the Word which saves. It is thus that the Gospel preaching can be a divine power saving those who believe. Consequently, the apostle is the man who is to make God present and active through his words, and to that end, he is to incarnate in his words that life of God which animates him." [5]

It is this divine power of the Word which makes the teacher of religion a witness. His chief task is to be penetrated himself with this power and let himself be guided by it. Natural abilities, such as eloquence, gift of clear exposition, power to convince others, are no doubt very useful, but they are only of secondary importance ; only the capacity of bearing witness is decisive. St. Paul himself experienced this when all his gifts of eloquence and adaptability did not save him from meeting with failure, whereas a little later the simple preaching of Christ crucified produced wonderful results.

" When Paul first came to Corinth " writes M. Grossouw, [6] " he had quite recently suffered a setback at Athens which had somewhat discouraged him, but it taught him a lesson. At Areopagus where used to assemble the intellectual élite of a town which had still retained, or claimed to retain, the ancient patrimony of its glory, he had tried human wisdom and tactics. He had begun his speech with a few stoic sayings about the one God. He even adopted a literary style and quoted poetry. By this method he hoped to prepare the way for his real message : Christ who had died and risen again for sinners, Greek sinners in particular. But at the first really Christian word he uttered, interest disappeared. His listeners were not going to be caught. Some politely said they would listen another time. Others burst out laughing : the idea of a resurrection was simply absurd (*Acts* XVII, 22-34).

Paul never tried that method again. When he reached Corinth, where snobbishness and immorality rubbed shoulders, he acted differently : ' And I, brethren, when I came to you, came not in loftiness of speech or of wisdom declaring unto you the testimony of Christ. For I judged not myself to know anything among you, but Jesus Christ, and Him crucified. And I was with you in weakness and in fear and in much trembling. And my speech and my preaching was not in the persuasive words of human wisdom, but in showing of the spirit and power ; that your faith might not stand on the wisdom of

---

[5] Jean MOUROUX, *Sens chrétien de l'homme*, Paris, Aubier, 1943, p. 50.
[6] In *Christus*, pp. 27-8.

men, but on the power of God' (*I Cor.* II, 1-5). By spirit and power he does not mean his strength of will or firmness of character, but a supernatural efficaciousness due to the purity of his message of the cross and to the working of the Spirit of God in the hearts of his hearers. "

Now if this was Paul's experience in his preaching to the pagans, ought not we in our teaching of Christians to abstain from relying mainly on natural means? To be true witnesses of Christ we ought, even more than our listeners, be anchored in faith and convinced that there is in the Gospel itself a " divine strength to salvation " and that the word of God " shows forth its power " upon those who believe.

But this does not mean that we need just quote Scripture or refer to the words of Christ. Our teaching must be steeped in the facts of Revelation in such a manner that they convey their full meaning to the intelligence of our pupils and make vivid in their minds the life and teaching of Christ. For this purpose the teacher must have assimilated the doctrine of Revelation ; his faith must be manifested in his life. When the pupils see this transparent faith, they are unconsciously led to adopt the fervour of believers themselves, and they will welcome within themselves the Christ who is put before them.

The Curé of Ars is an example to be remembered. Although he had difficulty in getting through his theological studies, his catechism classes had remarkable results. It was precisely his sanctity which acted and spoke. Someone has said that he preached with his whole being and that his mere presence was a presentation of the truth. And when he spoke of Christ or Our Lady his listeners were under the impression that he was looking at what he was talking about.

CONCLUSION

How may we describe the fundamental attitude of the teacher of religion ? First, he must be convinced that his task is primarily divine, not human, that he is an instrument of grace, and that in the Gospel given to his pupils, the power of God is at work to enlighten and convince them. The teaching of religion can be looked on as a charisma, that is to say as a particular manifestation of divine power for the good of others, " the showing forth of spirit and power. " Therefore, the teacher must rely above all on this gift of God for the success of his work. Knowing that God speaks through him, he will trust, not in his own ability as a pedagogue, but in the all-powerful action of grace.

To be a perfect instrument of grace, the teacher must be penetrated with the truths of faith and live them fully. He must be the witness of Christ in the wider sense of the word, so that his whole person is a living commentary of the Gospel. The quality of his teaching will depend on his sincerity, that is, it will be in the measure of his personal holiness.

Since he is speaking in the name of God and bearing witness to Christ, the teacher must appeal to their authority and not give the impression that he is speaking by his authority (it is so because I'm telling you). He must be constantly referring to the words of Christ and make his audience feel that God is the final witness and the supreme guarantor of the truths of religion and that he himself is merely the channel of Revelation.

Besides this, he must rely on the working of grace in the souls of his pupils. The minds he is addressing are energized by the Holy Ghost. The teacher owes his pupils a great respect ; but he can also aim high with them, because their minds have been specially prepared to receive his teaching and because the truths of the faith, although profound, answer to a hidden call within them.

There is one criterion by which to judge whether a catechism class has been given in a supernatural spirit : does it lead to prayer ? Is there, at the end of it, a spontaneous desire to pray ? To pray, that is, to thank God for what has been learnt, and to ask Him for grace to be more fully convinced and to shape one's life more in conformity with it. If teacher and pupils join together in such prayer, is it not a sign that God has spoken by his voice ?

Of course, we are not suggesting that efforts to adapt the teaching to the age, milieu and intelligence of the hearers should be despised, nor that in explaining the Gospel one should take no notice of all those comparisons, analogies and stories which serve as illustrations. This adaptation is necessary, and its importance cannot be overstressed. Nevertheless, it is of secondary importance. The substance of the lesson comes before its adaptation. The chief thing is that the pupils should really receive the word of God. The master must ask himself whether his main preoccupation is to transmit this word and so make better Christians of his pupils, and whether in order to achieve this, he lives by faith and as a witness to Christ. This basic requirement shows the nobility of his task.

2

Man
Meets
God

Faith: Communion with God

Faith is man's response to God's message of love and
invitation. Faith has a triple dimension: (1) confidence in God
as living Father and source of all truth, (2) an intellectual
assent to God's message, and (3) a complete gift of
self to God. God is thus the witness, object, and finality
of man's response of faith. The religion teacher must
be careful to show that the response of faith is directed
primarily to a personal God, not to things or concepts.
Faith is communion with God in Jesus Christ.

The Aim of Religious Formation :
Faith as the Assent of the Mind
and Commitment of the Whole Person

by Prof. Dr. Franz X. ARNOLD

If it is true, as taught by St. Thomas Aquinas, that in the practical sphere the *aim* is the decisive factor, then practical theology in general and religious formation in particular are governed by the law of finality. It is not superfluous to insist on this point. Is not the present pedagogical situation characterized by a deep mistrust of any ideal of formation, any educational aim ? The failure in the 20th century of the pedagogical idealism of the 19th century, a too optimistic autonomous idealism inspired by Rousseau, led to a general distrust of idealism and, under pretext of realism, to the relinquishing of any specific aim in education which could not be adapted to ever-changing concrete pedagogical requirements. [2] To

---

1. Professor ARNOLD was born on the 10th September 1898 at Aichelau (Wurtemberg). He studied theology, classical philology and social science at Tübingen. Ordained priest in 1924, he exercised the priestly ministry from 1924 to 1928. Since 1928 he has held various positions in the University of Tubingen (" Repetent, " " Dozent, " " Professor, " " Rektor "). He is at present professor of the pastorate and dean of the Faculty of Theology. Prof. ARNOLD has published important articles in the *Encyclopédie catholique pour la Chine*, in various periodicals, especially in *Die Theologische Quartalschrift*, which he has edited since 1939. His principal works are : *Dienst am Glauben* (1948), *Grundsätzliches und Geschichtliches zur Theologie der Seelsorge* (Points of doctrine and history of pastoral theology) (1949), *Seelsorge aus der Mitte der Heilsgeschichte* (1956), now printed in the ' Lumen Vitae ' editions : *Proclamation da la Foi et Communauté de Foi.* — Address : 20, Aus dem Vieweidle, Tübingen (Germany) (Editor's note).

2. See Wilhelm FLITNER, *Allgemeine Pädagogik* [3] (1950), pp. 128-133. Also, *Erziehungswissenschaft und kirchliche Pädagogik :* Sammlung 6 (1951), pp. 631-645, esp. 643. — E. WENIGER, *Die Pädagogik in ihrem Selbstverständnis heute :* Sammlung 5 (1950), pp. 740-752, esp. 747 ; 6 (1951), 8-19, esp. 11-15. K. FRÖR, *Erziehung und Kerygma* (1952), p. 63.

relinquish an *essential* pedagogy in favour of a *situation* pedagogy proved all the more dangerous when it extended to *Christian* education. [1]

We are not merely referring to *theoretical* considerations of isolated pedagogues but to ideas which have already to a large extent invaded *pedagogical practice*. For example, is not a ministerial scheme " for the reform of secondary education " in one of the German States in 1955 the outcome of a coherent conception of man in our Western world. And even if this idea existed, faith is wanting " for the education of children according to a definite conception. " It is assumed that education acts only as a " powerful aid in the present concrete circumstances of the child. " The goal of education is thus abandoned. It is the conviction of all Catholics interested in pedagogy that education is impossible without an *aim* and that the work of formation and religious education in particular must tend towards a definite goal. In spite of this, or just because of it, the organizers of this meeting on ' Catechesis in Our Time ' have rightly placed at the outset theological reflections and an examination of conscience on " the aim of religious formation. " My subject is already a reply to this question and is as follows :

I. " FAITH IS THE AIM. THE MINISTRY OF FAITH IS THE FUNCTION OF RELIGIOUS FORMATION. "

It is not without reason that we give ' *faith* ' as the aim of religious formation. It was already the attitude of Johann Baptist Hirscher when he began in 1820 in the periodical " Tübinger Theologischer Quartalschrift " the literary work of his life : " The duty of the pastor of souls is to preach faith. " We are also in open opposition to the exclusively intellectual and moralizing theology which has been grafted on to religious pedagogy since 1800. The 18th century's conception of religious formation is well expressed in such terms as " the *teaching* of religion " and " *teacher* of religion. " These terms evolve, not from revelation, but from the deistic religious philosophy [2] under the influence of which religious instruction

---

1. W. KOEPP, *Die Erziehung unter dem Evangelium* (1952), esp. p. 197-199. W. UHSADEL, *Evangelische Erziehungs-und Unterrichtslehre* (1954), pp. 37-47. Eugen WALTER, *Das Ende der Ideale : Katechetische Blätter*, 76 (1951), pp. 353-362 ; 408-411.

2. F. X. ARNOLD : *Grundsätzliches und Geschichtliches zur Theologie der Seelsorge* (Freiburg 1949), pp. 88-97, esp. 94.

was no longer regarded as the kerygmatic ministry of the Church towards the action of the *Faith*, which takes place between God revealing Himself by His word and the catechumen called to the obedience of faith.

Religious instruction was purely a matter between men : an affair of master and pupil. ' Religion ' was a ' school subject, ' a matter of ' teaching. '

This brought repercussions on the *contents* of religious instruction. Minds convinced of reason's almightiness tended towards a rationalistic religion above confessional oppositions and having a universal value, " religion within the limits of reason alone " as Kant said in 1793. The result was that religious pedagogy in the 18th century no longer sought in the contents of religious instruction the specifically Christian element but the truths common to all religions and identifiable by reason. The mysteries of Christianity became " theoretical truths ; " the Incarnation, Passion and Triumph of Christ were no longer represented in the catechism for their theological content as revealed in the history of salvation, but as inspiration for the mind and models for a higher morality. It is not surprising that the catechist lost his role of herald of the Divine message and became a " teacher of religion " and the catechumen his ' pupil. ' The success of catechetical instruction was expected to result from the *method* instead of from the living contents of the message. It was perhaps the intention, in virtue of the absolute trust of the 18th century in the almightiness of reason, to lead the pupil by the Socratic method to discover everything by his own powers, or else to inculcate the necessary religious knowledge by means of books ; in either case, the didactic goal was religious *knowledge* and moral education. This was the result of rationalist determinism, the intellectual concept of formation and the moral attitude of the period. [1]

This intellectual and moralizing ideal is not confined to the past. True, a powerful reaction against the 18th century impoverishment of the Christian message was set on foot by men such as Sailer, Hirscher, Möhler, Scheeben, Casel, etc., and it is also true that the liturgical movement and the kerygmatic revival have re-introduced a theological way of thinking into the life of the Church and catechesis. Yet it must be observed that, talking generally, catechetical instruction fails to reveal the essence of Christianity and to distinguish it clearly from natural religion. [2] Consciously or unconsciously,

---

1. *Ibid.*, esp. p. 94.

2. F. X. ARNOLD, *Glaubensverkündigung und Glaubensgemeinschaft* (Düsseldorf 1955), pp. 10-13.

and more than is necessary, the *aim* of religious formation remains the transmission of religious knowledge and moral teaching.

This, however, is not the true aim of religious instruction. Obviously sound knowledge is necessary. But the real objective and the specifically Christian aim of religious teaching is not knowledge, nor the cognizance of the things of faith in itself and for itself, but faith as the way of salvation, a supernatural and preeminently active reality, as the foundation of all justification. What St. Paul wrote to Titus is applicable to the catechist of all times : " God's servant, sent out as an apostle of Jesus Christ, with the faith of God's elect for his care ; they were to acknowledge that truth which accords with holiness, and fix their hopes on eternal life. It had been promised to us long ages since by the God who cannot fail us ; and now, in due time he has made his meaning clear to us through the preaching with which God, our Saviour, has seen fit to entrust me. " [1] In other words, the catechist does not simply seek or desire the attention of his audience as a spiritual lecturer, or their comprehension as a professor, their approval as a leader , nor even their respectful submission. He seeks and demands nothing less than faith, this ὑπακούειν of the whole man, this welcome, this eagerness, abandon and surrender, which is not the answer to *his* message in itself but to the divine mandate and its contents. If the catechist called for anything else but faith, if he sought or expected anything less, he would no longer be a Christian catechist. He is not intended merely to instruct, teach, convince, move. He, like St. Paul, is " committed by Christ to the ministry of *faith* among the elect of God. "

II. POSSIBILITIES AND LIMITS OF THE CATECHETICAL MINISTRY OF FAITH (PREACHING THE FAITH AND ACT OF FAITH)

This ministry implies the knowledge of the connection between preaching the Faith and the act of faith, a clear view of the true role of preaching in the dawn of faith, a clear appreciation above all of the limits assigned to catechetical action on the part of God as much as on that of man. Are we not tempted to assume that our teaching itself effectively creates faith and therefore also union with God ? This would mean an over-valuation and misunderstand-

---

1. *Titus*, I, 1-3.

ing of our function as catechists. Indeed, faith comes from hearing and hearing from preaching. [1] But the ultimate ground of faith can be nothing created, not even the Church's preaching. The Christian believes in the Church, not for herself, but because of God Who is revealed in Christ. Faith is primarily an action of God, a supernatural gift from Him. Mysterium stricte dictum. No one, says the Vatican Council, can assent to the preaching of the Gospel, as he must to obtain salvation, without the light of the Holy Spirit. [2] Faith itself, even when it does not become active in charity, is a *gift of God*. [3] And yet — again to quote the Vatican Council — the assent to faith is not " a blind act of the mind. " Faith does not exclude the secondary role of the human reason, but includes it. In it are not only divine but also human elements : the moral act of hearing and obeying, the adhesion to truth and the voluntary act of choice, psychologically very human and possible, according to St. Thomas, by the ' operatio ' of knowledge and love, by which man, moved by grace, utters the ' yes ' of faith. Faith therefore is a gratuitous divine intervention and a free human decision ; it is a matter between God and man.

The catechist must take into account this *fundamental connection* and subordinate his action to it. He must not leave aside or underestimate in his preaching the fact of this encounter of man with God. On the contrary, he must consider the two realities between which occurs the event of faith : the revelation of God and the free assent of the catechumen. What then is the catechist's role ? He is an instrument : a service, a ministry, the " diakonia of the word. " He proclaims the word of God. He calls men to decision. He seeks to provoke the encounter between the student and God, to be the mediator. He is between the two. The catechist is not God's substitute but the ' intermediary ' between God and man ; and together the divine and the human action culminate in the highest fruit of the spirit : faith. The catechist must be convinced that the encounter of God and man is the essential thing, that his role is secondary, instrumental, an indispensable but very modest *service*, leading to the final event between God and man : *faith*. If he had higher pretensions, the catechist would affront the majesty of God and man's personal dignity.

---

1. *Romans*, X.
2. Denzinger 1791.
3. *Gal.*, V, 6.

III. NATURAL PREPARATION :

THE ' PREAMBULA FIDEI ' AND THE GOAL OF RELIGIOUS PEDAGOGY

Faith is a supernatural gift of God but also an assent and a personal decision of man. It commits the *whole man*. Hence the need to approach the *whole* man. To serve the Faith is to serve man. The stronger our conviction of the gratuitous nature of faith and the supernatural end of all religious formation, the stronger will be our belief in the *natural preparation of faith*. This preparation is not entirely ensured by the *direct* presentation of the positive message. During the crisis of adolescence, supernatural motives often recede to the background. The soil must therefore be prepared from the bottom upward : receptivity must be encouraged, this capacity for reception by reason, will and heart which we call " potentia obedientialis. " The religious fate of a man, even baptized, largely depends on whether this readiness to receive the call and the word of God grows or diminishes with his spiritual growth.

There are natural conditions, ' forerunners ' of faith, called in theology " preambula of faith. " They are partly *rational*. There exists a knowledge of the existence of God and a possibility of revelation *before* faith : a natural knowledge of God, the fides humana. Man may know by reason that it is not *unreasonable* to believe. Here religious pedagogy must assume the task of fundamental theology. It may be found even more important today to ensure the affective and moral forerunners of faith, for the spiritual life seems to centre more on the *will* and the *heart* than on the understanding. In our times the attitude of will and heart is perhaps a *more frequent* obstacle to faith than intellectual difficulties. He who has not the *will* does not obtain faith. Just as decisive is the connection between purity of faith and purity of conscience. There are *moral conditions* indispensable to faith : a will to listen with respect, a humble and grateful acknowledgment of a personal need of redemption, an unselfish acceptance of sacrifice. On the other hand, laziness and unsteadiness, pride and a wordly spirit, passions and immorality are obstacles to the obedience of faith. The wreck of a conscience, said Sailer, very often brings about the wreck of *faith*. Therefore a zeal for purity of faith without a zeal for purity of conscience is a half zeal often more harmful, for its followers do not act, its adepts do not obey, it is a faith without love : the *foundation* is forgotten in the desire to see the *crowning* of the edifice. [1] This is a moral lesson for religious formation.

To attend to rational, affective and moral attitudes is to prepare the understanding, the will and the heart for the message, to obviate certain obstacles, to bring into play the propensity of the mind and the will in favour of faith.

Let us not, however, lose sight of the fact that our action does not *procure* faith but only prepares the way for grace and for assent, the two factors of faith.

IV. FAITH, INTELLECTUAL ASSENT : THE FAITH WHICH ACKNOWLEDGES TRUTH

This acknowledgment implies an assent of the *mind*, but also a commitment of the *whole man*. Faith is the " sacrificium intellectus ' expressed in the classical phrase " Credo ut intelligam " (I believe in order to understand) and " fides quaerens intellectum " (faith seeking to understand) ; in these formulae, Anselm of Canterbury encloses the unity of experience of faith and nature. In each, it is a matter of understanding, of intelligence. Faith — according to the definition in our catechisms — is " to hold as true " certain events, truths and doctrines. In this sense St. Paul writes, " We believe that Jesus Christ underwent death and rose again " [2] " that God has raised up Jesus from the dead. " [3] The apostle speaks in many places of a ' knowledge ' of the truths of the Faith : Epistle to the Romans : " We know that Christ, now that he has risen from the dead, cannot die any more ; death has no more power over him. " [4] Second Epistle to the Corinthians : " Knowing that he who raised Jesus from the dead will raise us too. " [5] There is no denying that these truths surpass human reason. But, in spite of their transcendence, they contain " a hidden idea which can be grasped by our reason enlightened by faith and comprehensible even although partially and imperfectly. " [6] Our faith is determined by historical events : facts of revelation and the history of salvation. There is no mystery of the Christian religion which is

---

1. J. M. Sailer, *Vorlesungen aus der Pastoraltheologie*, 4, (1820), II, p. 387 et seq.

2. *I Thess.*, IV, 14.

3. *Rom.*, X, 9.

4. *Rom.*, VI, 9.

5. *II Cor.*, IV, 13.

6. Gottlieb Sohngen, *Die Einheit in der Theologie*, p. 297.

not historical. Creation and Revelation, the Fall and Redemption, the Incarnation and the Parousia, are all historical. This is very important for catechesis. The catechist does not transpose historical realities of Christianity into ideas and doctrines ; he communicates to his hearers, not an abstract Christianity, but a living, acting, historical Christianity ; [1] the truths and mysteries of which he speaks are connected with events of the past. These facts in the history of salvation and the mysteries which they express demand the catechist's intelligent assent. By its very nature and aim, catechesis is bound to impart a ' knowledge ' of these truths as positive and complete as possible. The *fides historica* of theology is also of capital importance in catechesis ; as faith which " holds as true, " it cannot be eliminated from the final goal of all religious formation.

Yet religious formation cannot rest *satisfied* with it. Nothing is achieved by a *purely* historical faith, a mere adherence of the mind to historical facts. Revelation is not so much objective statements as a personal call ; it seeks the acknowledgment and the profession of truth : the witnessing of the New Testament, the ' Confessio ' of St. Augustine or the profession of faith of Bellarmine, which throw man on to his knees in adoration ; hence the introduction of the Creed in the service and liturgy of the Church. It means also that the truths of faith are not only — in the Aristotelian sense — the object of the act by which we " hold them as true, " but that the believer is seized — in the New Testament sense — by the *reality* contained in the truth and takes an effective share in it. [2] The New Testament also speaks of ' welcoming the Word of God ' as a paraphrase of faith. According to the general doctrine of the New Testament, human action is reduced to the acceptance of God's gifts, and man of himself has no possibility of going to God, but on hearing the message, man is free to choose for or against. [3] The natural man, says St. Paul, does not perceive what comes from the Spirit of God, it is indeed, foolishness to him. " [4] There only where God speaks and gives understanding by the Spirit [5] does the choice fall to man ; the divine summons of the Gospel gives man the alternative of decision. [6]

1. F. X. ARNOLD, *Katechese aus der Mitte der Heilsgeschichte* : Katechetische Blätter, 1956, pp. 227-235, esp. 232.

2. Goottlieb SOHNGEN, *Die Einheit in der Theologie*, p. 343.

3. *Ag.*, VIII, 14 ; XI, 1 ; XVII, 11 ; cf. *James*, I, 21 ; *I Thess.*, I, 6 ; II, 13 ; *II Cor.* III and VI, 1 ; *II Thess.*, II, 10.

4. *I Cor.*, II, 14.

5. *I Thess.*, I, 6 ; II, 13.

6. KITTEL, *Wörterbuch zum N.T.*, vol. II, p. 53 ; GRUNDMANN, sub voce δέχομαι.

V. FAITH AS A PERSONAL DECISION
AND THE COMMITMENT OF THE WHOLE MAN

This choice is more than an assent of the mind, more than " holding as true " certain events, facts and doctrines. A catechesis more or less reduced to the *contents* of faith would lose sight of a fundamental element, beyond the material objective of faith, an even more decisive element from a religious point of view : faith as an *act*, as a personal *choice*, is for the man whom God's word has reached the most powerful supernatural reality, binding him to Christ, Who is redemption personified. Does not the religious situation of our times demand that catechesis and preaching before and together with the faith, veritas quae creditur (faith : a truth which we believe), not only suppose as known the fides *qua* creditur (the act of faith by which we believe), but insist on its whole value ? It is this faith which catechesis needs if it is to restore the Christian view of Life to modern man, under the sway of scepticism, nihilism and despair.

Undoubtedly the intellectual element of faith expressed in the words " to hold as true " is an essential element in the faith-trust and in the trust of faith, of which we are about to speak. Here an important question arises : Is it possible to " hold everything as true " and yet have no faith, in the biblical sense of the term (πιστεύειν) ? To believe we need, besides the essential " holding as true, " the *personal* element and the *fact of trust*, in the biblical sense of πίστις and ἐλπίς : a faith free from all fear, because it has been said, " Why are you faint-hearted ? Have you still no faith ? "[1] This faith is attentive to the Saviour's exhortation : "Be not afraid : It is I. "[2] This faith is free of all anxiety ; for it has been said : " Men of little faith, why is this anxiety in your minds, that you have brought no bread with you ? "[3] and " How is a man the better for it, if he gains the whole world while losing his own soul ? "[4] Of this *living* faith St. Paul says : " It is faith that *brings life* to the just man. "[5] Referring to this saying, which was to become the leit-motiv of Martin Luther, St. Thomas taught in the Middle Ages that " Faith is the beginning and foundation of salvation " ; it is the " life of

---

1. *Mark*, IV, 40-41.
2. *Matthew*, IV, 23-26.
3. *Matthew*, XVI, 8.
4. *Matthew*, XVI, 26.
5. *Rom.*, I, 17.

the soul. " [1] " Faith in the Passion " — not the Passion itself —
" gives their efficacy to the sacraments. " [2] In the same spirit the
Council of Trent describes faith as " the foundation and root of
all justification. " And of this faith which justifies, the Council
says : " If to this faith are not added hope and charity, it does not
unite us perfectly to Christ nor render us living members of His
Body. " [3] It is a ' dead faith, ' which the Council distinguishes clearly from the ' living ' faith ; a ' formless faith ' (fides informes), of
which Peter Lombard, the author of this expression, says that
" the demons and false Christians have it also. " [4]

The Council of Trent intentionally dwells on this aspect of the
' *living* ' faith. Martin Luther and the German Reformation insisted
that something *else* happened in faith, that it was not only an intellectual acceptance by man of certain truths and certain events in
the history of salvation. The reformer had so little concern with the
" holding as true " that he thought it should be excluded from the
concept of faith. [5] His interest lay exclusively in an affective, personal and voluntary trust, fides in the sense of fiducia. Thus in his
" Kurze Form des Glaubens " [6] of 1520, he expresses himself in
these terms : " There are two ways of believing. The first consists
in believing of God, that is, believing as true what is said of God, as
I believe what is said of the Turks, of the devil, of hell. This faith
is more a science or a discovery than a faith. The other way is to
believe *in* God : not only do I believe as true what is said of God but
I place my *trust in Him*, I resolve to enter into relations with Him,
I believe without doubt that He will be, and will act with me, according to what is said of Him. I could never believe in this way
in a Turk or in any man, however good he might be. For even if I
am willing to believe that a man is pious, I would not for that reason
confide in him. Only a faith which *trusts* absolutely in God, in life
and unto death, makes the Christian and obtains all from God.
This faith no evil nor tortuous soul can obtain, for it is a *living*
faith. This little word ' in ' (believe in God) is so true. Observe that
we do not say : ' I believe God the Father, ' or *of* God the Father,
but *in* God the Father, in Jesus Christ, and *this* faith is due to God
only. " The " Confession of Augsburg " is in the same strain :

1. St. THOMAS, II II, 9, 12, ad 1. ; q. 16, a. 1, ad 1.
2. St. THOMAS, III, q. 62, a. 1, ad 2 and *Sent.* IV, d. 1, a. 4, sol. 3, ad 3.
3. DENZINGER, no. 800.
4. *Sent.* III, dist. 23, 4 ; *P. L.*, 192, 805.
5. Erich SEEBERG, *Luthers Theologie in ihren Grundzügen*, Stuttgart, 1940,
p. 129.
6. Eine Kurze Form des Glaubens, 1520 : O. CLEMEN, *Luthers Werk in Auswahl*,
Berlin, 1933, II, p. 47 et seq.

" The faith to be taught is not that which the demons or the godless also possess, who also believe that Christ has suffered and has risen from the dead, but the true Faith, which believes that through Christ we obtain grace and forgiveness of sins. " [1]

Fortunately these extreme opinions formulated in the heat of controversy are offset by more balanced Protestant statements. The apology of the Confession proves it. It also upholds the Protestant conceptions against " opponents for whom faith consists in knowing or having heard the historical narratives concerning Christ, " " but who say nothing of the true Christian faith which Paul always mentions and by which we become good in God's sight. In the Apology this faith is ' not *merely* the knowledge of the historical birth of Christ, His death, etc., the demons also know that — but the conviction and unshakeable trust of the heart : I, with all my soul, I hold as certain and true, the words of God by which, with no merit on my part, I obtain forgiveness of sin, grace and all salvation through Christ the Mediator. And in order that no one may imagine that this is *merely* an historical knowledge, *I add* : Faith consists in that my whole heart receives this treasure in itself... in that a heart can trust in it and surrender to it. " [2]

A modern Catholic theologian justly remarks, with regard to this passage : " Neither the Protestant nor the Catholic doctrine has any interest in playing the card of faith ' holding as true ' against that of faith-trust, or vice versa, as if the one radically excluded the other. " There is " no difficulty in using the Catholic ' and ' and saying : Faith which holds as true and trusts. " [3] There is no doubt that one requires the other, and neither would be what it ought to be without the other.

Unfortunately, the Catholic ' and ' disappeared long ago, especially from catechism lessons on faith. As I said above, teaching on faith in the atmosphere of the Reformation and Counter Reformation, and owing to Bellarmine's attitude, had taken a direction which was perhaps suited to the period, but which from the point of view of catechesis did not give the Catholic dogma of faith its full value. St. Peter Canisius had described faith as " light of the soul, gate of life, foundation of the blessedness and grace of God, which helps man to apprehend God and His revelation firmly. " For Canisius the act of faith and faith as the way of salvation are

1. *Die Bekenntnisschriften der Evangelisch-Lutherischen Kirche* [2], Göttingen, 1952, pp. 79, 23.

2. *Ibid.*, p. 169, 48.

3. P. Dr. Thomas SARTORY, O. S. B., *Was verstehen wir katholischen Christen unter Glauben?* Una Sancta, 10. Jahrg. 1955, pp. 2-17, esp. 5 and 1.

in the foreground ; on the other hand the great controversialist, Bellarmine, is content to bring in evidence the " professio fidei " to give the contents of faith and to defend the old Faith against the new.

Since then, catechism lessons have dwelt too much on the intellectual element ; they define faith as " holding as true, " which it certainly is, but not exclusively, nor primarily. It was, and still is, a great pity that catechism and catechesis, during these centuries of an intense crisis in beliefs, should prefer to suppose, rather than to bring out in strong relief, the irreplaceable importance of the option of a personal and confident faith.

The time has come to remedy this impoverishment and unilateral aspect of catechetical teaching. For however important and indispensable may be the science of the content of faith and the science of " fides quae creditur " for the faith of trust and faith flowering in charity, the supreme *objective* of all religious formation remains indubitably this faith which *dares* in God, which puts all its hope in God ; this faith which moves mountains and accomplishes miracles of charity, [1] this audacious faith which knows no nihilism but remains firm in the midst of dangers because it has been said : " Fear not, I have overcome the world. And behold the victory which has overcome the world : our Faith. " [2] This bold faith, which no earthly perplexity can defeat, because it knows that God is sufficient in all things and all difficulties, that " nothing is impossible to Him, " that His unequalled majesty shines more brightly when man and the world are at the end of resources and reason ; this faith, which " hopes against hope, " [3] because it knows that every disaster brings in its train man's submission to the Invisible and therefore a new beginning, a new possibility of liberty, vitality and strength ; this faith, entirely fixed on the future of God, stronger than all the threats of the world, than all armies and all kingdoms ; [3] this faith, founded on Christ crucified, a scandal to the Jews, to the Gentiles foolishness, but for us, the elect, the strength and wisdom of God ; [4] is the Way of salvation, the most powerful supernatural reality, the luminous goal of all religious formation. May I say in conclusion that the ministry of this Faith is the most urgent duty of all pastorates and catechesis in our troubled times. [5]

---

1. *Matt.*, XI, 23 ; *Luke*, XVII, 6 ; *Matt.*, XXI, 21 ; *I Cor.*, XIII, 2.
2. *Rom.*, IV, 18.
3. *Hebr.*, XI, 33 et seq.
4. *I Cor.*, I, 23 et seq.
5. F. X. ARNOLD, *Dienst am Glauben*, Das Vordringlichste Anliegen heutiger Seelsorge, Freiburg, 1948.

Faith, Man's Communion with God

by François Taymans d'Eypernon, S. J.

When the Christian prays, he knows that he is entering into communion with God. Is he as conscious when he believes, that it is God Himself Whom he encounters and to Whom he surrenders himself ? Too often the act of faith seems to be an undertaking on the part of man alone, the result of reasoning and will.

The aim of these few pages is to show that faith is attached to the whole supernatural life, like the threshold is attached to the house, or, to speak in terms of living things, like the root to the tree, inaugurating that reciprocal presence of God to man and man to God in which all beatitude consists.

Faith is a communion with God, not only because it involves above all belief in God and because belief in God is, according to M. Blondel's formula, to accept that He should be for us what He is in Himself, but also because the light of God and the attraction of grace are to be found in man at the very origin of belief, and because the motive for the believers is, again, God, Who bears witness in man, according to the Apostle's word : " qui credit in Filium, habet testimonium Dei in se. "

It is therefore in all its elements that faith appears as communion with God : in the *object* which is to be believed, in the *subject* which believes, in the *motive* for which one believes. It is always an active presence of God which attracts, raises, supports man at the level of the Divine mystery.

---

[1] See the biographical notice in *Lumen Vitae*, VII (1952), p. 341. This article, which the author has newly introduced for our readers, is taken from a larger study which the *Nouvelle Revue Théologique* (February 1954) has published under the title of *Les énigmes de l'acte de foi*. We thank Fr. MATAGNE, editor of the *N. R. Th.*, for having kindly authorised the reproduction. — Address : 23, route de Mont-Saint-Jean, Louvain, BELGIUM (Editor's note).

I. THE OBJECT OF FAITH

The Christian sometimes complains that he finds in his *Credo* nothing but a mosaic of truths to be believed. In reality, everything is seen to be divinely unified in the outpouring of the *God of love* Who gives Himself to man by Revelation. *In fact all the dogmas, however much they contrast in appearance, are aspects of one truth.* This truth is God present in the world, to save and beatify mankind. All else which is divinely revealed in Holy Scripture, is only assented to by faith insofar as it refers to God and inasmuch as under divine action man is disposed to tend towards the enjoyment of God. There is therefore among the objects of faith a truth which to a certain degree contains all the others, which gives each of the revealed dogmas its final meaning and decisive significance ; a centre of convergence because it is the centre of diffusion and this truth is *God, our beatitude, Deus salus nostra.* God Who beatifies us but Who, in the actual order of things, cannot give us happiness without first saving us and liberating us from sin. God the Saviour reaching down to His creature in order to attract it to Himself. As soon as he encounters God on his way, as soon as he understands by means of grace (and he cannot understand without it) that God is not solely the supreme Being, the creator of all to Whom all returns, but the God of love Who seeks His creature in order to transform it into Himself and to open to it the eternal springs of perfect joy, man is saved ; he is already destined to beatitude, even if he is still ignorant of many of the redemptive gifts of this God Who rewards.

The God Who saves and beatifies us is the same Who causes us to share in His very life, the life of the Blessed Trinity, Who gives Himself to us through His incarnation in the womb of the Virgin Mary, Who redeems us by His life, death and resurrection ; He Who sends the Spirit to dwell in us and make us one in Him, Who blots out sin, Who is the fulness of grace, the Head of the Church, the source of all sacramental life, the Judge of the living and of the dead, Who diffuses in His eternity of happiness the simple gift, still wrapped in mystery, of faith and charity.

God the Saviour ; it can well be seen how all the truths of our *Credo* find their centre in this truth, how all manifest one aspect of this merciful love to which even sin and hell bear witness in their own way, being the painful deprivation of this beatifying God. For in Hell the damned are not deprived of the presence of God the creator, but are for ever without the beatifying presence of God.

One object, the primary one, without which the rest fall away in dust but in which they find consistence and meaning.

One object, yes, but also a *living* object.

For, if the first and central object of faith is God the Saviour, can we look on it as a scene which is static in the monotony of the centuries ? There is here not only a question of the *happy meeting* of the living God and the man whom God calls to life (and that alone would suffice to compose the parts of a drama in which all is life and action) ; it is a question of admitting, with the whole of tradition, that the life of faith is a *perpetual movement* which carries the person of the believer towards the God of love, manifested in Revelation.

This point of view, already adopted in the time of the Fathers and taken up again in the Middle Ages by St. Thomas among others, [1] makes the richness of the act of faith apparent by revealing three inseparable aspects of it, three aspects whose solidarity composes the whole of the interior life of the believer. Faith is an act by which we admit God and all that He reveals *(credere Deum)*. Faith is an adhesion to God because He Himself witnesses to the truth He reveals *(credere Deo)*. Faith is finally a movement which carries the believer continually towards this God, the meeting with Whom constitutes an appeal and towards Whom he must always tend until eternal life *(credere in Deum)*.

When St. Thomas tells us that faith is the beginning of eternal life in us [2] he means that this beginning is a seed which should grow in the light and warmth of the life of hope and charity until perfect maturity, which is eternal happiness. Now this movement, following the meeting of man with God, has this particular character, that not only does man if he is faithful grow in faith and love, but that God in some way grows in man. All the truths which the Christian receives develop in him. In proportion as he lives in them, they become more luminous, better understood, better loved, more united to each other and with the whole of life. They, therefore, truly grow in him.

Instead of comparing the faithful to a walker weary of a scene which he has contemplated for too long a period, it is better to say that he is the adolescent in whom the rising life which transforms him from year to year, month to month, progressively reveals the extent of its movement and the fascination of its beauty.

---

[1] II^a II^{ae}, q. II, a. 2, c.
[2] II^a II^{ae}, q. IV, a. 1, c.

II. THE SUBJECT OF FAITH

The act of faith is endowed with a certitude which surpasses all human certitude. The Church is not afraid to employ the superlative to qualify this firmness of adhesion : *Certissima est fides*. This act is, however, free. It depends on the loving and voluntary ardour of man raised by grace. It is together and indissolubly an affirmation of the mind and a free act of the will.

We will not delay to prove that this is so ; the official teaching of the Church is very clear on this question. It shows the full face of the faith with its harmonious features, while protestantism on the one hand and rationalism on the other have only seen the profile. But, in the light of this supernatural reality, human psychology becomes more accessible to us and as it were translucid in its most natural action. There are living certitudes which only develop in man thanks to the intimate collaboration of mind and will. There exist living certitudes such as only the active presence of a will full of love can engender, because this faculty possesses the secret of good, carried as it is by all the energy of its being, towards man's beatitude. No doubt it does not judge, the mind judges for it. And yet the mind would be incapable of this judgment if this will were not there communicating its fire, which becomes light in the mind.

The experience of daily life shows us that this is so. Man, in most of the situations in which he finds himself drawn to make a worthwhile judgment, only succeeds in this delicate but truly human task because there is in him, in his reason, when it judges, a force which is capable of overcoming his hesitations, a force whose object is goodness. He can only pass judgments as to the beauty of an heroic action, fidelity to contracts, the charm of a life consecrated to art, the urgent necessity for establishing friendly relationships between nations, if his mind is open to such things. The power which opens, enlarges and raises the mind to appreciate true goodness is the will tending towards goodness and acting on the mind.

It is therefore not sufficient to say with Pascal that the heart has its reasons which reason does not know. We must complete it by adding that the reasons of the heart soon become those of reason when the heart is one with the reason which moves it. Since it is a matter of living certitudes, for those of the moral order and therefore religious ones are living (certitudes which only rise up in the mind by the force of a free will), can one be surprised that the act of faith which opens the doors on the whole of religious life should be both quite certain and free ?

It is in this way that a man judges when he judges the things which concern his intimate and profound life. If he arrives at understanding and expressing without hesitation the holiness of Christ, the beauty and unsurpassed grandeur of His doctrine, the holiness and divinity of the Church, the permanent sign that she is for us of a Redemption which is being carried out, he can do this because his will, completely transfigured by grace, opens and enlarges his mind and renders it capable of appreciating divine things.

The whole interior life is thus unified in the act of faith. It can easily be seen that it is an act of the whole person, not merely an act of the mind alone nor of the will alone, but, as we have said, of the two together. And we must also add that it is not only an act of the spirit but of the spirit and the senses together. For, just as the mind dives into the life of the senses to find nourishment for its thoughts, so the will dives into sensibility to find the efficacious springs of its energy.

This does not cease to be true when it is a matter of faith. Revealed truth comes in fact to man through signs, and these signs are sensible ones. God's message, whether made known to us by Scripture or by the Church's living tradition, is expressed in terms which are understood by the senses. Think of the influence on man of the style of literature used by God in addressing him. [1] No one can deny that the poetry of the psalms exercises an influence on the orientation of the mind and will towards divine truth or that the sight of the blood of the martyrs has contributed to conversions and inspired the courage of believers.

Was it not when listening to the *Magnificat* that Claudel suddenly realized the unique value of the Christian religion ? And is it not also through the splendours of art that a Huysmans or a Joërgensen have been invincibly conquered by the truth contained in symbols ?

Yes. It is indeed the whole of man which is exercized in the act of belief : man, head and heart, soul and body. This can be understood when we comprehend the central mystery of revealed religion, the Incarnation of the Word. God become sensible is perceived by the whole man ; He is seen, heard, touched, and by means of all these perceptions the divine is born in the heart and spirit.

Faith is not therefore the act of one faculty, nor of insulated faculties, but the product of the harmony, and, to borrow a word which Maurice Blondel has made familiar, of the *synergie* of all the faculties motivated by grace. The psychology of the act of faith imitates at its own level the life of the Divine Persons. There is a perfect distinction among them, and all Three are reciprocally immanent in a total circumincession. The same can be said, taking

---

[1] We are here speaking of the influence of literature on those who read the Bible without considering the problem of inspiration, which is completely outside the scope of the present article.

the laws of analogy into account, of man's faculties. Formally distinct, they are all immanent to each other in the sphere of their activities.

But if it is true that the faculties which posit the act of faith are not insulated, it must also be said that *the persons who believe are not insulated either*.

It is doubtless quite true that faith is a unique experience and personal to each, and it is also indubitable that it makes man more of a stranger on earth by making him already a denizen of Heaven. But what is this apparent ostracism ? Is it not the very condition of a better and more intimate mutual comprehension, a closer embrace of the entire universe ? Faith, doubtless, causes each one to lose many illusions, rooted in the mind and very dear to it. *But all meet together in the heart of truth.* What does it matter if God is received in a unique way by each when it is God Himself Whom each encounters and God becomes all in all. What is ineffable in personal experience is an enrichment for all since all, meeting at the same source, can admire the variety and beauty of its outpourings.

It is no longer, certainly, at the level of purely human experience that the encounter takes place and the imperishable bonds are knit but in *God*. But who will say that for this reason they have lost their force and charm ? Each one is a member of a Church whose principle of unity goes beyond man, because it is God in Whom all are welcomed. Father Mersch, in *La Théologie du Corps Mystique*, [1] has shown in a masterly way that the divinisation of the Church imitated the very mode of the union in the incarnate Word of the human nature to the Divine Person. It is not the Word Who limits Himself in His descent to take on the contours of humanity ; that would be a frightful heresy. But the human nature assumed " in consortium divinae naturae " lives by another life, the life of the Divine Person, subsists in it and acts in it and through it. Thus the Church, the Mystical Body of Christ, by an assumption which is doubtless not of nature but of grace, is interiorised in Christ. And every movement of faith, hope and charity in each of its members takes its source, develops and spreads in Christ. In this sense it must be said that the faith of each is the faith of the whole Church. Not only because the doctrine which is taught and received is the same for all but because the act of faith of each one is the work of the same Spirit Who is the Spirit of Christ and the soul of the *Church*.

---

[1] Vol. I, book III, chap. X, pp. 284-293.

It is therefore easily demonstrated that there is no isolation, no barriers between Christians, however personal may be their experience as believers.

III. THE MOTIVE OF FAITH

In order the better to understand what follows, let us first study from a practical angle the state of soul of the believer and of those who do not believe in the presence of a mystery in our religion, that of the Blessed Trinity for instance. The unbelieving philosopher can study the development, the mystery as a whole and the details of the theological explanations which Christian tradition has given of it. He can understand with as much penetration as the Catholic theologian the metaphysics of the Trinitarian relationship. The content of the revelation is thus made familiar to him. Yet, he does not believe. Let us set before the same truth a Christian who is ignorant but animated by a lively faith. She knows nothing about the metaphysics of the Trinitarian relationships. She is ignorant of the rudiments of theological explanations, the content of revelation seems far less accessible to her than to the pagan philosopher. She, however, believes with her whole heart.

The difference in these states of soul is obvious. While for the philosopher revelation consists in a system of religious thought, for which he may profess a sincere admiration but which has for him no more title to proclaim itself true than has the Hindu Trimûrti or the Buddhist Nirvâna, for the believing soul, on the contrary, this truth exists and is living.

Faith, although always based on knowledge of the mystery, is not primarily, not even necessarily, linked in its progress to the increase of knowledge of the nature or the essence of the mystery, although of itself and normally the life of faith engenders a more perfect understanding of the mystery. The value of the act of faith depends on the intensity and totality of the adhesion to the truth, recognised in the light of grace, as belonging to the order of existing things.

But what forms the foundation of this certitude of what is real and actual ? It is no doubt the work of grace, but grace, and in the case which we are considering, the light of faith, must show some particular thing. And as it does not create the intrinsic evidence of the content of Revelation, which remains veiled, what can it show which causes the certitude of the reality of the mystery ? To

117

answer this question we must call to mind that intangible fact in our tradition, that is to say, that only the authority of God in revelation is for us the objective and absolute guarantee of the Divine truth. Theology makes this authority the formal object of faith, that is to say, the supreme reason which gives our assent its consistency and value. Every mystery is therefore credible to us, that is to say, given us as being real and true, because it is directly and adequately penetrated by the Divine intelligence, which guarantees its existence by communicating it to us through Revelation. Revelation therefore offers two aspects which cannot be disassociated : the communication of the truth and the divine guarantee of it.

It would seem at first sight that the believer should therefore remain always and for as long as faith lasts, a stranger to the mystery. To know is to make one's own, and identify oneself with, what one knows. *Cognitio fit per identitatem subjecti et objecti.* But the believer can never be identified with a mystery. That would be not believing, but seeing. How then can he arrive at it ? If he cannot identify himself with the mystery, he must identify himself with divine intelligence in which the mystery has its being and its intelligibility.

Faith is above all this *communion of created intelligence with the divine mind.* Scholastic tradition as a whole has consecrated this point of view in an apparently paradoxical expression : *auctoritas Dei est simul id quod creditur et id quo creditur.* To attain the object revealed by faith we must first of all attain to the divine authority of the Revealer, which is none other than the infallibility of the knowledge of God and the supreme truth of His evidence. [1]

The authority of God as Revealer is not, certainly, the authority of one man speaking to another ; it is not only the authority of God the Creator, manifesting by created things, like reflections, His power and goodness. It is *the evidence of God, the Author of the supernatural order, addressing Himself to man in a wholly new way, to teach him a truth which is also wholly new.* It is therefore through grace, which raises man's intelligence to the level of God's, and by grace alone that the authority of God the revealer can become the formal object of supernatural and divine faith. [2] This elevation is, as we have said, a communion establishing a connaturality of grace between the created intelligence and the uncreated Spirit.

---

[1] Cf., among others, SUAREZ, *De Fide*, disp. III, d. 6 and 12 ; CAJETAN, II^a II^{ae}, q. I, a. 2 ; JOHN OF ST. THOMAS, *Cursus theologicus, De Fide*, art. II, 137-194 ; BILLUART, *De Fide*, diss. I, art. I.

[2] SUAREZ, *De Fide*, disp. III, d. 6, n. 8.

Light of faith, since, in default of the intrinsic evidence of the mystery, it identifies us with the very source of the latter, with the infallible mind of God.

God's authority as it has just been described undoubtedly forms the final motive for faith's assent. This motive appears to be such that it ought to cause the disappearance of any other good reason for belief. And St. Thomas says that this is so and all tradition repeats the same thing : " No one believes if he does not realize that he ought to believe. " The objection, in its ingenuous form, certainly does not lack weight. But once more it must be said that the difficulty comes from an arbitrary separation of elements which are in reality indissolubly united. In reality, God's authority and our personal reasons for belief are two aspects of the same life of faith. This is what we must now explain. Speaking of God's authority, we may look at it from two points of view which are both equally true ; from the objective and static point of view, that is to say, as evidence of revealed truth given once for all. God's authority is in this case similar to that of a witness who produces a letter in which his testimony is written down. But it can also be thought of — and in the act of faith of each Christian, it should always be thought of in this way — as a dynamic reality, which has become an element in subjective life, like an actual initiative on God's part addressed to the believer's soul. It is very true that Christian Revelation is public, that it has been made once and for all and that it ended with the death of the last of the Apostles. God is the guarantor of this Revelation and His testimony transcends the centuries and remains the supra-temporal motive for the faith of all who are called upon to believe.

But this same authority should become the formal element in the personal act of faith of the believer. It is therefore necessary that the latter should, so to speak, make this authority of God his own, realizing that God is speaking to him and inviting him to believe. The Rev. Fr. Dhanis has very clearly deliminated this dynamic aspect of God's evidence in the act of faith. [1] The authority of God on which the whole of the exterior and objective Revelation rests, becomes in each soul like an invitation by grace, a solicitation from the living God addressed to each in order to bring him or lead him back to the Faith.

If we consider, on the other hand, the personal reasons for believing, we must admit that, however enlightening may be the object-

---

[1] *Révélation explicite et implicite*, in *Gregorianum*, vol. XXXIV, 1953, pp. 229-232.

ive proofs of the fact of Revelation, however numerous and convergent the marks of the divine value of the supernatural message, these proofs and signs whose solidity forms the foundation for a prudent judgment of their credibility, a judgment which makes man realize that it is reasonable to believe, they still have not, in themselves, the force to induce the assent of faith. It is the time to recall Christ's saying: " *Nemo venit ad me nisi Pater qui misit me traxerit eum.* "

Among these motives, there is one and only one which is decisive, whatever form it takes : it is that God calls us to believe and that it is not only reasonable but necessary that we should respond to His call. Every other reason may fail. And there are cases in which no other reason appears ; the faith of the child, for instance, or even that of the adult, ill instructed in questions of apologetics, who has not, as one says, a reasoned faith. But this motive is always present. No one can believe who does not realize that he ought to believe. No one engages himself in practice in adhesion to revealed truth, if he does not see that he is giving himself to God, to God Who invites him to believe. And this motive, as soon as it comes to birth in the conscience, appears thoroughly sufficing, and entirely reasonable. For man to surrender to God's invitation is the most rational act of his life , an act the foundation for which is supremely evident.

It is therefore easy to understand how, in the act of faith, the authority of God and the personal reasons for belief do not only agree with one another but call for each other and are mutually dependent. The same God, Who has given the Revelation, interests Himself in every soul to bear witness to the truth in it and to invite it to believe. " *Qui credit in Filium Dei, habet testimonium Dei in se.* "

So in the personal act by which man surrenders himself to God, all the forces meet together and are in harmony, those of God Who attracts by inviting, and those of the man who responds by believing.

CONCLUSION

Among the gospel narratives in which the awakening or reawakening of faith is described to us, there is one which shows, perhaps more explicitly than the others, the genesis of this action of grace : the story of the meeting of Jesus with the disciples on the way to Emmaus (Luke, XXIV, 13-35). The faith of these disciples who were going along the road was apparently extinguished. Their interior disillusion is expressed in the dialogue with Christ by the use of the past tense : " *Nos autem sperabamus.* " The meeting with Jesus on the road does not lead at first to any manifestation of the Master's identity. He is a traveller, like the others to whom they tell their trouble, because he is ready to listen compassionately and because it is a comfort to discharge the burden of their suffering on to someone else. But He begins to talk and without being aware of it the two disciples find themselves irresistibly drawn by the attraction of His presence so that they beg Him to stay with them : *coegerunt illum.* They have not yet recognized Him however. But later, when they have in the sign of the breaking of bread realized the evidence that it is He, they understand the sway which He had already exercized over them when He was explaining the scriptures to them. " *Were not our hearts burning within us when He spoke to us on the road ?* " (v. 32).

This narrative seems to us admirably to describe the different phases of a regeneration of faith. The sway of Christ the God and Saviour which is exercized long before we realize it is the efficacious attraction of grace. Under the influence of this still obscure but continually active force, the search goes on under the aspect, not of the interest of curiosity, but of expectation, a desire to find what we guess already to be the whole of life. This call — for we may speak of it thus — this appeal of God makes the whole problem appear from the point of view of being actual and personal. It is not merely a matter of solving in the abstract a moral or religious question but of finding for oneself the road which leads to the light.

Once the term has been reached, which is the recognition of the divine value of a revelation guaranteed by God Himself and manifested by signs, that which has preceded the evidence, the road to this faith in the word of God, appears to the mind as the work of this God Who has been found. And in the same act by which he surrenders himself in a definite adherence, the believer perceives the objective and subjective motive for this adherence : God, Who both attracts him to the truth and guarantees it.

Thus we perceive that all who believe have this quite personal motive for belief which is their own vocation to the Faith and that this motive is no other than that which gives the act of faith its interior consistency and being, since it is one and the same God Who tells the truth and attracts to it.

Faith: Its Growth and Development

The growth and development of faith can never be charted the way one charts the history of something that matures according to fixed laws. Yet, generally speaking, grace follows nature. By better understanding the visible evolution- of nature, the religion teacher can come to appreciate better his role in aiding the growth and development of faith in those whom God has entrusted to him.

Faith and the Psychological Development of Children and Adolescents

by André GODIN, S. J.

"Faith, visualized not as the fact of being a Christian, but as the demands of growing into Christ : this is the essence of Kierkegaard's attitude."
(G. FESSARD, *Dialectique des Exercices*, Paris, 1956, p. 226).

When the philosopher or the theologian undertakes to define Faith and analyse its component parts, they very often have no idea of the astonishing variety of historical ramifications and the multiplicity of psycho-social factors which condition its concrete existence.

The present statement, intended as introduction to psychological problems (in no way will we deal with pedagogical matters), comprises a *first section* describing briefly *what Faith must be* to remain faithful to its theological essence (and theological definition) — *a second section*, the most important, will present *certain evident facts of positive psychology* concerning the origins and the main stages of development of a psychic nature in regard to Faith *in children of normal environments* — finally, *in the third section* we endeavour to compensate for the lack of truly scientific documents and studies concerning *the child deprived of a normal home* by giving *some impressions and observations made by educators*, underlining their importance as well as the particular difficulties encountered and the *definite investigations to be* undertaken in this domain.

---

1. This is the opening paper at an international meeting, called by Mgr Carroll-Abing at Fribourg (Switzerland) in June 1957 to study the problem of religious Education for children deprived of family. — Address : 184, rue Washington, Brussels, BELGIUM (Editor's note).

I. NATURE AND CHARACTERISTICS OF THE
THEOLOGICAL VIRTUE OF FAITH [1]

From the theological point of view, Christian Faith is a gift of God (a supernatural virtue) which, on His testimony, invites and helps us to adhere to the mystery of salvation through Christ and to the means of achieving this within the Church.

Faith is a threefold supernatural affirmation : as to its principle (God effects it within us), its contents (the revealed truths), and in its destination (the vision of God promised to the adopted sons).

To quote the words of a contemporary theologian [2], Faith, the theological virtue, is both an *attitude of soul* and an *assent of the mind*: an attitude which turns wholly to God, the Saviour, in answer to His call (in this respect, Faith is not actually distinguishable from love and submission : " Fides per dilectionem operatur ") — an *assent of the mind* where the central motivation (the testimony of God) establishes the supernatural certainty of revealed truths, obscurely visualized in the dogmatic pronouncements and lived by those who hope for salvation through God alone, looking beyond the signs by which He reveals Himself.

Such, briefly summarized, are the main-springs of our theology of Faith. Let us add a few consequences on the level of descriptive psychology, choosing them as the resultant of positive psychology (inquiries and empirical observations) which we shall present immediately afterwards. We must bear in mind *five psychological characteristics of living faith* which we will loosely connect with five periods in the development of adolescents and children — beginning with those characteristics which presuppose the most advanced psychological maturity.

1) Living the Faith is always in some manner *an experience of love and de-centration:* Another is the *principle* of my adherence, and is also its end. This goes for the personal attitude as for the

---

1. This article does not deal with the *contents* of faith and has left out entirely the problem of religious instruction insofar as it deals with the transmission of revealed truths. It is deliberately that we have adopted the dynamic and progressive aspect of the *attitudes* within the faith. The actual doctrinal aspect is evidently essential, but it is more directly dependent on the *intellectual* powers of the child and does not lend itself to the differentiation which the child deprived of the benefit of a home deserves from the point of view of his *affective* losses.

2. AUBERT R., *Le problème de l'acte de foi.* Louvain, Publications Universitaires, 1950², pp. 691 and ff.

assent of the mind. Therefore to attain to mature faith, it would not suffice to take on an attitude of courage, energy, constancy, or even proselytizing. These natural virtues are in themselves too shallow to support the virtue of faith. Love is needed here : an acceptance of the action of others and of subordination to it, which is taken up and assumed by the agapé, by the gift of God. Truly, the commitment to faith calls for courage, will-power and perseverance, but it is also the acceptance of a risk derived from an experience of love.

Regarding the assent of the spirit, it is necessary to point out that the " reasons for believing " are not, humanly speaking, so compelling that it is possible to speak of evidence excluding all doubt. We would stress this point because it seems that a certain " rationalist exigency " in the nature of an obsession (frequently found in our modern culture with its element of anxiety) leads souls away from the faith and from the risk involved in an ultimate commitment.

This kind of attitude, as also the intellectual assent, calls for psychic dispositions which, as a rule, are only found towards the *final stage of adolescence* [3]. Previously — or in default of this maturity — the theological faith is present and active (as it is from baptism) but it is impeded in its psychological manifestation of the plenitude of its fundamental characteristics.

2) Faith lived always brings, to a certain degree, *the knowledge of sin*. It is in God *our Saviour* that I believe, and the abyss of sin itself is only known to me through the generosity of the divine call. To attain to adult faith, therefore, an exact morality, an irreproachable conduct and a pure conscience do not suffice. Doubtless, religion calls for good works, but these accomplished in a spirit of egocentric sufficiency cease to maintain the contact with God, while sin itself, bringing home the need for forgiveness, can better develop it.

We think that the point of psychic maturation which corresponds to this state of faith is normally reached at the age of *puberty*.

3) Faith lived remains an *acceptance of the mystery :* an obscure meeting with God *beyond those signs* by which He reveals Himself and saves me. Christ Himself is God, but the unfolding of His historical life appears to me as the emblem of divine charity. Faith

---

3. In this connection see ALLPORT G. W., *Becoming*, New Haven, Yale U. Press, 1955, p. 94.

enlightens me as to the significance of the Church, the same applies to the sacraments whose efficacy lies in the faith. Symbols are an essential part of religion as lived, just as were the parables announcing the Good News. The awakening and development of the " symbolic sense "[4] that aptitude to read a spiritual meaning within a material sign conditions the faith psychologically and protects it against the " magic " tendency. The sacramental signs themselves are not " magic " ways of transforming our personalities : they are meant to be approached and received in a spirit of faith — that is to say — as mysterious contacts between the saving action of God and the free will of men. And though their effect is not in proportion to our dispositions they do not bring us into relationship with God after the manner of a talisman, without any spiritual activity on our part. It seems that the development of the symbolic function required to see beyond the material sign is usually arrived at towards the ages of 11 or 12 years in boys, while in girls it comes a year earlier.

4) Lived faith brings with it a *sense of expectancy, of hope:* the saving power of God does not cause an upheaval in the established order. His immanent justice is not immediate : it is none other than the long-term victory of His love.

Infantile anthropomorphism and " animist " causality [5] only allow for an imperfect prayer of faith which brings no immediate or visible triumph of the good man over the bad, or over adversity, or on the fatality of secondary causes. We must know how to wait : faith impels us to think in *terms of eternity*, transcending the time limits of our human desires. Through faith we call on an infinitely good God, but without subordinating Him to the requirements of our immediate necessities.

Normally, it is from 8 to 12 years that the anthropomorphic and animistic characteristics disappear, as do those which enclose in short-time provisions, which inevitably stamp the psychology of the faith lived by the youngest children.

---

4. For further information on the awakening and development of the symbolic function see GODIN A., " The Symbolic Function," in *Lumen Vitae*, Vol. X (1955), n⁰ 2, pp. 277-290.

5. In addition to the scientific experiments mentioned later, profitable reading on animism and magic thought will be found in the short, suggestive article by SCHURMANS J., " Santé mentale et formation religieuse à l'âge pré-scolaire " in *Santé mentale et formation religieuse* (Brussels, Assoc. Cath. d'Hygiène mentale, 5, rue Guimard, 1955, 57 pages).

5) Finally, faith lived usually coexists with *a joyful assurance, a happy security*, and *a longing to share with others :* all of which brings to mind the state of a child within its family where a twofold tenderness guides him firmly and warmly together with his brothers and sisters towards maturity (" in mensuram aetatis plenitudinis Christi ").

The fundamental affective structures, the nature of which depend on the *6 or 7 first years* of life, play an important psychological part in active faith. *Frustrated anxiety, fear on the defensive*, or *conquering aggressivity* do not tend towards the plenitude of faith : these human characteristics of psychological existence, reactive and compensatory, can eventually uphold lines of conduct which *outwardly* have a positive function in the practice of religion and in the individual development of faith. But, based on egocentrism, they are destined to collapse (as are all attitudes wherein remain traces of idolatry), so that the call to true charity may be heard. Faith is not within us to compensate for our psychic deficiencies ; as a gift of God, it is a call and a help to place our free will under the aegis of love and of charity.

II. PROGRESSIONS (STAGES OF PSYCHOLOGICAL DEVELOPMENT)

1. *Early Childhood (2-8 years).*

Dating from Pierre Bovet [6], no doubt is left but that the awakening of religion in which active faith finds psychological roots comes via the parents.

This can be understood in three ways which complete each other, but are of unequal value : 1º The sociological and to a certain degree *exterior influence* of the parents. It is, for instance, noticed that the majority of children of Catholic parents remain Catholic, and those of Protestant parents remain Protestant, in those countries where various Christian forms of religion co-exist. This fact also explains the answers obtained by Brother Étienne [7] to the question : " Within your own circle have you met Christians who have helped you by their example ? Where ? How ? " From 14 to 15 years, 4th

---

6. BOVET Pierre, *Le sentiment religieux et la psychologie de l'enfant*, Neuchâtel, Delachaux, 1951 (2d éd.).

7. Frère ÉTIENNE, " Une enquête sur la morale ", in *Catéchistes*, 1956, nº 1, p. 44.

and 3rd Forms (804 replies came from Catholic schools) school friends headed the list (23 and 28 %), adults followed (21 and 18 %), priests (9 and 12 %), etc., and finally parents (3 and 6 %). The influence of parents is here understood in a very superficial sense, whereas it is in effect far more durable and profound.

2⁰ The *conscious image* of the Father (or the Mother) has a bearing on the ways in which the child will ultimately visualize God. Thus Allport [8] relates the case of a child of six, in a great state of anxiety, who suddenly refused to say " Our Father. " His reason was that God being so good could not be a father, as his was a drunkard and a traitor. " He had not as yet, " writes Allport, " passed from the concrete image to the abstract notion fitted to a more advanced stage. "

3⁰ But there is an intimate, deeper and *less conscious way* through which parents indirectly influence the religious awakening of their children : it is in the manner in which, through their own mutual relationship and that extended to the child, they satisfy his affective needs. What the child has to learn on the *authority* of God, on *His care* for us, on *His unceasing forgiveness*, is not primarily learnt in an abstract way through the catechism. If all goes well, he has already lived, felt and seen all this. The " *attributes of God* " are discovered through living with the father and mother. If there is discord between the father and mother, the foundation for the intuitive assimilation of religious values is lacking. The doctrinal concepts will reach the intellect but only with difficulty penetrate the psychic depths and equally so the awakening of the soul's acquiescence.

Within this line of thought, let us read over the accurate and profound views of Dr. Oswald Schwartz [9] (adding a word of commentary on the religious aspect of the matter) : " *The mother* normally gives the child the feeling of being at home in the world. She is *the main source of security*. The child must know that in spite of his failings, weaknesses and errors, he can always have recourse to her. Maternal love has often been described as the unconditional acceptance of another being. In effect, the child always wants to be accepted and loved by someone. Lacking this, when he reaches manhood, he will for ever be seeking, without ever finding, this comforting experience. The true meaning of marriage may even

---

8. ALLPORT G. W., *The Individual and his Religion*. New-York, Macmillan C⁰, 1950, p. 31.

9. SCHWARTZ O., *Psychologie sexuelle*, P. U. Fr. Paris 1952. — Introd. F. Duyckaerts, p. XXII.

escape him : he will endeavour to find security and complete acceptance from his (or her) partner in life, and will not find what his
infantile heart claims ; the time for maternal love is past. " Or
else, he will endeavour to obtain from an abnormal devotion the
unconditional and affectionate acceptance of which his childhood
was deprived. This gives rise to a possessive piety towards God,
an insipid and sentimental attitude to religion, which far from
being favourable to normal development, fixes it permanently
in its infantile limits.

Schwartz goes on to say : " *The father represents those values*
which give life its significance. He has to lead the child to the threshold of adult responsibilities by giving him confidence in himself,
burdening him with tasks neither too heavy, nor too light. He is
the one who will teach how to act. His approval or reproof will be
neither arbitrary nor capricious... The child whose early life has
been devoid of this gently stimulating paternal influence runs the
risk of never being capable of giving himself to a determined undertaking. He will increase the number of those anguished souls who
find no way of justifying their existence and refuse to dirty their
hands. " It is also possible to note (for instance in a young girl
who has had to endure excessive indifference on the part of her
father) a strange feeling of discomfort which will last her all her
life in her dealings with God. Or else there is the playfulness of the
little girl trying to " get round " her father by loving and affectionate ways, which prolongs itself in an attitude of " power-politics "
toward God, an attitude which can later show itself to be fallacious
and plunge the young woman into depression and religious despair.
It is a fact that many false religious dispositions owe their origins
to the unsatisfied or exasperated needs of the child in regard to his
parental relationships.

How can we represent the progressive ascent towards God as
originating from the very first years of parental relationship ? In
three ways which we will just simply state.

a) *Through a participation in the religious attitude of the parents.*
It is the most effective way and that which gives the best results
where religious pedagogy is successfully carried out within the
family. The child senses after the manner of a reflection, through
the *authority* of the father, or the *kindness* of the mother, the *source*
of a higher authority of a greater benevolence, to which the parents
occasionally make reference in the course of daily life.

b) *By outstripping certain affective structures* which cultural
education instils into the child, thus creating new requirements :

longing for beauty (admiration), need for order (cleanliness, neatness), desire for creative and constructive activity, etc. These are merely stages of a good education, but they have an influence on the type of philosophy lived by the adolescent and the adult, and they also affect the mode of approach to God, salvation and the hereafter.

c) *By supplementing parental limitations.* Bovet (o. c.) has particularly emphasized this point, perhaps even too much so. It is evident that when the child perceives that his parents are not all-powerful : that his mother can be arbitrary or unfair, his father weak and untruthful, or again that there are certain contradictions (however small) between the scale of values within his family circle and those by which he is judged at school, he feels obliged to call on some omniscient, omnipotent and perfectly good being to whom he can have recourse as to his secret witness (even at times against his parents) to achieve a fair judgment. It is evident, of course, that this third mode of access to God is neither the only one, nor perhaps the most important. Taken on its own, it would oblige us to the following conclusion which is obviously erroneous : the greater the parental deficiencies and limitations, the more the child has need of God. If this were so, those who have no parents would turn into beings desperately clinging to God. Evidently, such is not the case ; the true recourse to God does not tend to an egocentric desire for affective compensations. The greater the basic equilibrium achieved within the first years of life, the better the possibilities of a broadening out of the richness of the divine message in the adolescent and adult.

From the pedagogical point of view, therefore, God should never *be made use of by parents in their task of education* as a means of bringing pressure to bear through religion (" If you are naughty, the priest will come and take you away "), as an auxiliary to weigh down the child's sense of wrong-doing (God sees everything... that is all the child's misdeeds), as a sterilizer of intellectual curiosity (" Why is it raining ? Because the good God sends us rain "). These are only caricatures of religion and without future in the true development of the child. Equally, religion must never be allowed to serve the child as a means for *evading his duties and obligations as a human being:* he must not be permitted to bully his little sister because at night he " says his prayers like a little angel, " nor must visits to the Blessed Sacrament nor good marks at the Catechism class be allowed to obliterate the fact that the boy is lazy or given to domineering his school-mates.

130

The gravest difficulty in matters of religious growth comes from the affective structures of those early years. The anxious child, or the child suffering from a complex of fear, guilt, or compensatory ambition, not only does not arrive at the fullness of true religion lived " for the service and glory of God, " but he misunderstands the religious message taught him. And this misunderstanding influences the smallest details of the lessons on religion. We have shown how young children who (through home privations for the most part) suffer from an anxiety complex, have a very different appreciation of the biblical story of Abraham and Isaac, than have others. For them, identifying themselves very thoroughly with Isaac, this episode (meant to demonstrate the protection of children by a God who rejects the sacrifice of the first-born) carries a different message and produces a new source of anxiety [10].

2. The Second Stage of Childhood (8 to 12 years).

We can obtain some idea of the evolution which ordinarily takes place in children of these years through the works of Clavier [11], Gesell [12] and, at least indirectly, of Piaget [13].

Clavier and Gesell present very convincing gradations showing that the child passes from absolute anthropomorphism (God wears a robe, picks flowers, lives in a terraced house, etc.) to a mitigated anthropomorphism (a man who cannot be touched, whose house is filled with angels, etc.) and finally to a certain spirituality (God is everywhere, lives in our souls, is invisible, etc.). In equal degrees of schooling, girls are ordinarily ahead of boys by about one year, as they are in temporal matters. The themes of power and life, in the first place frequently associated with divinity, give way little by little to those of justice and finally of love. From the age of five when the child easily makes God responsible for every unexpected event (especially of a punitive nature) he passes on towards 7 or 8 years to the discovery of a certain dualism in the religious world (heaven and hell, God and the devil, etc.) and then on to a degree of scepticism charged with curiosity and leading to progress in purifying his notion of God and of His attributes. Fear which seems

---

10. This is a summary of the inquiry published under the title ' Isaac at the Stake " in *Lumen Vitae*, Vol. X (1955) n⁰ 1, pp. 65-92.

11. CLAVIER H., *L'idée de Dieu chez l'enfant*, Paris, Fischbacher, 1926².

12. GESELL A. et ILG F. L., *L'enfant de cinq à dix ans*, Paris, P. U. Fr., 1953².

13. PLAGET J., *La représentation du monde chez l'enfant*, Paris, P. U. Fr. 1947. *Le jugement moral chez l'enfant*, Paris P. U. Fr., new edit., 1957.

to reach a maximum towards 8 or 9 years and then continually decreases (if one judges by the overall statistics) until the age of 12 and after. But, of course, the anxiety-ridden children develop badly or fix on certain attributes of God which misrepresent the true Christian message.

But it is specially through Piaget that we acquire a precise knowledge of the mechanism of reaction to an immediate immanent justice. In ordinary little stories, the theft of apples, for example, if the planks of an old bridge, rotten with age, give way and the little thief falls into the water, the young child easily sees (" animistic ") intentional intervention. This animistic interpretation decreases gradually from the age of 6 (86 % of the children) to the age of 12 (34 %). But in a class of intellectually " backward " children of 13 to 14 years there were still 57 % answers of the animist type. We know what long preparations were needed in the days of the Old Testament for the religion of the chosen people to lose the conviction that God punishes the sinner already in this life (see the teaching of the Book of *Job*) and gradually to grasp the notion of the infinite patience which is the outcome of Divine Mercy. God does not govern our world of men by a succession of miraculous interventions. And anyone expecting to see the punishment of the wicked in this mortal life is liable to fall to doubting God as his experience of life develops. It would probably be possible to demonstrate — through research following a method similar to that of Piaget — that frustrated children remain more attached than others to this childish animism and to a way of prayer which places God at the disposal of their immediate needs. Conversely, children brought up in an atmosphere full of love and trust can put up with absences more and more prolonged, not only on the part of his parents, but also of God, of the God reached through faith.

3. Pre-Puberty (12-14 years).

Towards the end of the preceding period, we see many children turning towards the more ritualistic aspects of religion and piety. Well-performed gestures, a fixed number and order of prayers, the punctual accomplishment of the rites : such is the spontaneous religion of many 10-year-old children. The well-founded works of Mathias [14] and of McDowell [15], can give an idea of the slow

---

14. MATHIAS W. D., *Ideas of God and Conduct*, Teachers College, New-York, Columbia U. Press, 1943.

15. McDowell J. B., *The Development of the Idea of God in the Catholic Child*, Washington, Cathol. U. of America Press, 1952.

progression towards higher spiritual notions of prayer and religion, disentangled from the " magic " aspect of the materially effected rite and tending to the accomplishment of the liturgical gestures in a more profoundly symbolic spirit (" Is not a sacrament the outward sign of an inward grace ").

A rather remarkable fact, pointed out by Mathias, is that the children who take the longest to discard the attitude of fear towards the Divinity are those coming from non-practising families. It is also noted that the increasing spiritual notion of God is negatively co-related with the teachers' remarks on the submissive and adapted behaviour of children within the school ; it would seem that certain children's precocious personalities converge simultaneously to an accentuated maturation of the image of God and a spirit of opposition to conventions.

On his part McDowell shows that the consciousness of human liberty asserting itself before God (" God cannot force us to do what we do not wish ") exceeds 50 % of the 11-12 age-group and reaches 75 % at 14-15 years.

It seems too that the fact of having badly negotiated the earlier stages entails a prolongation of those attitudes towards a redoubtable God who is to be placated through the performance of certain rites, and whose attributes of avenging justice far overshadow the love and mercy He bears us.

4. Puberty (14-16 years).

Researches and investigations within this age-group reveal the strong " moral " aspect of religious considerations. The predominant religious obligations centred on morals (with a very definite bias on sexual problems) and on the sense of guilt play a considerable part in the affective ties which bind the young man and the young girl to religion (especially in the Sacrament of Penance) unless, on the contrary, they contribute to a turning away from religion. In this connection, reference can be made to the investigations of Fr. Delooz [16], of Brother Étienne [17], of the French research published under the title " A qui irions-nous ? " [18]

---

16. DELOOZ P., La foi des élèves de l'enseignement d'État en Belgique, in Nouvelle Revue Théologique, Louvain, january 1951, p. 37.

17. Frère ÉTIENNE, o. c., p. 40.

18. A qui irions-nous ? Inquiry into the meaning of Christian life (950 answers, 15-18 year old youths in France). Centre d'Études Pédagogiques, 15, rue Louis Davis, Paris, 1956. The wording of the questions oriented the replies towards ambition and wealth in so far as they are the principal obstacles to a Christian life.

Ausubel has demonstrated that children coming from abnormal family circles have a tendency to linger within a rigid form of morality (at times rejected with violence) and consequently their religion seems to center on a deep sense of guilt.

It is, of course, extremely important that man should adhere to God as the sinner awaiting forgiveness and salvation from Him alone. Nevertheless, it seems to us that religious pedagogy should particularly be on guard against the following points : religion and moralism (or morals) should not be treated as identical, religion calls for good morals but these are not automatic guarantees of a true Christian religion — direct the psychic sense of guilt on to other and more varied matters of conduct, sexual ones are of themselves, and naturally so, very prone to a sense of spontaneous culpability — an attentive and carefully-handled education helping to discern the sin in actions and the sin in thoughts (making the distinction between " thoughts " and " consenting " to thoughts, which the scrupulous fail to do, and this is just the age when moral-religious scruples develop) — finally, a well-balanced assimilation of the two notions of authority and love (in God) combining in an ever-ready pardon, in which the malice of sin is appreciated in the light of God's goodness, not the generosity of God measured to the importance of our sins (as in all those whose religion remains stamped with a more or less conscious egocentrism).

5. *The Adolescent (16-18 years).*

We have dealt, in the first part of this article, with the outcome of faith at the end of adolescence and in the adult soul. This is the age when the problems of religious doubts arise : intellectual doubts (in students), or more insidiously under the pressure of social conditions (in the young working-class adolescents who discover a world practically closed to the supernatural). From the pedagogical point of view, we think it would be unwise to lay great stress on what is sometimes called " Christian evidence " and that one must allow for a certain element of doubt corresponding with a certain degree of speculation even in the midst of adherence to the faith. Recent investigations by Fr. Delooz [19] show that in a group of 1 200 girls between 16 and 20 years old, the purer the motives for belief, the greater also is the tendency to doubt — while there

---

19. DELOOZ P., *Une enquête sur la foi des Collégiennes*, Éditions du Foyer Notre-Dame, Bruxelles. *Une enquête sur la foi des Collégiens.* Éd. du Foyer Notre-Dame, Bruxelles, 1951 (2d ed).

is no connection between doctrinal errors in matters of faith and the frequency of doubts.

Concluding this second part, we would again stress the importance of the first years of life on the ulterior development. On the psychic level (the only one, as we have previously said, which is the subject of strictly positive and scientific research) the general law of recapitulation must always be taken into account : the entire past affects our way of living the present moment. Any disturbance or deficiency at one stage or other continues to bear consequences and to influence all the others, either by obstructing the development (these are the worst cases) or (at the least) by inducing ways of living or feeling intended, at best, to compensate for the deficit. This is why those earliest influences are the most important and the hardest to rectify in later life.

III. DIFFICULTIES INHERENT IN CHILDREN
DEPRIVED OF FAMILY LIFE

We would have liked, in this final section, to base ourselves on well-founded positive research, as in the preceding one. Unfortunately, this is not possible, we will have to limit ourselves to a few empirical observations more in the nature of impressions received by educators. We will use these both as an opening for the discussion and as an incentive for further research which, however, are bound to be difficult.

1) *The characteristics of the bereft child*, in secular matters (intelligence, nervous energy, affectivity, etc.) are actually much better known than they were thirty years ago. The works of Jenny Aubry, Bowlby, Goldfarb, Spitz, Theis, etc., have thrown considerable light on the critical periods and disastrous consequences which the deprivation of a family, especially of a mother, occasion.

In the religious domain unfortunately, we can only go by certain impressions which, though fairly unanimously agreed, are not easy to connect with specific evaluations and co-relations. We can here refer to articles by Fr. Cruchon [20] and Madame Donatil [21], and

---

20. " Manque de personnalité des adolescentes dans les manifestations de leur vie religieuse " (summary of the report by P. Cruchon, S. J.) in *La Religieuse d'Action Hospitalière et Sociale*, Paris, November 1954, p. 267.

21. DONATIL-BARMARIN R. M., " The Doctrine of Divine Love : a Psychological Difficulty Met with by Catechists Among the Children Deprived of Family Influence ", in *Lumen Vitae*, vol. X, 1955, n° 4, pp. 564-568.

two interesting reports on the role of the father in the volume " *Vaterproblem* " [22].

Madame Donatil has stressed the difficulty of transmitting the doctrine of divine love to children deprived of a home. She shows too that the mere absence of parents (actual orphans) is not so harmful as the permanent impression left on children who have been ill-treated, or have been witnesses of their parents' unworthy conduct (drunkenness, debauchery). Father Cruchon speaking of a reformatory for delinquents (girls), establishes the following religious characteristics : — conformism allied to a certain degree of superstition — motives of self-interest in religious behaviour (to win good opinions) — extraordinarily good imitation of a teacher one has " fallen " for — excessive emotionalism leading, at times, to pseudo-vocations of a purely sentimental nature encouraged by dreams of promotion.

While gathering material for this report, we asked M[lle] Colette Lauwers, who gives much of her time to the religious training of the children of a large Belgian home for orphans (Brugelette), to pay special attention to those children whose family circle was disunited or non-existent, setting aside the mentally-deficient or other seriously unbalanced cases. These are her findings from the religious view-point : — The " Omnipotence " is the most impressive characteristic for the 7-10 year-old, and the fear of the Great Judge — where the subject of love is assimilated, it is in connection with those joys and good things one is actually longing for — one frequently hears talk of " the end of the world " (longing to escape ? need for security ?) — there is also a particularly vivid identification of God with the person who teaches religion. Among the older girls in many cases it seems that moralism (system of social restraint imposed by daily life) actually replaces religion properly so-called ; when they go out to work and achieve freedom, it also means that they discard all religious practice. The element of " Sin " which rests on lack of discipline. plays a great part ; confession also is looked upon in certain cases as a means of regaining favour... with the community. However, there seems also to exist on quite a different plane and in a certain measure a hidden conception of God detached from any organized religion, but they do not succeed in really making it a part of their lives. The prayer attitude remains essentially one of " requests. "

It is not difficult to relate these characteristics with the main

---

22. *Vaterproblem in Psychotherapie, Religion und Gesellschaft*, written and published by Dr. Wilhelm Bitter (note especially the contributions by A. Köberle and O. Haendler), Stuttgart, Hippokrates Vg. 1954.

stages of psychic evolution, the basic features of which we have retraced in the second part of this article. However, it seems advisable to try to ascertain in what measure these traits are due to the absence of a family ; under what aspect (no mother, no father, no settled home circle) ; at what age ; lacking what possible substitutes, etc.

2) *Are there nothing but deficiencies ?* Observing first that many of the characteristics mentioned in the documents cited above are also evident among a great number of children brought up in normal families, it would seem that perhaps they are just more frequent or more marked among children lacking families, without for all that showing a really qualitative difference...

But, from the religious point of view, is there nothing to be gained by a boarding-school education ? Following certain opinions one could place on the " credit " side : — a diminution of class prejudices, the starting-point of a more universal charity regardless of social spheres — less culpability due to scruples (obsessional), this often comes from an over-rigid supervision which is not usually the case with children living in communities — a greater degree of submission in the sphere of mutual aid, at least when it is provided for by the rules or by the institute.

3) *The difficulty of being more precise* comes, first of all, from the great number of substitutes which, psychically, are placed at the disposal of children deprived of parents. Every child classed as orphan (socially) is not a psychic orphan. Symonds [23] has described various substitutes which automatically come into action to preserve effectively the child from the harmful effects of the loss of parents : identification with a substitute (an uncle, an older friend, a member of the staff of the institute), idealization of the deceased parent (here again, the orphan is privileged compared with the child of unworthy parents who have abandoned him or from whom he has been legally separated), etc. The actual occasion, natural or imposed, when the child becomes an orphan has, of course, considerable importance. Madame Favet-Boutonier [24] has given detailed descriptions of four such occasions producing completely different psychic results. This is the sort of research our group should undertake in order to assess subsequently the effect the loss of the family has on the awakening of the religious sense and on the assent to the fullness of faith.

---

23. SYMONDS R., *The Dynamic of Parent-Child Relationships*, Teachers College, Columbia U. Press, 1949, pp. 104 ff.

24. BOUTONIER J., " L'enfant orphelin ", in *Conférences de l'École des Parents*, Paris, April 1950 (No 7).

Psychological Conditions of Adult Faith

by Antoine VERGOTE

INTRODUCTION :
THE IMPLICATIONS OF A FREE CONSENT
TO THE WORD

Faith is a free consent to the Word by which God gives himself to man. In return, faith frees man from his bonds. Like truth itself and any true relation between two subjects, it both presumes freedom and leads to it. Religious faith, as a human act, is this paradox of initiative and welcome, of purpose and receptivity. Man opens himself to the creative Word, and the Word dilates man and awakens him to a freer consent. Faith, in releasing man from his bonds, arouses in him a more docile attention to the Other.

This double rhythm which is the pulse of encounter and exchange presumes a first rise of freedom. The measure of a man's inner freedom is that of the freedom which revelation brings him. It is his encounter with the Other which liberates him from his egocentric attitude. But then that encounter must take place.

Now only a man psychologically adult seems able to apprehend in reality the other as he exists in himself and to love him for what he is. Even this is only a paradigm used to convey the development of man and his relations with others ; the creative desire is but an ideal towards which human love tends.

This adult age is indeed of a psychological order. If in our society aptitude to marriage is a sign of adult age it is neither on the ground of a physiological maturity or simply of social working conditions ; it is an accepted fact that marriage presumes a certain degree of

---

1. Monsieur l'abbé Antoine VERGOTE was born at Courtrai in 1921. He won Doctorates in both Theology and Philosophy at Louvain University. In 1954 he was appointed Conference Master and in 1959 took charge of a Course at the same University. He lectures on epistemology and religious psychology. He is also a member of Societies of psychology, philosophy and psycho-analysis. He has published the following articles : Le IV⁰ Evangile, la psychologie d'Aristote et de S. Thomas, Freud et la psychanalyse, Angoisse et religion. — Address : 8 rue Jean Stas, Louvain, BELGIUM (Editor's note).

experience of life and human balance, but little is said of a capacity for love. It is taken for granted, and is expected to follow automatically the physiological maturation and a certain self-control which is the fruit of a good education. Yet the effective encounter with another and the ability to know this other as himself, essential conditions of a happy union, are not necessarily within reach of a well-bred and physiologically grown man. This encounter is part of human history, and its eventualities are foreshadowed by the past history of the subject. Similarly, the encounter with God is not immediately accessible to man. It is cradled in a human history, which prepares and determines its effective possibilities. Our psychic development is a determining factor in our eventual apprehension of the living God.

Far from us the attempt to limit the amplitude of human possibilities to an adult equilibrium. But with due regard to the inventive wealth of childhood and the dynamic and avid wonder of adolescence, we still must admit that genetic psychology is guided by a just presentiment when it gives its preference to adult age. Certain of its behaviourist criteria may well be severely criticized, like that of adaptation to reality, or social output. Man is not in himself an accomplished being, and certainly not a social function, and it would be fatal to keep religious psychology within the confines of a positivist psychology which runs the risk of stifling all our present anthropology. Fervent adherents of psychotechnique are a serious threat to the advent of adult faith ; for instead of raising in man a free consent, always personal and original, they seek to hedge him round and encircle him in their economic concepts. True faith will always be a spiritual childhood, the attitude of belief will always find renewal in the rise of ever revolutionary youth.

This warning against psychology need not however dispense us from examining the psychological conditions of adult faith. The knowledge of the one living God is possible in a man as tormented and neurotic as Bernanos' country priest. But we must agree that the psychological fragility of man corrodes both his human and religious gift. The psychologically adult age conditions the plenitude of faith. This is what we intend to prove, by examining faith in its relations with the two elements which characterize adult psychology : affective autonomy and social responsibilities.

Our study will follow at every stage the double movement which operates between human psychology and religious commitment : the advent of a new phase in the attitude of man towards his existence and towards his world may each time influence his religious faith and enlighten him on the inadequacy of his past acceptance of a provisional truth. Thus human experience can prepare an adjustment of faith and throw light on new virtualities. Faith is inserted in history as well as human existence.

I. AFFECTIVE AUTONOMY
AND SPIRITUAL CHILDHOOD

a. The believer is a child of God. Unless adult man returns to the state of childhood and becomes like a child, he will never enter the Kingdom of Heaven (Matthew 18, 1-4). For the believer is he who, from the heart of his humanity accepted and recognized, calls the living God : « Father ». Before the redemptive teaching of Christ, no man had dared to address God-All-Other as such. In this word, he acknowledges himself to be man and not God, and at the same time he opens himself to a Word which transcends him. From now on God is his God, and he is son of God just as the Son of man. It is his glory to be son of God because he has given up his will to be a god. As St. Paul says : faith is obedience. The glory of the Christian is to be glorified by the Father, after having accepted with humility his human impotence. Christ first, the Christian after him, are marked by the dialectic of the Cross.

Obedience to the Word, accepted dependence, trust in the power and the protection of the Living God ; are not these Christian virtues, these modes of existence incompatible with an adult psychology ? For adult man is independent, he is critical, and he is creative. The paradox of Christian existence is a problem for many of the faithful, who, unable to face it, solve it by a denial of spiritual childhood. Or else, which is not less frequent even if it is less flagrant, they take refuge in a false spiritual childhood, which is the immediate transposition of a human infantilism.

b. In no human sphere is the danger of infantilism greater than in the sphere of religious faith. Seeking to introduce, in the heart of the religious attitude, interpersonal family relations, it often fails and in the relations with God slips into filial attitudes which derive from a simply human childhood. Christian dogmatic itself may present the illusion of truly religious relations, while in reality there exists only a prolongation of a human attitude.

The close dependence of the religious attitude on the first family formation may also influence the dialogue between God and man. Psycho-social research on religious behaviour has confirmed this truth daily experienced, that early formation in the family exercises a predominant influence on adult religious practice. On the most varied cultural levels, the assimilation by the child of the religion of the parents predetermines his future religious behaviour. The main reason is that the family, in its very structure, presents many striking analogies with the religious institution, thus preparing the entrance of the child into it. [1] There is a symbiosis between family and spiritual appartenance.

Family structure can be said to be virtually religious. [2] Moreover, in a Christian family, feasts, ceremonies, values and principles are on the same religious and familiar scale. This family draws its cohesion from the religious tradition which it shares and transmits.

A serious study of the psycho-social reality of the family would therefore elucidate why parental influence is so predominant in religious behaviour. [3] Its ambivalence is sufficient to prove it. Rooted in the family constellation, the religious attitude is more likely than any other behaviour to retain the infantile characteristics of its prime emergence all the more so that its dogmatic content goes back to it as its birthplace. There is a certain insistance, apparently mystical, on the desire to be in all things a child of Mary, which renders a hollow sound. This attitude, which is uncongenial to the solid Christian who is embarrassed by its false confidences, does not deceive an experienced ear. It is an easy caricature of spiritual childhood.

c. Human childhood is stamped by its essential prematuration. At its birth, the child finds himself absolutely dependent on others. And if he is soon aware of the loving looks and smiles of his parents, his affection for them remains essentially narcissic, in the technical sense of the term. He loves those who care for him and feed him. His tenderness as his demands are addressed to those who surround him with kindness, and maintain him in affective peace and joy. The others, who are deaf to his sollicitations, he expels from his world as bad ; he leaves them out of his universe. But, towards kindly persons, he is, according to Piaget's formula, in an affective syncretism. [4] He possesses no explicit conscience of himself or of

---

1. See A. T. Boisen, *Religion in Crisis and Custom : a Sociological and Psychological Study*, New York, 1955, p. 35 ss.

2. G. Murphy in : G. Lindzey, *Handbook of Social Psychology*, New York, 1955, pp. 601-623.

3. See the two enquiries : G. Allport, G. M. Gillespie, J. Young, *The Religion of the post-war College Students*, in *Journal of Psychology*, 1948, 3-33. And the investigation carried out by the Institut français d'Opinion publique, published in : *Informations Catholiques Internationales*, 15 Dec. 1958, p. 13.

4. This phase of indifferentiation has been described by many psychologists. See on the subject : Piaget, *Les relations entre l'affectivité et l'intelligence dans le développement mental de l'enfant* (Course at the Sorbonne), Paris, 1954, pp. 57-59.

others. His subjectivity embraces others and the world of objects, as far as they are good. Neither he nor others are private subjectivities, as all happens within a perfect reciprocity of which pleasure is the regulating principle.

But man must grow beyond this egocentric attitude. In the beginning his affectivity is awakened and formed in and through his vital needs, which seek enjoyment and conservation in life. This affectivity, however, contains the germ of the knowledge of the other which is called love, and which it will only reach after a prolonged expansion. The child has no access to the point of view of another. The original affective undistinction has no knowledge of it.

Religious attitude is inscribed in its affectivity and follows its curve, even when it begins to introduce the child, in an obscure manner, into the presence of the All-Other. The child sees his god in the image of his father and attributes to him the essential qualities of his father. They are on common ground, are made of the same stuff, which is familiar to an affectivity which embraces all encounters within his own perspective. For the child, God co-exists with the father. Adult man may remain attached to this first experience of the other, and seek in every man a father who would respond to his always unsatisfied demands. Or he may cling to the paternal image of his God, seeking to satisfy his vital and affective needs, which remain like open wounds, even under cover of a successful social career. In this case, God is the captive of the egocentric universe of an anguished and starved affectivity. He is not apprehended in his own being, no more than the father is for the child.

The classical example, often cited by depth-psychologists, is that of a man internally consumed by a feeling of insecurity. He may fulfil important functions, but there is a weak spot in his system and his lack of certitude throws him into an intolerable state of abandon. There are stiles in the field of his existence which only others can help him to cross, day after day. It has been noted that this type of man clings sometimes particularly to Providence. When he prays, he is no longer alone. With God, he hopes to do all he feels unable to do. He loves to dwell on this permanent support which accompanies him in all the trials of life. Besides, traditional prayers echo his own history. « The Lord is my shepherd. He is my rock... ». In his thought, and in all interior conflicts, he experiences the value of his trust. Are not men strong because they pray, because God is with them ?

At other times, religion may appear to them as immensely sad, and deadly dull. They long to rely on their own strength. Their dependence on others is a burden and they find no permanent relief in the kindness of their Father in Heaven. They are lonely in their solitude, and no one can deliver them. They are burdened and oppressed, and the yoke of Christ does not alleviate the yoke of their own existence.

Indeed, apart from moments of intense desires of human peace, religion brings them no true joy. It fails to be an independent dynamic value, and only a value lived and experienced can be a source of creation and joy. Religion enslaved by desires of security and human serenity may help to make life more tolerable ; reduced to a human end, it can still transfuse a dim light of its own truth. But in the form of a function, not an autonomous value, it cannot transform man through divine truth.

A human image is always interposed between God and the man who is not affectively autonomous. This is why crisis-born vocations so often turn into vocation crises. As soon as the subject is delivered from his infantile affective needs, he abandons religious life. Even conversions follow this rule. Let me recall the case of a young convert, who, in a state of deep depression, and left to herself, discovered the Church, Mystical Body of Christ. The vitality of Christ continued in humanity, sensibly present in the Sacraments, building up the great human family. This Christian truth, she had discovered in a lightning experience, which lasted a few weeks, and filled her with an extraordinary joy and plenitude. An authentic conversion, obviously. Yet, it was only a fugitive light in a state of twilight depression. This reality of the Mystical Body, admirably apprehended and experienced during a few weeks, responded too naturally to an immense desire for vital warmth and tenderness. Under the sway of a new depression, the creative joy of this young faith became singularly blurred. Long months of bitter disappointments and consecutive rebellions were to follow, before she found her way again to this new vital centre, discovered at the summit of an exasperated affectivity.

d. The encounter with the living God takes place in a theocentric faith and demands the displacement of the centre of interest and the point of view. A self-bound affectivity knows only its own point of view and brings everything back to itself. No true dialogue can occur, because the urgency of his affective needs withdraws man from the thoughts of the Other, even though it has a power of attraction. The religious life of men affectively non-adult runs the risk of wasting itself in a limited number of purely human functions.

Adult faith, fostered by an affectivity liberated in some measure from itself, will be a dogmatic faith. It will seek God as He is in his own being, as He has uttered Himself in His Word. God can be our salvation, in the measure in which man communes with life strange to him, beyond his human needs. But this living God, far from fulfilling his desires, will often deceive them. He satisfies man, but against man's own demands.

Enquiries have proved that the adult often abandons dogmatic faith. [1] This is particularly true among protestants, as dogma as well as form of worship are largely left to their own choice. It would be interesting to study the direction of this movement towards a liberal faith. We may presume that it reveals the uneasiness of the adult in the face of a doctrine too imbued with infantile imagery. The trouble is that the non-dogmatic God remains to a large extent the God of man's own conception, according to his own desires. Affective autonomy may therefore bring about a religious crisis. This is a salutary crisis, as the renunciation of the desire of God prepares the discovery of divine paternity. Affective autonomy, as feature of adult psychology, appears at first sight contrary to the psychological conception of childhood and of obedience in faith. At certain times indeed it stands in effective opposition, but in reality it is its condition.

II. INSERTION IN THE SOCIAL BEING AND SPIRITUALITY OF ADULT MAN

a. Professional and family responsibilities form and express psychological maturity. In them, the absolute and undetermined aspirations of youth find their reality and their efficacy. Less « idealist » in sentiment, adult man is capable of gauging reality by the measure of values, and by his personal decisions, he can introduce in the landscapes of social life the notion of the last ends. Youth is almost uniquely concerned with the future ; it moves in the temporary, and derives from its still undefined possibilities the freshness of the detachment which is its charm. Adult man founds a family ; it is the great work of his life. He has gone beyond the solitary indecision between hope and reality. He can commit himself, because stability is the condition of realization. More detached from his « ideal, » he takes his responsibilities and lives no longer by procuration.

---

1. ALLPORT, *The Individual and his Religion,* New York, 1953, pp. 40-44. An enquiry carried out among 500 American university students reveals that the majority have remained religious and believe in a God, but only a quarter have adhered to theological dogmatic, and more than 56 % reject the church in which they have been brought up.

He has not for all that relinquished his creative will. In attaining psychological adult age, he has found a true and institutional channel of invention, and he precisely escapes the paralyzing alternative between accommodation and revolutionary dream of happiness. The adult who has not attained a certain degree of maturity refuses to commit himself in any definitive undertaking ; or else he superimposes on small daily events a wild aspiration towards total happiness. He may stifle his ideal in accommodation, or leave it on the nostalgic horizon of his short-sighted daily round ; but he does not really take possession of it. As all neurotics, he lives in a constant to-and-fro between the real and the imaginery.

b. Man may retain internal division, and it happens that a cleavage occurs between his psychological transformation and the evolution of his religious attitude. More often however the profound change caused in him by social and professional responsibilities challenges anew his religious attitude. It may not reach a crisis, but there is always a definite conflict between the new mode of existence of the adult and his religious attitude. Statistics indeed set the problem of the astonishing evanescence of religious practice at adult age. The enquiry conducted by J. H. Fichter [1] shows the religious profile of a medium American community as such : great religious fervour during adolescence and post-adolescence ; lapse in religious practice after the age of 20 ; between 30 and 39, the abstention is more marked ; after that age there is a progressive improvement. C. W. Telford, [2] who has studied the religious attitude of 1000 University men before and after their military service, concludes on a levelling on a lower scale. Among the most fervent, fidelity is on the wane, among hostile subjects, there is a real discovery of religion ; from this collective compromise results a decrease of religious life at adult age.

c. The significance of these figures is obviously not univocal. Many examples tend to show that the creative expansivity reached by the adult often throws him into conflict with the demands of a practised faith. Social contact with non-Christian conceptions, and above all the feeling that Christianity is absent from the human world, may gradually develop in him intellectual doubts on the truth of Christianity. And there is another doubt, more insidious and more total, which invades him in virtue of his human maturity.

---

1. J. H. FICHTER, S.J., *The Profile of Catholic Religious Life*, in *American Journal of Sociology*, 1952, *58*, 145-149.
2. C. W. TELFORD, *A Study of Religious Attitudes*, in *Journal of Social Psychology*, 1950, *31*, 217-230.

He acquires sometimes a sense of the inefficacy, and consequently of the illusory character, of religion. In so far as he is fully man, he finds in himself and in human values the spring of his creativeness. Is faith of any use to him ? We cannot ignore the pertinency of the question , because so far, faith has greatly helped him to become a man.

This feeling of the inanity of the religious attitude is often strengthened by the experience of a pronounced conflict which makes the attitude of faith appear in all its difficulty. For many, abandon and self-effacement before the All-Other, essential tenets of the attitude of faith, seem incompatible with the creative and expansive surge. Some do not reason out this conflict, yet it is at the heart of their existence. Passivity and humility are felt to be a menace to the self of one who achieves realization. And, unless he remains on the human slope of the religious question, the believer must accede to this stage of receptivity, to this contemplative component of Christianity. To believe is to allow God to will in us, and in us to accomplish our salvation, at times almost against our will. Faith is together intellectual assent and personal trust.

d. The conflict may be singularly aggravated by an excessive stress, in certain forms of Christianity, on so-called passive virtues. Humility, obedience, chastity, seem at times to constitute the most essential Christian attitude. These qualities — real without the shadow of a doubt — appear to certain Christians as very irritating Biblical themes, in so far as they express a depressing human impotence. « The poor of Israel, those who weep and thirst for justice »... shining truths which have shed their paradoxical eloquence ! Because they are associated with psycho-social attitudes of weakness and secret resentment, unwelcome failures and inefficient desires ! Psycho-social research on the formation of religious sects have very clearly proved that those who are attracted by the sects are the restless, the unhappy, the emigrants and those who have lost caste. [1] The sect seems to offer them a fatherland where they are admitted and recover their value. Separated from others, and blessed by a privileged and absolute religious experience, they rediscover in the sect the social status which society as a whole denies them. Psycho-sociological analyses clearly reveal the secret motives of a sectarian attitude prevalent in certain Catholic circles, which is distasteful to lay adults. This sectarianism finds expression in the eclipse of active virtues such as creative generosity, of initiative,

---

1. See for ex. W. R. Catton, *What Kind of People does a Religious Cult attract?*, in *Am. Sociological Review*, 1957, 22, 561-566.

responsibility, the courage of one own's conscience, truth in affirmations of scientific order, loyalty and truthfulness in politics and in relations with non-Christians.

It is a lack of humanity which is found also in the tearful tone of certain prayers, in accents of false complaisance of devotions centred on the symbol of the heart. No inspired text produces this uneasiness, at least if it remains inserted in the context of its primary and paradoxical experience.

If Christianity appears at times to make a man less virile, it is not due to the exigencies of Christ or of St. Paul which have the power of provoking and scandalizing the man of the world. They contest his humanist creativeness and may provoke his revolt but never lead to a state of « ennui, » for they invite no connivance with human weakness. Therefore the present re-discovery of inspired texts must bring about a more authentic encounter of man with God. Human deficiency will no longer obscure to this extent the interrogation of man by the living God.

e. Lay spirituality in the Church of to-day corresponds certainly with the effort of the adult believer to establish harmony between his faith and his social commitments. If there exists a trans-temporal history of salvation, which the Christian must accept in humble obedience to the Word, this history is yet objectively unachieved. It remains to be done everywhere in the human universe, in a praxis which penetrates the history of man. True faith is not solely a trusting welcome of salvation ; it is also an active service in the Kingdom of God. And if it is the great task of adult man to build human society, it is a no less greater one to build the city of God. It is the adult's double task ; to build up the Church, and also to propagate the Christian sense of the realities of the world and of the profession. This vocation calls for all his human qualities. It can only be fulfilled by men who have reached the adult age of social and constructive realism.

In his prayer, St. Paul faces the God of the Covenant, and answers to his mission. He did not find God in the interior of the soul but in an historical call. [1] God placed him in front of an unachieved world. Is it not this call, rather than that of the God appealing to the heart, which adults are more apt to hear ?

The situation of the woman-mother is somewhat different. If the woman is not affectively troubled by anguish or misery, by the family burden, maternity may be for her a privileged religious

---

1. See L. Cerfaux, *L'Apôtre en présence de Dieu,* in *Recueil Lucien Cerfaux,* Gembloux, 1954, T. II, pp. 474-475, 478.

event. She experiences a reality which transcends her. Maternity introduces her into the mystery of life, which is beyond her and which yet enters into her. The child born of her body, she receives as a gift. Whatever she does to prepare birth, the child is not her work in truth. She accepts him in wonder. And this acceptance is for her like an initiation into the religious mystery of the origins of life.

Can this be the reason why woman in our civilization practises her religion better than man ? It cannot be the only reason... But without doubt the interior consent to her femininity and her maternity places her in an attitude of receptivity which prepares her to the contemplation of the absolute. Man, on the contrary, through the very process of his psychological « maturation, » is inclined to resist the religious invitation to the abandon of himself. And only a proper spirituality of believer in the world allows him to live his life of man and Christian without compromise. By himself applying religious values to human history, he is able to meet them and accept them.

CONCLUSIONS

We have mentioned only two factors which affect the problem of faith at adult age. Another worth considering is the experience made by each adult of human resistance to religious ideal, experience of which the issue is called : the realism of maturity. This also challenges his religious attitude. Another point for study is the desire for the integration of the personality which all psychologists acknowledge as a major process of psychological maturation ; the religious attitude, by the fact of its absolute value, cannot remain outside this movement of unification. Laying aside for the moment these new aspects, we will draw the conclusion of our present considerations.

In the story of humanity in the course of ages, there are several possible centres of living faith. The child, the adolescent, and the adult each enter these centres in their own way, and realize original possibilities. But these centres are not juxtaposed, simply and purely. There is a history of the individual, and therefore a history of his religious attitude.

The psychological growth of man goes through this rupture of the affective symbiosis existing between him and the universe, above all between him and others. While he frees himself from the affective attachment which is the mainstay of his existence and thus conquers his affective autonomy, he at the same time loses an image of God and a religious practice which were the prolongation of his affective childhood. This affective infantilism is frequently dressed in noble evangelical terms which may be deceptive, but it is radically opposed to spiritual childhood.

This rupture does not constitute a spontaneous movement towards a humanly and religiously adult attitude. To turn towards the living God as He is and has revealed Himself requires a radical transformation of the religious attitude. The term conversion may apply, even if it extends over many years, and even if God has already revealed Himself to the adolescent under His true name.

This theocentric conversion may be very inhibited by a non-adult psychology. Faith indeed transcends in some way the individual inherence into a psychology which absolutely ignores the disparity of the other. But the plenitude of faith remains conditioned by the human substance in which it is rooted.

Knowledge of the other imposes on the adult a responsibility towards others. He knows how to assume them. Thus he inserts himself in the concrete texture of the world which is in the making and to which he brings the fruit of his initiatives, however humble.

This commitment is of course incompatible with a belief in a God who marshals the course of things, so the faithful are seen to have recourse to their God mainly in cases where they are powerless in face of events. But if circumstances do not require them to bring into play their religious attitude to foster their human desires, they are torn between their attitude of trust and their human creativeness. A false accentuation of passive virtues aggravates the conflict.

Only a spirituality able to combine the attitude of faith with the sense of human creativeness will maintain its position at the level of adult psychology, and bring man to the synthesis of two attitudes which at the outset seem to repudiate one another.

3

Transmitting God's Message

Goals

The goal of religious education is the transmission of
God's message in order to educate to a mature, living faith.
The religion teacher must present God's message
not merely as a *truth* demanding assent, or as a
truth having value for his hearers, but as a *personal call*
inviting the hearer to a deep, personal union of faith
in Christ with God.

The Aim of Religious Education :
Deepening and Cultivating the Life of Faith

by Marcel VAN CASTER, S. J.

INTRODUCTION : CRITERION OF A GOOD METHOD

The reformation of religious methodology is an encouraging fact, attracting the attention of all those engaged in education. Some are anxious to seek out certain practical ways of improving their teaching : for instance, the use of intuitive means and supervised exercises. These questions relating to method are, however, in the best contemporary manuals on catechesis subordinated to considerations on the content of the Christian revelation. But even this matter of the message to be delivered is not the first to be elucidated before judging a method.

As its name implies, method is ' the means to an end. ' The criterion of a good catechetical method is its aptness for attaining the true end of religious education. What is this end ?

I. THE AIM OF RELIGIOUS EDUCATION

For years, happily, there has been a reaction against instruction divorced from life. The fact is insisted upon that education should be a preparation for life, and a full Christian education must take into account every aspect of the Christian's life. The religious aspect, the subject of religious education properly so-called, consists in the life of grace which should transform the whole man. In this scheme of education, religious instruction has not an immediate aim

---

[1] Address : 27, rue de Spa, Brussels, BELGIUM (Editor's note).

similar to the direct objectives of other branches of education. Circumstances may require that the catechism class deal with part of what should, by rights, devolve on the family, the parish or even a youth movement. But religious instruction has a definite aim of its own.

This instruction does not deal directly with exterior practices, which might be the effect of routine traditionalism. The life of the spirit is an activity of knowledge and love. The Christian learns in the religious course to know God personally in as deep and fruitful a manner as possible, so as to love Him with his whole soul, as He is. Since God calls us to a supernatural knowledge of Him, expanding in love, the proper aim of religious teaching is to deepen and cultivate the life of faith.

A theoretical knowledge, which would allow an unbeliever to obtain full marks in an examination, is not enough. An exhortation to religious practice without a consciousness of its significance, without supernatural inspiration, is deficient in essence. Pragmatism which is indifferent to truth constitutes as great a danger as religious knowledge divorced from action. It is a question of an indivisible activity : of a living knowledge which leads to a conscious commitment. Religious teaching should awaken and encourage the act of faith which develops itself into ' Christian mentality ' and inspires the whole behaviour of the Christian. [1]

A systematic analysis of the life of faith will lead us to suggest some methodological applications.

II. THE LIFE OF FAITH

God makes Himself known supernaturally by the coordination of two means : an exterior manifestation, which we call revelation, and an interior influence, which consists of the virtue of faith. The life of faith is therefore a double gift of God which man accepts and with which he collaborates with his whole soul. Our faith is our reply to the word of God.

---

[1] Among modern catechists who have dealt with this aim of religious instruction, we may quote : F. ARNOLD, *Dienst am Glauben*, Freiburg, 1948, 92 pp., and his article in *Lumen Vitae*, III (1948), pp. 448-509 ; J. COLOMB, *The Inner Milieu of the Catechism Course, ibid.*, V (1950), pp. 351-9.

1. The Word of God is a Living Gift.

This living reality must be discovered in contexts so familiar they have become dead letters. The sources of revelation are Holy Scripture and Tradition. They are not viewed in their true light when they are treated as ' documents relating to certain abstract truths. ' Faith sees in them God Himself speaking, with words, but especially with facts and finally in a complete manner through the Person of His Son. Words have only a subsidiary rôle in explaining the meaning of the facts and the Person of Our Lord. The content of revelation is in fact the providential design of salvation in Christ.

It is above all in carrying out His plan of salvation that God reveals to us who He is and to what union He calls us. The revealed fact is set before us and explained by the living messengers of God. Christ acts through His Church. The latter bears witness to Him, in the authority of its hierarchy and in the life of its members.

The same applies to the *virtue of faith*. It is not a lifeless ornament for our souls, but the working of Christ in us, a communication of His capacity for knowledge. A supernatural light and strength are infused into us by the Holy spirit. The life of faith consists therefore in cooperation with God acting in us so as to enter into His revelation.

2. Our Reply is an Active Welcome and a Penetration.

In order to be ready to believe we must be open to receive the word of God, *welcome* it without stifling it, accept it as the seed which must germinate and produce fruit (Cf. the parable of the Sower, Luke, VIII, 11 and St. James' admonition, I, 21).

The life of faith consists then in *penetrating* into the living truth which Christ communicates to us. Knowledge and commitment are indissolubly united in one action of which we can distinguish three aspects :

a) *The Christian sense : Credo Deum, sicut Christus eum revelavit.* — The object of our faith does not consist of ' pronouncements ' but of persons and personal relationships. It is not indeed a matter of knowing ' what ' is true but of ' Who ' God is and what our relations with Him are. '' This is eternal life, that they may know Thee, the one true God and Jesus Christ Whom Thou hast sent. '' (John, XVII, 3) To know Jesus Christ is to know

God personally, and the supernatural union with God in Him to which all men are called. This plan of salvation is the basis of the whole conception of Christian life. Penetrating this truth, we learn to perceive and judge all ideas, standards and situations " with the eyes of Christ. " We develop in ourselves the Christian sense of God and life.

This Christian mentality presupposes not only a knowledge but a personal commitment, as appears in the fact that the Christian sense is a transformation of our whole intellectual activity. We must give ourselves to Christ so that He makes us think like Him, in collaboration with His grace. Moreover, the intimate knowledge of a person can only be acquired if it is sustained by love. And above all, none can fully know God Who is Love without a love which comes from conature with Him ; for " God is love. " (*I John*, IV, 8).

b) *Confidence : Credo Deo, qui locutus est per Christum.* — The reason which makes our faith absolutely certain is the witness of God, which Christ bears. The interior light which enables us to enter more and more deeply into the meaning of revelation does not here on earth remove all the veils of the mystery, but in spite this relative obscurity, we are absolutely sure of possessing the truth, because we have trust in God, speaking through Christ. Therefore to develop the life of faith is also to make this trust ever more conscious and faithful in spite of all difficulties. When many of His hearers turned away from Jesus because of the ' hard saying, ' the head of the Apostles gave us a fine example of this confident faith : " Thou hast the words of eternal life. And we have believed and have known that Thou art the Christ, the Son of God. " (John, VI, 69)

The confidence which establishes the certitude of knowledge reaches its full development in the commitment of the whole person reaching out to the union which is the aim of our lives. " I know Whom I have believed. " (*I Tim.*, I, 12)

c) *The commitment : Credo in Deum, qui est finis meus in Christo.* — God has revealed Himself as our supernatural end. He has unveiled the mystery of His plan of salvation in Christ. To believe is to make the object of our life union with God in Jesus Christ. Here it is that thought and action are most intimately linked together. The life of faith as knowledgeable activity is the deepseated attitude of our soul, by which we recognize in the fullest sense of the term that the aim and meaning of our life is to encounter God in Christ. This attitude can only be completely real if it is the motive power of all our actions ; thus an active faith is the first requisite of a Christian life.

Our primary duty consists in completely adopting this Christian attitude. It has been sufficiently emphasized that faith without works is a dead faith. We may dare to remark as forcefully that works without faith are dead works. St. Paul repeats this in many ways, echoing a profound saying of Jesus which is too often misunderstood. Men who cared little about adapting their mentality to that of the divine Master and who were too much occupied with external works came and asked Him one day : " What shall we do that we may work the works of God ? " Jesus answered them ': " This is the work of God, that you believe in Him whom He hath sent. " (John, VI, 28-29) This orientation will be manifested in all the actions of the Christian, which thus witness to his living faith.

Here we come back to what was said at the beginning of this article. The aim of religious instruction is to promote the faith which is an active knowledge, a voluntarily cooperative mentality, an orientation of thought and action pledging the whole being. To deepen and enrich the life of faith consists in developing the transformation of our thought in its Christian sense and perfecting our trustful commitment towards union with God in Christ.

III. METHODOLOGICAL APPLICATIONS

Since the life of faith is a reply to God's word, the method lies in presenting the doctrine as the word of God and assisting the understanding and cooperation of the pupil to respond to the call of God.

It will therefore be advisable to emphasize this character at the outset of the religious course, making it clear that an active attitude of faith is expected. The different parts of the course will then clearly fall in their proper perspective.

1. *Presenting doctrine as the word of God* — The first element in the method will consist in putting the pupil in contact with the *sources* of revelation, as the Church interprets them with the authority communicated to it by Christ. Hence the importance of quoting Holy Scripture textually, but also of explicitly referring to living Tradition. The latter includes the expression of faith in certain doctrinal texts, in liturgical prayer and in the lives of Christians approved by the hierarchy, especially those of canonized saints.

The catechism, as distinct from Sacred History and Liturgy, is a theological text emanating from ecclesiastical Authority. This summary of doctrine, completed in the higher classes by very full excerpts of theological thought, has therefore an essential place in the method which must present doctrine as the word of God. But it is important not to separate it from the other witnesses to revealed truth. Amongst these, the liturgy fills an eminent place, although we must avoid exaggerating its didactic function. The Pope has found it necessary to recall recently the exact meaning of the principle : *lex orandi, lex credendi*. The law of prayer is determined by the law of faith ; it expresses the faith precisely because it is part of faith, to which it remains entirely subordinate. It is not the complete expression of the faith, for the whole of

Christian life is not simply a liturgy. The most important thing is to show that God speaks to us through the realization of His plan of salvation, revealed in the inspired books and explained in all the authentic manifestations of Christ's life in His Church.

2. *To help the conscious and committed ' response '* — Since faith is intellectual knowledge, the method cannot neglect any of the appropriate means for making truth understood by the intelligence and retained by the memory. Points of departure in the senses and imagination, precise notions, rational proofs and textual memorization are not to be despised, but there is the danger of insisting too much on them and neglecting to appeal to the other faculties whose help is needed for the life of faith. The mind itself can only know in a supernatural manner by means of the infused virtue of faith. This supernatural capacity raises all our spiritual modes of knowledge onto the ' Christian ' plane. The method must therefore bring all these possibilities into play. We may single out a few which are particularly important for a total response to God's word.

The sense of reality connotes both what Newman called the faculty of ' realizing ' the meaning of truth and what our contemporaries understand by ' an existential vision ' of life in, the best sense of the term. The religious lesson is continually dealing with something which is happening, or rather with a contact which is being established between one person and another. The method cannot therefore be content with a systematic theory, nor with providing technical details of external behaviour, but must cause the pupils to be aware of an actual event, containing an appeal from God and asking a response from the whole man.

The sense of values is in the same line of thought. Faith makes us know God as He is and as He wills to be for us. Our union with Him is the supreme value of our lives. The scale of all other values is established in relation to it and therefore a method which seeks to develop Christian mentality will appeal to the supernatural sense of values.

In order to convey to others an aspect of our existence and give it its true value we must ourselves have had a certain amount of experience.

Religious experience takes on different forms according to environment and temperament. It can be a positive preparation or an expectant waiting, even for non-Christians. The matter of knowing how the method of instruction of Christians can appeal to their supernatural experience sets a very delicate problem,

156

but it is the most important one from our point of view. The Christian cannot know experimentally the presence and interior action of God insofar as they are supernatural. All the masters of the spiritual life teach us that we must not depend too much on ' sensible ' consolations or desolation. However, the flavour of the supernatural goods which God communicates to us can be experienced to a certain degree. [1] By beginning our lesson with an invocation to the Holy Spirit together with our pupils, the Holy Spirit who works in us — *da nobis recta sapere et de Ejus semper consolatione gaudere* — by recalling what they have experienced of the divine action in their souls, on the occasion of a meditation on the person of Our Lord, when there is an invitation to a generous action, a fight against temptation, a good confession or a fervent communion ; by making our teaching lead to an attitude of prayer, we integrate the religious experience of our listeners with our method of instruction.

Finally, and this sums up all we have been saying, *the sense of mystery*. When our mind has not been deformed by rationalism, each movement of ' comprehension ' with which it enfolds what it has conquered is completed by a movement of ' extasy ' in which it opens out to what is beyond it. It is a greater thing to wonder than to understand. A method which pretends to explain the truths of faith in complete clarity is going the wrong way ; the best way to proceed is to open the mind so that it can tend in faith towards the complete truth which is beyond us. For if the mystery remains incomprehensible to us, it has been ' revealed, ' that is to say, God has released it in part from its transcendence for us. He has made it immanent in His Son made man. He has made us capable of knowing Him in a supernatural manner. The Christian sense of mystery allows us to illuminate our whole life with the supernatural light of revelation.

The Christian mystery contains more than an incomprehensible truth, which however is enlightening. It is the design of God, manifested with our collaboration. The sense of mystery is therefore a disposition to fulfil our part in the divine plan of salvation. The method which calls upon it, places the religious course completely in the true Christian spirit. [2]

---

[1] Pius XII, *Humani generis* : " Doctor Communis censet intellectum altiora bona ad ordinem moralem supernaturalem pertinentia aliquomodo percipere posse, quatenus *experiatur* in animo affectivam quamdam connaturalitatem cum eisdem bonis, dono gratiae additam. "

[2] See *The Spirit of the Religion Course, Lumen Vitae*, VI (1951), pp. 431-8.

All these suggestions convey that the method which suits religious instruction is that which develops the life of faith, knowledge and commitment. Everyone knows that we only get to know a virtue perfectly by practising it. The principle of the indissoluble unity between the knowledge of the truth and the active resolve to make of it the inspiration of one's life goes for all parts of Christian doctrine. The Message of Christ is only fully welcomed by those who enter consciously into the mystery of salvation in which God draws them.

CONCLUSION

He who came to bring us the divine revelation is the Master of both teacher and pupils. Jesus took as the aim of His teaching His disciples' faith and employed the best method to attain it. The religion teacher has not to substitute himself for Christ, Who continues to teach His faithful Himself by the light of His earthly life and by His action in souls. We are only His instruments. Our primary preoccupation must therefore be to make our pupils understand that Christ is their Master. Our ulterior effort will consist in imitating Jesus in His way of teaching.

Our Lord's way is not as simple as is sometimes believed. He did not confine Himself to employing images to make His doctrine perceptible to the senses. His parables were an instruction ' in mysterio ' for the purpose of enlightening those who wanted to believe and hiding the divine mystery from those who refused their faith. For the same reason, His style was often paradoxical. The divine Master taught mainly by His actions (miracles and example) and by the radiance of His person, rather than by words. His manner of expression was less notional than vital, less relative to things than to persons, less ' clear ' than suggestive, less static than dynamic. His teaching was external but first and continually interior : He gave the grace to respond to His message.

The people and the surroundings to which He addressed Himself were different from ours ; to imitate Him does not mean to copy Him literally, but to encase His teaching in a form adapted to our pupils at the same time keeping faithfully to its sense and spirit.

Teaching, Formation and Initiation

The Triple Task of the Catechesis

by Marcel VAN CASTER, S.J.

INTRODUCTION

THE CATECHETICAL RENEWAL

Let us situate our study in the renewal of the catechesis of the XXth century. That will enable the reader also to situate himself in this renewal : and how does he stand ? In which direction and towards what improved synthesis of essential elements is he asked to advance ?

One can discern three periods in the maturation of the catechesis since 1900. According to the country in question, these periods have succeeded one another sometimes slower, sometimes faster, and exchanges have taken place between countries. If on the whole there is evidence of a chronological evolution, we are dealing above all with three crystallizations of a psychological development.

First Period.

Attention is first drawn to the truths and realities of fact belonging to the *object* of the faith. Specified and systematized, these traits constitute the « Christian doctrine, » which is codified in the official text of the catechism. The catechesis, then, conceives itself as teaching this doctrine, and especially as a means of making the text of the catechism well understood.

Now, the beginning of the XXth century is particularized by its renewal of « didactic » methods for profane teaching. From now on, efforts will be made to benefit religious teaching as well, i.e., by intuitive and active methods ; not starting from a formal text ; treating it as a resumé of the lesson, etc.

---

1. Address : 184, rue Washington, Brussels, BELGIUM.

In spite of these didactic improvements, the teaching of truth « in itself » even though followed by practical « applications » dissociated too apparently (or did not bind organically enough) doctrine and life. It was necessary therefore to dispel the uneasiness of a doctrine that was cut off from life.

Second Period.

The accent was therefore placed on « life. » The divine revelation is not only truth « in itself, » but it is also truth « for me. » The catechesis is now centered on the *subject*, who must « live as a Christian. »

If, previously, dogmas had already been presented as « motives of action, » it is now the very vitality of Christianism which is all important, and attempts are made to persuade the catechized to participate actively therein. This need of the catechesis finds valuable support in various « movements » that are developing in the Church, but without unity having been achieved. They are movements of action : liturgical, pastoral, grouping of youth, catholic action. They are also movements of ideas : theology of the Mystical Body, biblical exegesis, liturgical spirituality, psychological studies, sociological research.

As invariably happens, certain of those promoting the reaction simplified exaggeratedly, or altered the directives given for the formation of a christian life as they affected the interests, capacities and activities of the individual. Thus, some of them went perhaps to another extreme : a life cut off from doctrine is as defective as a doctrine cut off from life.

Others, better advised, put to profit the above mentioned movements of ideas and action by basing their religious formation on a sound doctrine, one more centred on the role of Christ, ever-living Mediator ; on a doctrine that depends more on the bible and the liturgy, the presentation of which takes clearly into account the psychological growth and the sociological milieu of the individual.

Such a union of doctrine and life seemed a valid solution. All that was necessary was to strive unceasingly for its perfection within its own boundaries. But on closer inspection, it was found that the principal element remained almost entirely in the shadows, viz., the very nature of truth and of life, with which the catechesis is concerned.

Thought, from which will be born the best fruits of the catechetical renewal, is now given to the essential nature of the two components of the problem — the object and the subject, and as to what makes their union in the catechesis so unique.

The primordial object of the revelation is an interpersonal relationship : it is God who speaks to us ; it is God who makes Himself known to us in outward signs. The catechesis must transmit the Word of God. Its first duty then is to be faithful to this Word.

Fidelity to the very character of the contents : God who calls us to enter into communion with him in Jesus Christ. ' Existentielle ' reality, demanding that the catechesis be, to a certain extent, the announcement of an event. It will present the doctrine as the veritable interpretation of this event.

Fidelity to the right forms of the Word of God. They are multiple. The catechesis must make them all known in absolute authenticity. Living sources will have priority over abstract codifications. It is not enough to say in « our » way the equivalent of what God has said ; we must say what God says « as » He Himself says it.

And finally, fidelity to the *actuality* of the Word of God. God speaks in the act itself of the catechesis. That is why the catechesis must be above all an « initiation into the mystery of God who speaks to us » and especially God who speaks to us in Jesus Christ in His Church. The first initiation, or the most complete one, should make the listener enter into a real dialogue with God.

Thought given to the other component of the problem gives rise to the same demand. Man, to whom the catechesis is addressed, is called to enter and progress in *the faith*, which means giving a welcome to the Word of God. Above all, the catechesis must take into account the interpersonal character of the knowledge of faith.

*
* *

It is this, then, that we must study and consider in all its aspects. It is the veritable synthesis between truth and life , the justified arrangement of the three levels or dimensions of the catechesis : instruction, formation and initiation.

Let us see that what is in process of development and maturity in the « third period » is not an element of the same type as that already employed for instruction and formation. It is a « new » dimension (or too little perceived in preceding periods) the dimension of the « meeting » that of the actual dialogue and that of the conscious interpersonal contact.

In the catechesis, a doctrine and life cut off from a meeting with God is just as inacceptable as a doctrine cut off from life or a life cut off from doctrine. Instruction and formation cannot be separated from the initiation. It is the latter that determines the degree of validity and the methods of use of the others. It would be wrong to wish to establish a theoretical instruction and a practical formation with the idea of adding an initiation into the dialogue with God. Catechetical methods must be thought out again beginning with the « initiation. » For example, how to present and how to help the understanding of the « signs » by which a person makes himself known. In a catechesis faithful to the Word of God, it is always a question of initiation, to which instruction and formation are subservient.

This evolution is like the gradual blossoming of what was nearly always found, at least implicitly, among the best catechizers and catechists. It continues through the action of the Holy Spirit in the life and thought of the Church, great joy to those who participate to the full, but a warning to those who persist in too partial a point of view. It brings to light the insufficiency of a teaching predominantly intellectual and the insufficiency of a formation predominantly moral . At the same time it shows the need for an initiation, on the theological level, into the « meeting » between God who speaks, and man, who believes, in Jesus Christ in His Church.

I. THE CATECHESIS AND ITS ESSENTIAL TASK

What do we mean by « catechesis ? » Over and above the Christian context this vocable derives from the Greek verb signifying : to make resound in such a manner as to give back an « echo. » In the Christian context in the first centuries, where two or three stages of predication could be discerned — the first announcement of the Gospel to non-Christians, the preparation of catechumens for the sacraments and the more complete communicating of the doctrine to the baptized (converted) — the catechesis laid special emphasis on the stage following the kérygma.

To-day, certain people would be inclined to define the catechesis as a scholarly interpretation of the doctrine, distinct from predication, that exists in a more sacred framework. We use the term both in its complete and sacred sense. *Catechesis* is all activity connected with « making resound » the Word of God : in other words, the activity which makes known the divine revelation and aims at awakening and developing faith. How does the triple task of the catechesis correspond to its own goal ?

The general object of the Church consists in imparting and developing a Christian life, consciously lived ; for such a life renders glory to God and men find salvation therein. Now according to Paulinian terminology, to live as a Christian is to live in and with faith. A living faith is both *knowledge* and *commitment,* both of which entrain a *conversion* and are consummated in *communion.*

Within this general plan (a living faith being equivalent to the whole of a Christian life and forming the objective of all ecclesiastical action) the main goal of the catechesis is faith as a knowledge, knowledge that is not purely theoretical but knowledge that does not exist without conversion, knowledge which is already a communion of thought. But specifically, it is in the function of the aspect of *knowledge of faith* that all in the catechesis must defer and be judged. Not only knowledge of the contents of faith, i.e., the « sediment » of the revealed truths : but knowledge following the very nature of faith.

We shall be more precise about the knowledge of faith later. Let us show how the task of the catechesis responds to its own goal.

Task of the Catechesis.

The knowledge of faith is awakened and developed solely by a communication of the Word of God. The real task of the catechesis is to *communicate the Word of God* with a view to spreading faith. Now one can discern three levels both in the Word of God and in the knowledge of faith. The catechesis, by placing itself at each of these levels will have a triple task to perform.

We shall give a brief description of these three levels and shall do so in the order which will be the easiest to follow. We shall, however, have to inverse the procedure when defining the reciprocal relation between the three catechetical roles.

The divine revelation is based upon fact and truth. Level of objectivity. Knowledge of faith is objective. The catechesis has a task of instruction or teaching.

The gospel discovers for us a new scale of values. Level of subjectivity ; careful now : we do not talk of subjectiveness but of the stand taken by the subject in face of a value which appeals to his liberty. Knowledge of faith is personal, free, appealing to the subjectivity ; it constitutes the Christian scale of values adopted as the new « mentality » of the subject. The catechesis has the task of forming the Christian mentality.

The Word of God induces an entering into a conscious relationship with Him. God says that He invites man to live in communion with Him, in Jesus Christ. Level of intersubjectivity. For various reasons, the knowledge of faith is interpersonal. The believer realizes that God is speaking to him. In its fullest sense the « knowledge of God » is acquired in the meeting with God. Also, Christian faith is a participation in the known activity of Jesus Christ, activity communicated by Him to His Church, in order that those who « live in Him » know this life and that their life consist in « knowing » the Father and Him whom the Father has sent. The catechesis has a task of *initiation* into the mystery of God who gives Himself to us in an existing and efficient Word ; it is an initiation that is an invitation to share actively the knowing activity of Jesus Christ in His Church.

Anthropological Thought.

The trilogy of instruction, formation and initiation recalls the three anthropological categories of to have, to be, and to be with.

1) The instruction (or teaching) permits the acquiring of « knowledge » which comes under « to have, » data man absorbs and masters. Also, one says in regard to objects, facts and abstract truths « become aware of » and one hears talk of the conquest of science. If one applies this category to religion, one must be cautious. It is true that man can and does possess certain religious knowledge that instruction imparts to him. But he will never be the master of the knowledge of God ; he will never be able to say that he has acquired all of it ; he will never feel that he has God in his possession ; this would be the exact counterweight to the real religious attitude.

2) Formation concerns « the being, » the human subject himself, his development, his own values of thought and action. Education does not consist of clothing a man with good ideas and habits — as with an overcoat — but in aiding his spiritual growth ; in other words e ducere, to help a living creature to express outwardly what they are already imperfectly and what they must strive to express under the stimulation of the milieu.

And once again, there exists a real religious education or formation, but it is not solely concerned with man in his human environ-

164

ment. It helps the Christian to become more Christian, and that by making him more aware of the gift that God has freely bestowed upon him, and by causing him to respond to the divine grace within him.

3) The *third anthropological category* is the most important : that of the « being with, » that of the person-in-communion-with-others. As remarked by Gannaz [1] of those persons with whom one enters into a relationship, one no longer says « make the acquaintance of » but rather « become acquainted with. » By using the term « initiation » for acquaintance, which is entering into a relationship, we neither understand an « initium, » a beginning of an apprenticeship, nor a simple approach to any kind of mysterious reality, but the « inire » — the access and process of advancing into a more and more interpersonal relationship, which by its very intimacy, and because of its stretching beyond a purely individual life, is in some measure mysterious. If a communication of human life has a mysterious quality about it and if an intimate relationship between men needs an initiation, how much greater must be the mystery of God the Creator, and how remote from simple teaching must be the supernatural meeting with Him.

When God speaks to man to establish him in a life of communion with Him, the task of imparting this revelation will be an initiation par excellence. This appellation must on no account be reserved for the preparation of the sacraments or for general prayer. It is applicable to the entire catechesis which permits an ever deeper penetration into the mystery of God who speaks.

II. RECIPROCAL IMPLICATIONS IN THE CATECHESIS

The evolution of the catechesis in the XXth century might give the impression that it is instruction that should take the lead in formation, and that the latter, developing according to its own rhythms, will be crowned, if all goes well, by an entering into contact with God — a very transitory contact in any case. This is inexact. The reverse is more likely to happen.

The contact with God is not to be found at the end of an impersonal instruction and an anthropocentric formation. To begin

---

1. *Catéchistes*, 47, p. 221.

with, there is no revelation of abstract ideas ; on the contrary, the latter are the results of the reflection on the living knowledge accorded by God in a contact with Him. In the catechesis, the entering into contact with God takes place at the beginning (eventually after a pre-catechesis) : As soon as the catechist really shows a sign of God, it is God making Himself known in this sign and who is leading man into a dialogue with Him.

Also formation is not so much a condition as a concomitant effect of the meeting with God. If the welcome of the Gospel demands that man not withhold himself from God nor be distracted from God (the parable of the sower), one must not hope at first to obtain a conversion that from worldly values will swing to Christian values, for it is the gospel as the Voice of God calling to enter into communion with Him in Jesus Christ that will permit the conversion. In the catechesis, initiation has more than a formation value, it is supernaturally transforming.

Initiation is the « absolute » task of the catechesis, concurrent with which are two « relative » tasks. Instruction and formation are in the service of initiation and must therefore take their orders from it. Occasionally they may receive the emphasis but can never stand as absolute entities without reference to the dialogue with God.

So much then for religious information. It is indispensable. The Christian religion is based on facts that form the very object of instruction. The divine revelation contains a doctrine that the Church has made explicit with the aid of the Holy Ghost and which must be taught. Compared with other forms of the ministry of the Word of God, such as the homily initiating prayers and the exhortation directly aimed at a moral formation, the catechesis when dealing with schoolchildren and adults who have begun to reflect upon religion, will be clearly instructive. See what is said on this subject in the Declaration of the French Episcopat in 1957. (*Lumen Vitae*, XII, p. 672)

This however does not signify in any way that this instruction is absolutely identical to profane teaching, nor that it can be solely developed as an enrichment of the intelligence. This instruction is in the service of the initiation. It must not be forgotten in spite of the temptations that will be encountered to neglect the initiation. For many catechists and professors, teaching as an absolute entity is easier than the far more delicate process of initiation. The same temptation exists for those in charge of administration. It is true that a certain organization renders great service to the preservation and even development of life. And religious teaching is more susceptible than initiation to become organized. Programmes, manuals, methods, examinations, diplomas, all those can be useful — but, one must avoid the great pitfalls that beset the development of an organization for the teaching of the catechesis.

We are all aware of the danger of an organization that stifles inspiration, of the rules that kill the spirit, of the method that arrests initiative, of the conformity that replaces the living witness, of the routine that renounces research for improvement.

What we have said about teaching can be said about a religious formation. Neither one nor the other is of value in the catechesis except in its « relation » to the initiation.

The reciprocal implications of this triple task are presented as a rhythmic movement. It starts with the global phase : initiation in which neither instruction nor formation is yet clearly discernible. The movement passes through an analytical phase : explanation of instruction, specific formative activities, moments of halt in prayer. It ends with a synthetic phase : the Word of God is truly proclaimed and greeted with a clear understanding of its significance and transforming supernatural effect. This synthetic phase reached the first time is equivalent to the superior global phase in relation to a more searching analysis and to a richer and more coherent synthesis.

The dose of implications — if one can use such a term — will vary with the dominating factors involved : bible, liturgy, witness of life, doctrinal statements, and according to the catechetical milieu : family, school, liturgical assembly ; providing that school catechesis is not reduced to teaching and that doctrine is not removed from the family or homiletic catechesis.

A good auto critic will make us ask questions on the triple tasks of the catechesis : Have I followed the programme, shed light on the truths, suggested applications, spoken a language that listeners have understood, appealed to their activities, etc. ? Have I above all, been careful to make my auditors realize that it is God who speaks to them, and have I helped them to listen to God and to reply to Him ? In other words : have I, in giving instruction and formation « initiated » into the mystery of God who speaks to us, in Jesus Christ in His Church ?

41

III. RECAPITULATORY TABLE - CONCLUSION

Word of God	Facts and Truths	Scale of Values	Lived Relation
Knowledge of faith	Adhesion to a doctrine	Transformation of a mentality	Realization of a meeting
Anthropological categories	Objectivity to have possession of certain data	Subjectivity to be development of the personality	Inter-subjectivity to be with participation in a communion
Catechesis	Instruction	Formation	Initiation

The catechesis :

— initiates the meeting which permits a participation in the supernatural relation that God starts when speaking to man.

— forms a Christian mentality which consists of values on an evangelical scale.

— teaches a doctrine that specifies and groups the facts and truths belonging to the divine message.

Initiation to Life With God

by Klemens TILMANN

1. Distorted Image of Christian Life.

A typical formula of the now past catechetical period is the reply found, with an occasional variant, in a great number of catechisms. After a first question : « Why are were here below ? » and the answer : « We are here below to do the will of God and thus get to heaven, » the catechism asks : « What must we do to get to heaven ? » The reply is : « To get to heaven we must — 1, believe, 2, observe the Commandments, 3, make use of the means of salvation. » This reply contains a number of positive facts, and on it rest principally the three main divisions of the catechism, the Creed (1), the Commandments (2) and the means of salvation (3). This order can boast of a long tradition. It comes to us from Auger (1563) and was used very extensively in Deharbe's catechisms (1847). [2]

On closer investigation, this reply avers itself awkward and dangerous. It presents Christian faith and Christian life and our personal relationship with God exclusively as a duty, therefore a burden. Seen thus, Christian life is no longer a life of redeemed children with their Father ; the joyous and grateful reply to the marvels operated by divine love ; the initiation to Christ ; nor, finally, our spiritual progress through the action of the Holy Spirit living in us as a new source of life. In this context, God is not seen, nor His initiative, love and grace as the beginning of Christian life, but only the obligation, the duty, the command and, through their instigation, the operation of man.

2. Effect on the Formulae for Examination of Conscience.

The dangers of this false outlook on Christian life are manifest

---

1. See biographical note in *Lumen Vitae,* XI (1956), p. 605. — Address : Klugstrasse 91, München 19, GERMANY (Editor's Note).
2. WEBER, *Zurück zu Deharbe?,* in *Katechetische Blätter,* 1947, p. 67.

in the forms for examination of conscience based on such a conception. These set forms follow the order of the Commandments. Generally speaking, the commandment of love and the precepts of the Gospel have no place in them. Furthermore, there where he should examine his relationship with God in the light of the First Commandment, the Christian often finds a series of questions which overlook the essential points. Here is an example drawn from an official diocesan publication:

First Commandment : Faith and Prayer. Have you wilfully entertained doubts on the faith ? Have you spoken lightly or ridiculed the faith, the Church, the clergy ? Have you approved of such talk ? Have you through regard for public opinion omitted to defend the faith or the Church ? Have you read, passed on, or encouraged others to read books or writings against the faith ? Have you attended meetings or associations of sects opposed to the Church ? Read their books or publications ? Have you renounced your faith — perhaps through joining societies proscribed by the Church (free thinkers, freemasons, leagues for incineration); by contracting a civil marriage only, or a mixed marriage in front of a non-catholic minister ; by omitting to bring up your children in the Catholic faith ; by apostatizing or abandoning the Church ? Have you committed sin through superstition (card shuffling, chain-letters, astrology) ? Have you given up saying daily prayers for any length of time ? Have you omitted prayer altogether ? Prayed without attention or respect ?

All these questions, even the last three, refer to the fulfilment of commandments and obligations. There is absolutely no inquiry into our living relationship with God. This formation is positively frightening when we know that Jesus expressly condemned such a mentality in the parable of the pharisee and publican. The pharisee, who had observed all the commandments and even exceeded them, therefore, according to this form of examination of conscience would not have found any sins, and yet he is declared not justified: this means that such a mentality and such a form of examination leave on one side the essential point and lead us astray on what is the will of God and on what we should be.

3. A Stage in the Process of Liberation : Education in Prayer.

The prevailing spirit of our catechetical teaching was to present the faith and Christian life unilaterly as the fulfilment of a duty, the observation of a commandment. Therefore, the consideration of the theoretical and practical initiation into prayer as an important part of catechesis was looked upon as a new and liberating factor. For initiation into prayer no longer consists, as it has done

170

up to now, in instructions on the duty and properties of prayer, but seeks to awaken to a life of prayer and enhance the value of its countless resources: invocations and colloquies, adoration and admiration, abandon and trust, contrition and love, joy and gratitude, etc. These are living manifestations, no longer the result of exterior commands, but that of the contemplation of God who reveals Himself and His works, and also of the interior movement of His grace. The child of God must be brought to speak with joy and gratitude to His Father, and he will then feel his interior life developing and becoming rich. There are many ways of fostering and building up a life of prayer: spontaneous prayer, prayers learnt by heart, prayer out of a book, interior prayer or that which accompanies communal recitation, responses to litanies, vocal or silent prayer, continuous or repeated, private or liturgical. Catechesis is now no longer satisfied with imparting notions, it has become the source of the practice of Christian life, the source of prayer. The advantage thus gained must not be lost.

4. A Néo-Testamentary Conception of Christian Life.

The further biblical thought penetrated into catechesis, the more did doctrine on Christian life gain in depth and vitality. In the teaching of Christian truths, abstract notions gave place more and more to the living God, who acts and calls us, gives Himself and converts us, illuminates, sanctifies and draws us to Himself through love. Since then, Christian life has increasingly been envisaged as a response to the living God. *For Christian life is essentially a thing quite apart from the punctilious observation of limiting commandments and the fulfilling of juridical defined obligations.* It is as different from this as a tree from a plastic model. The predominant factor in the formation of Christian life is not an extraneous law (the latter merely has the character of an outward guarantee), but a new principle of interior life which S. Paul defines as « the spiritual principle of life, » or « the law of Christ » (*Rom.*, VIII, 2 and *I Cor.*, IX, 21). It is the most vital and loving reply to the merciful, revealing and charitable God, a reply coming from the very depths of the human heart. It is life modelled on and lived in imitation of Christ. The observing of the great commandment of charity which *calls upon* us to respond to the proof of God's love. It is a new birth through baptism and confers membership with Christ. It is the Holy Spirit poured out in us. Therefore Saint Thomas Aquinas says: « The new law is principally the grace of the Holy

Spirit », merely repeating the teaching of S. Paul in his epistles to the Romans and the Galatians.

If we train children to envisage Christian life in this spirit, not only prayer, but the whole of Christian life itself will be freed from all narrowness, from all boring and depressing minuteness. The whole of their comportment towards God and towards God's creatures will reveal itself as the right answer to the nature and action of God and to His designs on creation. The questioning look of the Christian is not directed towards official instructions or duties to accomplish, but to the reality of the living God and of His creation. This is an invaluable gain.

If we would now condense this new acquirement into a short, simple and comprehensive catechetical formula, easily understood by children, adolescents and adults, we could adopt the formula: « *Living with God.* » God does not only want our faith, our prayer, our obedience; *God wants us to live with Him.* All who are baptized are called to this ; it is our purpose in life ; in it we find our happiness, our duty, now and for evermore.

5. *Concretely, What Is the Meaning of the Term* « *Living with God* » ?

The fullness and meaning of the formula « Living with God » is best seen when comparing the life of a Christian with God to the life of children with their parents, such as it exists in good families at the various ages. We here give the parallel.

The Child and his Parents	The Christian and God
1. The child sees his parents and knows they are there.	The Christian thinks of God and knows he is there.
2. The parents are more important than anything for the child ; whatever happens he wants to remain close to them (what cries when he is lost; what home-sickness).	Fundamentally, God is He who matters most to the Christian who draws his life from God and whatever happens wills to be united to Him.
3. The child knows that he is entirely dependent on his parents, that he receives everything from them.	The Christian knows that all the good he has comes from God and that he depends on His sustaining will as on His grace for every instant.
4. The child feels at home and safe near his parents.	In the same way : « hide me under the shelter of thy wings » (*Ps.* 16, 8).

172

The Child and his Parents	The Christian and God
5. He tells them his experiences.	He discloses his life to God in prayer and talks to Him about it.
6. He listens to what his parents tell him.	He listens to the word of God.
7. He thanks them when they give him something.	He returns thanks for the gifts of God.
8. He often asks with perfect trust in order to obtain what he wishes.	In the same way : « Ask and you shall receive » (Matth. VII, 7).
9. He says « Good morning » and « Good night. »	He prays morning and evening.
10. He imitates his parents, often in the very smallest ways.	He tries to imitate God « ... that so you may be the true sons of your Father » (Matth. V, 45). « As God's favoured children you must be like Him (Eph. V, 1). « Be merciful, then, as your Father is merciful » (Luke VI, 36).
11. He adheres to his parents' opinion on men and things. As he gets older, he asks for their advice when in doubt.	He tries to follow God's ways of judging and accept His thoughts.
12. When uncertain as regards a moral judgment, he asks himself : what would my parents say ?	He seeks to know what God thinks of his own actions.
13. Children are very obedient.	« to do Thy will, O my God, is all my desire. » (Ps. 39, 9).
14. He knows his parents think of everything for him and seek his highest good.	He is sure that everything helps to secure the good of those who love God (see Rom. VIII, 28).
15. He knows his parents keep their word and he rejoices.	The Christian puts his faith in the promises of God and lives in happy expectation.
16. He lets himself be led by the hand, and later by advice.	« by sure paths He leads me » (Ps. 22, 3).
17. He readily admits when his parents are right and agrees willingly.	He admits God is always right. « Thou hast right on thy side » (Ps. 50, 6).
18. When his parents are « cross » because he has done something wrong, he hopes they will calm down and asks their pardon.	« must Thy jealous anger still burn unquenched ? » (Ps. 78, 5). « to my sins be merciful » (Ps. 24, 18).

173

The Child and his Parents	The Christian and God

The Child and his Parents

19. He accepts the punishment deserved if he has been naughty.
20. If he is unhappy, he tells his mother.
21. He finds it quite in order that his parents should talk of things he does not understand or which do not concern him.
22. He submits if his parents require him to do something disagreeable.
23. Sometimes he shows his love by embracing them and kissing them.

The Christian and God

« Bethinking me still of the charge thou givest, I will mark thy footsteps » (*Ps.* 118, 15).

When he is troubled, he tells God. (see *Ps.* 87).

« by the full height of heaven above earth, my dealings are higher than your dealings, my thoughts than your thoughts. (Isaias LV, 8).

He is patient in trials and contradictions.

He knows how to pray with his whole heart and seeks, in Holy Communion, the most intimate contact.

Things and other people enter into his relationship with God.

24. The child lives on the bounty of his parents.

The Christian lives even more on the bounty of God.

25. He eats at their table.

He is fed at the table of the Lord.

26. He must give an account of the things he possesses, for instance, he cannot throw his coat away.

The Christian considers himself as a steward who must render an account of everything entrusted to him.

27. He knows that everything he finds in the house and garden reflect the will of his parents who have arranged everything.

« His the ocean, for who but He created it ? What other power fashioned the dry land ? (*Ps.* 94, 5). Moisture too for the forest trees, for the cedars of Lebanon, trees of the Lord own planting » (*Ps.* 103, 16).

28. If he works in the garden he follows his father's plan.

The Christian meditates on the plan of God and seeks to conform the world to it.

29. He knows that his parents love his brothers and sisters and want them all to be good to each other.

The Christian endeavours to behave towards all men as does the Heavenly Father « ... Love... that so you may be the true sons of your Father in heaven, who makes his sun rise on the evil and equally on the good... » (Matth., V, 45).

The Child and his Parents

30. « You wait till my father comes » says the child who is being unfairly treated.

31. The older children share the cares and know the mind of their parents.

32. According to their parents' views, they work at what is entrusted to them.

33. Good children pay attention to their parents' wishes.

34. They offer their services to their parents : « Can I help in any way ? What must I do now ? »

35. They have the greatest veneration for their parents.

36. They celebrate their parents feast day.

37. They give their parents presents.

38. They takes sides wholeheartedly for their parents' honour.

39. They endeavour to respond to the love of their parents and are supported by this love in every trial.

The Christian and God

« Do not avenge yourselves, allow retribution to run its course. Vengeance is mine, I will repay, says the Lord » (*Rom.*, XII, 19).

The Christian makes his own the care and designs of God on the world.

The Christian tries to administer whatever is entrusted to him according to God's views.

The Christian endeavours to pay attention to the wishes and designs of God.

He serves God : « Thy will be done. »

« I praise Thee... for the wonders of thy creation » (*Ps.* 138, 14). « Therefore Thou art magnified, O Lord God » (*Ps.* 9, 2). « None is like Thee » (*II Kings*, VII, 22). « I will proclaim thy renown to my brethren » (*Ps.* 21, 23).

We celebrate the Lord's feast days : « This day is a holiday of the Lord's own choosing ; greet this day with rejoicing » (*Ps.* 117, 24).

We celebrate the Holy Sacrifice and we give of our own goods.

« So that you should know, that we know that there is no other God save you. »

« The Lord's mercies have never failed me, what return shall I make to Him. » (*Ps.* 115, 12). « Gladly I take shelter under thy wings » (*Ps.* 62, 8).

We can here end this comparison. [1]

---

1. See *Katechetische Blätter*, 1960, Heft 1.

6. *Education of the Life with God in Catechesis.*

It is no exaggeration to say that to teach the child to live with God is the final practical end of all catechesis. Every instruction lends itself to this formative work, nevertheless some circumstances are more particularly favourable.

1) *The method of the first five minutes.* — For the initiation to prayer, the method of utilizing the first five minutes of the Catechism class, throughout the weeks and months, to speak in a practical way of one or other point in the life of prayer and show its application to daily life, has proved itself. We can proceed in the same manner to educate children to life with God. Each point in the comparison given above can be used as theme and be explained in a recollected way as is done in retreats or recollection days, and proposed for putting in practice during the week that follows.

If there are several catechism lessons in one week, in the subsequent lessons one will merely recall the resolution, eventually exchanging experiences or indicating a new line of thought. One week at least is necessary to carry out this exercise and turn it into a habit.

2) *The Teaching of the Bible.* — In almost all our catechism classes on the Bible, we explain the conduct of God towards men and men's response to the divine action: they listen, believe, obey, correspond to His plans, welcome His promises and rely on them, receive His gifts, give thanks and adore ; or else they turn from God, do not listen to Him, contradict or ruin His plans, end up in the greatest misfortunes, then are once more called by God and become converted. We see too how material things or men are entrusted to them, how they behave towards creation, try to understand God's plan and intentions and adhere to it, or make use of men and values to go against divine intentions ; how they are good or bad administrators, good or bad sons and daughters of the Heavenly Father. *In biblical stories, the reference is always to the action and the word of God and man's good or bad reply.* In our teaching, therefore, we will always repeat: This is how God acts and how we must respond to avoid falling into misfortune. Thus, in teaching the Bible, we always have the opportunity of speaking of the action of God and of our reply, in short, of *our life with God.*

But life with God is especially revealed to us in *the life of Jesus.* He is the perfect model, the Son of the Father, who knows the

Father, loves Him with a pure, unbounded love, considers the world and men as the work of the Father, knows and accomplishes all His desires, is only there for Him and to live entirely in Him. A very useful exercise, for personal meditation as for teaching the young, is to establish, for each paragraph of the parallel we have given above, a sentence or a corresponding episode drawn from the life of Jesus and in this way see how He lived with God.

We will quote a particularly significant example. It corresponds to Nos 7, 27, 28 and 38 of the parallel drawn, and even to a few more. When the disciples came back from their first apostolic mission, they related, full of joy, what they had done. But Jesus knew more than they did. He could see the work of His Father, and rejoiced at encountering the Father's action, expressing His great joy in these words: « O Father who art Lord of heaven and earth, I give thee praise that thou hast hidden all this from the wise and prudent, and revealed it to little children. » (Luke, X, 21.) This vision of God in exterior happenings and the spontaneous reply of His heart are a magnificent example of the life of Jesus with His Father.

3) *Making use of the Psalms.* We can also explain what life with God is by using the psalms, and certainly they do not only refer to the fulfilling of the commandments. We find there nearly the whole of life with God: praise and thanksgiving, adoration and homage, contrition and penance, petition and complaint, abandon and prayer, the offering of our whole life to the Lord, meditation on the works and actions of God, on his government, on his light, his graces, his protection and advice for each one.

Even children should be initiated to the psalms. If we carefully choose the psalms or extracts from them if we translate these accordingly and pray them with the children, they will learn, in a practical way, many things on the life with God which none of the commandments mention, although they belong to the life of the children of God with their Father. A « Psalter for Children » could be composed to be used for alternate prayer, some of which would serve at the beginning and end of the Catechism class, and others for specific subjects. No prayer rhyme, no repetition of the Our Father and the Hail Mary can replace words like the following, often heard and repeated in prayer: « ...earth in its turn should bless the Lord, » « every growing thing that the earth yields bless the Lord, » « Thy right hand supports me, » « Gladly I take shelter under thy wings, » « Lord of hosts, how I love thy dwelling-place !, » « He gives... food to the young ravens that cry out to Him, » « Moisture too, for the forest trees, » « In Thee we hope, » « The

Lord is my light and my deliverance ; whom have I to fear ?, »
« For his own worshippers the Lord has a Father's pity, » « Lord,
all the nations thou hast made must needs come and worship Thee,
so great Thou art, so marvellous in thy doings, Thou who alone
art God. »

These words bring children to an understanding of life with God.
They partake of the thoughts and sentiments of the psalmist and
thus develop a manner of living in which God is always present,
in which everything is seen from the viewpoint of God, examined
and accomplished with Him, received from Him.

7. *Lesson drawn from a New German Religion Textbook.*

The doctrine of life with God must hold a very special place
in the small religion textbook to be used before the German
Catechism in the second, third and fourth grades of the Primary
School. A trial edition for the third year is already in print. [1]
It gives, prior to First Confession, a positive moral formation and
an introduction on the way a child of God should live. The ten
main headings are repeated in the formulary of examination of
conscience. The first is *Living with God.*

The Child of God lives with his Heavenly Father

Jesus lived entirely with his Heavenly Father. He always thought
of Him, prayed and listened to Him. Everything Jesus did was done
for love of God. Whatever the Heavenly Father desired him to do, he
obediently accomplished ; even the suffering his Father sent him, he
endured with patience. He thanked God for everything and trusted Him
in all things. He knew himself always under the protection of the
Father.

Seeing the flowers and birds, he would think : It is the Father who
made them so beautiful and keeps them alive. When men came to him,
he would say to himself : The Father loves them, I will love them as
my Father loves them and show them the way to heaven.

Let us learn of Jesus to live with God. It is the greatest and most
important thing in this life. Let us often think of God, love Him with
all our hearts and be for Him a cause of joy.

---

1. *In Gottes liebe,* I. Kath. Schulkommissariat in Bayern, München 2, Max-
burgstrasse 2/III.

When we live with God :

We willingly think of God.
We often pay homage to God.
We give joy to God.
We willingly listen to the word of God.
We talk to God of everything that is in our hearts.

We thank God at once for any benefit.
We abandon ourself to God's guidance.
We pray to God with perfect confidence.

We often ask God : What will you have me do now ?
We willingly do God's will.
During work we say : « It is all for Thee, my God. »
We treat others as children of God.

In temptation we remain faithful to God.
After sinning, we implore God's forgiveness.
In any misfortune we remain firmly trustful : God arranges everything
    for our good.

We put up with difficulties for love of God.
We do not forget that we will only understand the ways of God in
    heaven.
We are happy that God loves us.
We rejoice in the thought of eternal life with God.

Reflect :   The child of God lives with his Heavenly Father.
            What does he think and what does he do :
            1. When something pleasant happens to him ?
            2. When he begins work ?
            3. When he sees his duty ?
            4. In sorrow ?
            5. In success ?
            6. When in doubt as to what to do ?
            7. In sickness ?
            8. When about to make a sacrifice ?
            9. When he sees a sin being committed ?
            10. If someone is good to him ?
            11. When he falls into misfortune ?
            12. When he sees someone in want ?

*Sentence to remember : Live with God : God wants us to think of Him
readily, to love Him, to do His will.*

Examination : How do I live with my Father in Heaven ? In what way
am I most forgetful ? What special points will I keep in mind more
particularly in the next few days ?

A hymn.

The content and form of this lesson show us what we can hope to instil into children 8-9 years-old on this theme. Obviously, all this is too much for one catechesis ; some of the points will take weeks to teach thoroughly.

8. *Initiating Infants to Life with God.*

When does the formation to this life with God begin. At the time of the first talk on God which the mother gives her child of three. The child should not at first be given a theoretical teaching, but he must right away learn to behave properly and in this behaviour he will grasp the truth. It may be an apple that will give rise to a first talk about God. The mother asking where the apple comes from goes on to speak of the Heavenly Father who has made all things and from whom all things come. « He now gives you this nice apple, let us thank Him : My God, I thank you for giving me this beautiful apple, I am longing to eat it. »

In this way the child already experiences the meaning of receiving and thanking. Soon, he will learn to ask and return thanks. Then he will hear that God sees us always, guides us, protects us, loves us, hears our prayers, rejoices in our good, etc. Thus the child of 3 or 4, taught by his mother, will quite naturally find himself living with God, assimilating this life with great facility as no sins are there to create an obstacle to the grace of baptism. The spiritual experiences and exercises of this age are an irreplaceable treasure for the whole life.

9. *A Theological Misgiving.*

Some readers will perhaps have certain theological misgivings on reading the above account, wondering if it would not be better to discern between the commandments and what is over and above them as, in any case, is done by many old-time moralists : they very definitely distinguish between « morality » which deals with universal obligations, and « ascetism » which is a matter of option. But from the exegetical point of view this is hardly tenable. There is no doubt that the commandment of charity is a commandment and therefore binding for all, and nothing surpasses this commandment. The encyclical of the 26.1.1923 declares à propos of the words : « You are to be perfect as your Heavenly Father is perfect » (Matth., V, 48) « This commandment is of obligation for every one, there are no exceptions. » We cannot therefore here distinguish between the obligations which are of command to be fulfilled through obedience and the concern of all men, and charity or tendency to perfection belonging to the sphere of freedom of choice and therefore a matter relating to the few.

The distinction we have formulated between « a commandment setting forth a duty to accomplish » and « a commandment stating a goal to reach » seems better. [1] It has been adopted by Häring in his book « The Law of Christ. »

« The commandments setting forth a duty to accomplish » are contrary to the « commandments stating a goal to reach » those which express a prohibition or an obligation to accomplish some specific action (generally speaking a minimum requirement) and they can be observed by any one who is so determined (example : the ten commandments, the commandments of the Church). These give the extreme limits within which Christian life can be lived and grow to the stature of Christ.

The « commandments stating a goal to reach » are those which actually oblige to do something but the complete observation of which, in opposition to the « commandments setting forth a duty to accomplish » go beyond what is actually possible, consequently remaining a future goal towards which to tend (commandment of charity, commandment of perfection Matth. V, 48, exigencies of the Sermon on the Mount, etc.) They derive from the necessity to give a living reply to the infinitely holy and infinitely loving God, who has made us His children and sanctifies us through His Spirit. » [2]

To reduce Christian life to the fulfilling of the « commandments setting forth a duty to accomplish » is, as we have seen, irreconciliable with the nature of Christian life.

Furthermore, *from the pedagogical point of view* it is necessary, with children as with adolescents, to place before them not just the minimum requirements but the whole of Christian life. Little ones accept it quite naturally ; in any case, it is the life of a child of God in its normal development. As for the older children and adolescents, they then have in front of them the goal which God intends them to attain and which appeals to their highest instincts, or which helps them at least to reach a good average.

---

1. *Katechetische Blätter,* 1946, p. 22.
2. *Lexikon der Katechetik,* Freiburg, Herder, 1960.

10. « *Life with God* » *in the Formula of Examination of Conscience.*

Every formulary and all the means we propose to children and adults for the examination of conscience should be headed : « Living with God. » If the first item in the list sets out some particular religious obligations, the majority of the faithful will be satisfied with examining themselves on this point. For instance, « Faith and prayer » : most of the faithful will say that they believe all that the Church proposes and will only find out if they have omitted their daily prayers or said them badly. They will examine themselves to see if they have transgressed a commandment, but will not look to see if they have lived as children of God and if they are not in arrears with God. But if the first heading is « Living with God » and a few of the items in our previous comparison are added, their attention will be fixed not on one special commandment, but on God and our relationships with Him ; they will ask themselves how they have lived with God. They will discover perhaps, that they have not taken God seriously, that they have secretly dismissed Him from their thoughts and practical values, have not relied on His Providence, have not thanked Him nor sought to know His views, therefore have quietly gone the way of unbelief without perhaps having failed in any specific commandment. In their contrition and firm purpose of amendment, they will not only return to the fulfilling of the commandments, but to the living God.

The same will apply when they examine themselves on their *indirect connections* with God, that is to say on their behaviour towards *creatures.* Here again, it is not so much a matter of keeping each commandment — but of adopting, in our contacts with the world and with men, the views and designs of God, of wanting to be his steward and servant, of imitating his sentiments in our dealings with our neighbours, of trying to arrange the world according to His view as a true son put in charge of his father's business for a time would do. This obedience, which goes far beyond that of special commandments, is a basic attitude, an essential element of all relationship with God. For in this way only does man really walk with God, pledges himself to God, loves Him and determines to turn his whole life towards Him. Then only is he really a son or daughter of God. Thus from this formula « Living for God » many Christians will find the true measure of their Christian life and really get to know their faults when examining their consciences.

11. *General Idea on the Ascetism of Children and Seculars.*

Finally, initiation into life with God is important for the progress of children, adolescents and adults in the ways of sanctity. When anyone asks by what means he can grow in Christian life, he is told most of the time that besides prayer he must make sacrifice. « It depends on prayer and sacrifice » is the answer. By sacrifice one more often understands a painful act, an act of self-denial. Progress then appears to consist in doing something disagreeable rather than something agreeable, in turning away from creation and the world and denying oneself.

But if we point to life with God as the means of making progress, as the field of exercise and battle (ascetism means « exercise ») we orientate men towards what is essential : conversion to God, and ever greater attention to and love for Him, a life penetrated with the love of God and our neighbour. The exercise is no longer that imagined sacrifice and victory over oneself which is a personal choice but, for instance, an effort of attention to receive with gratitude every good from the hands of God. The act no longer has bearing on the means of sanctity, but on the practice of religious life itself. In addition, the aim is now a positive thing and the sacrifice is hardly noticed being the negative side of a positive act.

Furthermore, in this way children and adults are not led to a form of escapism or flight from the world but to an acceptance of the world in a spirit willed by God and as such sanctifying, in order to realize therein the plans of God.

The world of human beings is the arena of our task, of our responsibility, by virtue of which we practice our profession as administrators and exercise the apostolate.

This ascetism is not an artificial imagined exercise, but the unselfish and faithful practice of the love of our neighbour and the carrying out of the divine mission of organizing the world. This attitude towards the world leads to personal sanctity because we partake in God's sollicitude for the world and consent to act according to his views. We become like God by sharing in his paternal care which wills his creatures' prosperity, peace and victory over corporal and spiritual miseries. This too requires sacrifices but not a seeking of them ; they are endured as is the negative side of a good action.

This is the root of a healthy ascetism. God does not require difficult things but good things whether they are easy or difficult.

God does not just want that we should turn from the world for we have a duty dictated by charity towards the world, an orientation whereby we love the world as God loves it and give it our services. Neither does God desire that we should repress our nature but that we should overcome our selfishness and our lower instincts.

The true ascetism of children continually finds *ways of living with God* and *occasions of doing good*. It does not neglect the practice of voluntary self-denial ; but the essential thing is to exercise oneself and endeavour to live unceasingly with God and to accomplish our task towards the world in the light of God. In this way the Person of God will more and more become the centre of our mind and purpose, of our sentiments and life, until we see God in all things, his love guiding us always and God becomes for us all in all.

Stages

The transmission of God's message divides itself into
three stages: (1) pre-evangelization, which addresses the
unbeliever and seeks to dispose him for God's message;
(2) the evangelization, which proclaims God's message to the
unbeliever and seeks to win from him a response of
living faith; (3) catechesis, which explains God's message to
the believer and seeks to lead him to full Christian maturity.

The Preparation of the Message

Biblical Research on the Necessity for Pre-Evangelization

by Alphonse M. Nebreda, S.J. [1]

Ancient Paganism and Neo-paganism.

Father Desqueyrat begins and ends his interesting analysis of the religious crisis of the present times [2] by stating — in contrast with those who repeat that « the world is becoming pagan » — that « our contemporaries never become pagans : pagans worshipped false gods ; our contemporaries having become unfaithful do not worship anything : neither false gods nor the true God. They are unbelievers and that is not the same thing. » [3] He returns to this theme in his conclusion : « The French are neither pagans (worshippers of false gods) nor christians (worshippers of the true God); they have no faith at all ; they do not worship. Therefore the so called missionary methods which were successful and still are effective in christian countries are useless in France ; novel methods must be used whether they are, called missionary or not, which will be able to succeed with non-believers : these are the difficulties of the French catholic apostolate of to-day. » [4]

---

1. Born at Bilbao in 1926, Father Alphonso M. Nebreda did his secondary studies at Santander and Salamanca. Having joined the Society of Jesus, he took a Licentiate in philosophy at the University of Comillas (Santander) and a Licentiate in theology at the Sophia University, Tokyo. He was director of the Japanese Language School at Yokosuka. At present Lecturer of Religion at the University of Sophia, he is also « chargé de cours » at the Gregorian University. He has written many articles of spirituality and religious psychology in several reviews, such as, *Hechos y Dichos, El siglo de las Misiones, Humanidades, Theological Studies* and *Missionary Bulletin*. Address : Università Gregoriana, 4 Piazza della Pilotta, Roma, Italy. (Editor's note).

2. A. Desqueyrat, S.J., *La crise religieuse des temps nouveaux*, Paris, Spes, 1955.

3. *Op. cit.*, p. 22.

4. *Ibid.*, p. 339.

I do not intend to discuss of the author's diagnosis. In general that judgement seems valid to me. But when, on the following line, Fr. D. adds : « A similar situation, we repeat, has never before been seen, either in France or elsewhere, » [1] I am forced to disagree with the author, for his description seems to apply remarkably closely to the attitude of the modern Japanese, particularly to the cultured Japanese.

This was the impression which I got when I came from Japan three years ago and read Fr. Desqueyrat's book for the first time. The reader will find my reasons for this feeling, set out briefly in an article in « Études » 1960, on the attitude of the Japanese intellectual facing the religious problem. [2] Meanwhile exceptionally valuable evidence appeared, and quite unexpectedly and in a different way completely confirmed my impression. Mgr Alfred Ancel, Auxiliary Bishop of Lyons, one of the most outstanding personalities among the worker-priests, has published his impressions [3] on his return from Japan. There he had personal experience for some months with the problems of that missionary country being in close contact with the missionaries to whom he gave several retreats. He viewed with concern the unexpected fact that in Japan the Church is confronted by a non-religious paganism, a materialistic paganism ; [4] and he confessed that the situation which he met in Japan had helped him to understand and to judge more clearly the neo-paganism of his own country. « When we speak of pagans, we think of Romans and Greeks of the Roman empire in the time of Christ ; but these pagans, as St Paul testifies himself, were religious. Hence there was in their soul, along with many errors and vices, a receptiveness to the message which the Apostles brought them. Thus, very often, in missionary territory, one is faced with religious pagans. There is therefore a receptiveness to the word of God. But Japan is not only pagan, it is extremely materialistic. There is no readiness to accept God. *I have thus encountered the same problem in Japan as I met in France in certain quarters of the urban working class.* When one finds oneself confronted with materialistic atheism one feels quite out of one's depth. » [5]

---

1. *Ibidem.*
2. *Etudes,* 307 (1960), pp. 361-370.
3. *Au retour du Japon,* in *Japan Missionary Bulletin,* 14 (1960), pp. 437-439. The title of the Japanese translation is more explicit (*ibid.,* pp. 531-532) : Nihon Taizai no Inshô (Impressions of My Stay in Japan).
4. *L.c.,* p. 437.
5. *Ibidem.* The italics are ours.

Doesn't this seem to echo Fr. Desqueyrat's statements but now applied to Japan ?

When we consider the newness and the « extraordinary complexity » [1] of this situation there is nothing surprising about the fact that the precise position of the problem and especially the working out of its solutions, « these novel methods, whether they are called missionary or not, which will be able to succeed with non-believers » of which Fr. Desqueyrat spoke, [2] are only at their preliminary stage.

But the problem is clear. We are dealing with a world closed to God's Message. How can we manage to open it ? Such is the difficult but necessary function of what is called technically *Pre-evangelization*.

Antecedents and Conditions of the Faith.

Fr. Liégé was able to survey the problem quickly and vigorously by approaching it in a double converging movement : the first considers things from the point of view of the heart of a man faced with the faith ; the other places itself at the point of view of the Word of God going to meet man.

Speaking of the faith, [3] after having explained its subjective and objective [4] antecedents, he sets out our problem [5] as follows :

« Is that deepening of personal life in which we recognized the remote subjective antecedent of the faith within the power of every man ? It is evident that numerous social, economical and *cultural* [6] conditions promote or hinder that deepening. It seems that many men of good faith do not accept the christian faith because of certain inhuman conditions of life, and this is true on a wider scale than ever before in our time of technical evolution. A double task demands our attention along with that of evangelization : to create an atmosphere of human truth in which people's attention is directed to what can be holy in their lives ; therefore, the material conditions of life must be bethered. »

---

1. Mgr ANCEL, *ibidem*.

2. *O.c.*, p. 339.

3. P.-A.LIÉGÉ, O.P., *La Foi*, in *Initiation Théologique*, by a group of theologians, Vol. II, Paris, Cerf, 1952, pp. 467-524.

4. *L.c.*, pp. 476 ss.

5. *Ibidem*, p. 485.

6. I have italicized the phrase so that it keeps its universal value with the sentences following seem to limit to a particular aspect of the phenomenon on the economical and social aspect. There are cases, like that of Japan, where more than the economical and social field, the whole culture in the broadest sense of the word, is not only on the margin of, but hermetically sealed to christianity. (Cfr e.g. : Thomas Y. TOMON, *The Church and Japanese Culture*, in Andrian HASTINGS

That task, which Fr. Liégé expressly calls « *pre-evangelization* » [1] is still better described, as we would logically expect, when speaking of the subject of evangelization, [2] the author exposes its conditions.

According to Fr. Liégé, evangelization is doubly conditioned : *in an immediate manner* by man's dispositions (that is what corresponds to what he calls its antecedents when speaking of the faith) ; *in a distant way* : by the atmosphere.

On this immediate conditioning Fr. Liégé writes :

« It is the work of pre-evangelization — not absolutely distinct chronologically from evangelization —, to work on human grounds to open them to the Message of the Gospel. [3] And a little further on, he reminds us that « the task of pre-evangelization can be very slow, above all if prejudices against the Church check it. » [4]

Speaking of the remote conditions, we find once more the ideas which the author states in the treatise on Faith :

« It is obvious that many human groups are in fact impenetrable to evangelization because of the inhumanity of their daily life which does not even give them the liberty of entertaining the religious hypothesis. » Therefore « the task of pre-evangelization cannot be dissociated from a collective fight for the transformation of social structures. » [5]

And the chapter ends with a formula which seems a key to our subject [6] :

« What we have just noted regarding social structures, can also arise in the field of the mental and cultural structures of certain human groups, although it concerns a lesser determinism and a less collective one. [7] Pre-evangelization will then consists of a purging of the intellectual climate by a presence of christian thought. »

(Ed.), *The Church and the Nations*, London-New York, 1959, pp. 136-162 (cfr especially pp. 136, 143, 161-162).

1. *L.c.*, p. 485.

2. P.-A. LIÉGÉ, O.P., *Evangélisation*, in *Catholicisme* (Encyclopaedia in seven volumes edited by G. JACQUEMET), Vol. IV, Paris, 1954, col. 755-764.

3. *Ibid.*, col. 761.

4. *Ibid.*

5. *Ibid.*

6. *Ibid.*, col. 762. Cfr A.-M. HENRY, O.P., *Esquisse d'une Théologie de la Mission*, Paris, 1959, p. 10, in which these « obstacles » are presented in a vigorous way.

7. If he had included in his vision the phenomenon of a complete culture appearing and growing on the margin of Christianity — as is the case in Japan — the author should simply have suppressed this qualification : « although it

More or less a decade ago Fr. Rétif among others wrote : « The Kerygmais fashionable »[1] and, on the protestant side, K. Stendal noted the same phenomenon.

Starting from that fact, Fr. Grasso in a masterly article had[3] the merit of bringing a double problem to light : « Does missionary preaching still exist nowadays ? And, if it does, is it still possible to-day to announce Christ in the kerygmatic way used by the apostles ? Or is it perhaps not true that the present conditions of missionary preaching are such that they need a different type of presentation compared with that which was used at the beginning of Christianity ? »[4]

It was high time that this problem of the greatest importance was set out explicitly. For both among theorists and in pastoral practice a dangerous misunderstanding was harboured. The lawful desire to stress the importance of the Kerygma and a natural reaction against certain old-fashioned forms of apologetics gave the impression that the essential problem was to preach the Message with all the purity of the primitive Kerygma. But very often, one forgot that one of the main features of the Kerygma was to oblige man to adopt a definite position with regard to it, by accepting or refusing it.[5]

Is the non-christian of to-day able to understand the Kerygma like this ? Before answering yes or no, one must first understand and know that one is called !

Fr. Liégé had rightly seen this when he wrote, about the adaptation of the Parish to human groups[6] : « There is more than a mere problem of language here, it is a matter of human experience, of feeling, of mentality. »[7]

---

concerns a lesser determinism and a less collective one. » The author, as one can see, is thinking first of all, here as before of situations of a French type, of more or less minority groups within the cultural community.

1. André Rétif, S.J., *Foi au Christ et Mission*, Paris, 1953, p. 7.

2. K. Stendal, *Kerygma and kerygmatisch*, in *Theologische Literaturzeitung*, 77 (1952), p. 715.

3. Domenico Grasso, S.J., *Il kerigma e la Predicazione*, in *Gregorianum*, 41 (1960), pp. 424-450, of which the first part is translated into French in *Parole et Mission*, 4 (1961), pp. 168-183.

4. *Ibidem*, p. 427.

5. Cfr the brief synthesis which, following Rétif, Grasso gives of the characteristics of the Kerygma : *ibidem*, p. 426; item, *ibid.*, p. 447; Liégé, *Evangélisation*, col. 756; Henry, *Théologie de la Mission*, pp. 18-19, 111, ss.

6. *Evangélisation*, col. 759.

7. *Ibid.*, col. 760.

After having answered the first question affirmatively — the Kerygma retains all its present interest both for the mission countries and for the dechristianized districts, Fr. Grasso passes on to survey the differences, which leap to the eye, between our times and the era of the primitive evangelization. [1] We shall only recall here the general outline of his analysis.

In the sight of the heathens, christianity nowadays lacks that novelty which, in spite of a thousand prejudices, fascinated the contemporaries of the apostles and their immediate successors. Nowadays, after twenty centuries, it appears to our modern pagans as « something old-fashioned and obsolete perhaps full of a glorious part, but to be kept as a museum piece. » [2] Prejudices against christianity have always existed, but those of to-day show themselves in a special light : in the days of Tertullian, « one condemned what one did not know. » [3] Now, one condemns what one thinks to know and this because of that knowledge itself. » [4]

Moreover, *objectively*, christianity of the present day shows a noteworthy difference. The presence of the Holy Spirit, with his palpable action and miracles, was much more marked and created a kerygmatic atmosphere which made an apologetic and theological presentation almost useless. [5]

The miracle of the Church is not sufficient to counterbalance these differences. Being of a moral character, it does not impress a stranger so much for he will inevitably dwell on the less supernatural aspects of the Church. The reality of sin in her makes it difficult for those who judge her from outside to see her holiness. [6]

---

1. Cf. *Il kerigma e la Predicazione*, pp. 427, ss.
2. *Ibid.*, p. 428.
3. *Apologeticum*, n° 40 : M.L.1, col. 478, ss.
4. *Ibid.*
5. *Ibid.*, p. 429.
6. A series of stock phrases repeated systematically by anti-catholic propaganda, sometimes a hundred years old, has not ceased — this is the case in Japan — to burn into the people's heart the caricature of an obscurantist Church, the enemy of progress, liberty and science; or of a capitalist Church bourgeois, imperialist and colonialist (cf. for Japan some recent pearls in Jos. J. SPAE, *The Religious Life of Japanese Catholics and Non-Catholics. A National Inquiry*, in *Missionary Bulletin*, 11 (1957), p. 549). If we have to use the argument of the moral miracle of the Church, that argument which was canonized by the Ist Vatican Council (D 1794) and was so dear to the New Apologetics, either as the « via empirica » (H. DIECKMANN, *De Ecclesia*, Vol. I, Friburgii, 1925, n. 601) or as « via ascendens a praesentibus ad praeterita » (L. BRUGÈRE, *De Vera Religione*, Parisiis, 1878, p. 104), I nevertheless think that in places such as Japan and especially among intellectuals, a delicate task of clearing away prejudices is an imperative preliminary.

It should also be stated that the scandal of the division among christians reduces the spiritual impact which the Church should produce if it does not annul it completely. [1]

From the point of view of those who preach the Message, there still remains another great difference. The Preachers of to-day, even in the psychological sphere, are no longer filled with that personal conviction which close contact with Jesus had given to the first heralds of the Gospel. [2]

Finally we must add the very common and deep-rooted prejudice in the mission lands that Christianity is the religion of the West, a foreign religion. [3]

Fr. Grasso can thus come to the following conclusion : « Hence the necessity of what is commonly called *pre-evangelization*. Before preaching the Gospel, souls must be prepared to welcome it, its expectation must be aroused. The problem of adaptation is still crucial and contemporary, as it has always been ; a kerygmatic presentation of Christ will not eliminate it. » [4] The necessity for pre-evangelization is most obvious in the dechristianized regions. Nevertheless beside the shadows there are also regions of light and hope, [5] and it is precisely on these that pre-evangelization will endeavour to establish its bridge-heads its footholds which prepare for the Message. But that work requires a constant effort of the mind and of the heart and needs the collaboration of all : theologians, psychologists, sociologists, ethnologists, etc.

What Fr. Grasso says [6] about the actuality of apologetics in the work of pre-evangelization seems fully justified. We could bring in many facts of our Japanese experience [7] which would confirm —

---

1. Cf. for Japan, a text which can sum up missionary's general impression : " Fr. Heuvers, who was rector of the Jesuit University in Tokyo, wrote : « When they opened their doors for the foreigns and sent men of progressive spirit away to study the situation in Europe and America, if at that very moment the Japanese had found a united Christianity, the country would be Christian to-day... " (T. Ohm, *Asia Looks at Western Christianity*, Freiburg, 1954, p. 54).

2. Cf. O. Cullmann, *Saint Pierre, disciple, apôtre, martyr*, Neuchâtel-Paris, 1952, pp. 194-195. Cf. Grasso, *l.c.*, pp. 430-431.

3. *Ibid.*, p. 432. This is so much so in periods, like ours, of strong revival of nationalism. To estimate the force of prejudice during the pre-war in Japan, cf. my article : *Cómo se convierte un Japonés. Una página de psicología religiosa contemporánea*, in *El siglo de las Misiones*, Dec. 1953.

4. *L.c.*, p. 431.

5. Cf. our article quoted above, p. 1, note 6.

6. *L.c.*, pp. 434-435.

7. The article of *Etudes*, Dec. 1960, pp. 369-370, gives a brief indication about that aspect as ideal stepping-stone to pre-evangelization in Japan.

2

if it was necessary — the contemporary importance of his thoughts. The criticisms and the evident antipathy against apologetics are, we think, directed less against that subject itself than against the *name* which has disagreeable associations for many and seems to focus attention on the negative aspect ; or else they aim at the *short-comings of a certain type* of apologetics. Fr. Grasso himself fore-warns us against easy and superficial apologetics. [1] It is obvious that to be valid to-day apologetics must have the characteristics of modernity which our world requires absolutely. [2]

We should like to call the reader's attention to a paragraph of Fr. Grasso's article which will serve as transition to penetrate to the very heart of the problem of pre-evangelization :

« Are we sure that the apostles presented christianity in such a keryg-matic way, as one could imagine by a mere reading of the *Acts* ? Let us leave aside the evangelization of the Jews which was made much easier

---

1. *L.c.,* p. 435.
2. Johann Peter STEFFES, in the introduction to the Vol. I of his monumental posthumous work *Glaubensbegründnung*, I, Mainz, 1958, p. XIII, ss, states our problem with deep accuracy. Admitting without reservation the essential part and the services rendered by apologetics, the author nevertheless exposes in a vigorous way the two main objections that can be urged against the apologe-tics of to-day : 1) An exaggerated regard for the normal abstract reason. This gives the impression of wishing to rationalize religion by assimilating it to an idealist and absolutist philosophy. Apologetics is suspected of claiming to prove christianity to anybody in its crucial presuppositions and its basic teachings, and this on the basis of an autonomous reason a heritage from the age of Enlighten-ment, so that the absence of consent can only be imputed to ill-will (*ibid.,* pp. XII-XIV). 2) A neglect of the revolutions of all kinds which have come about in almost all fields of knowledge : natural science, history of the religion, pre-history, sociology, anthropology, psychology, epistemology, etc. Apologetics can be compared with a lawyer who instead of seeking the objective truth, wishes only to save his client by any means. One doubts good faith of the apologist who pretends to know everything and that even better than anyone, and who thinks that by multiplying *distinctions* he will be able to dominate the situation and refute the opinions of opponents, without having understood them (*ibid.,* p. XIV).

For these reasons and because of the negative aspect of defence which accom-panies the name apologetics (*ibid.,* p. XVI), the author prefers to entitle his work *Glaubensbegründung* and to put as the subtitle *Christlicher Gottesglaube in Grund-legung und Abwehr.*

It is not my function to decide here if the reasons the author gives for aban-doning the name Apologetics — a name that has been canonized by twenty centuries of christianity — are sufficient. But leaving the problem of vocabulary out of account, it is obvious that the preacher will not forget the dangers and deficiences emphasized by Steffes, if he wants his defence to be valid for our time.

because Christ accomplished the messianic prophecies ; let us only consider the heathens. In his speech at Athens Saint Paul was surely far from having achieved success ; and yet he courted the goodwill of his hearers. His failure bears witness to the fact that the apostles themselves, filled with the Holy Spirit as they were, could not exempt themselves from pre-evangelization. » [1]

Kerygma and Pre-evangelization in the First Preaching to Pagans.

The study of the *Acts* inclines us to point out a path, which in spite of the enormous quantity of studies published on the subject, [2] still reserves surprises, especially for one who explores with the eyes and heart of a missionary.

Reverend Father Rétif sees the kingdom of the Kerygma [3] in the *Acts of the Apostles* — « a book bathed in the kerygmatic atmosphere. » [4] He distinguishes between Kerygma to pagans and Kerygma to the Jews. [5] In fact, however, he limits his study to the latter, and dedicates a mere few lines to the enigma of the preaching at Athens, « which presents the historian with a difficult problem. » [6]

Following the tempting route opened by Warneck [7] and Oepke, [8] Protestant research has stressed the importance of Paul's discourse at Athens. Rather than consider it as an abstract lesson on theodicy put by the author into the mouth of Paul, in the ideal setting of Athens, capital and symbol of Greek thought, [9] it must be given

---

1. Cf. GRASSO, *l.c.*, p. 431, with the quotations of Ricciotti and Dodd, notes 21 and 22.

2. Cf. a choice in Alfred WIKENHAUSER. *Introducción al Nuevo Testamento* (Spanish translation), Barcelona, 1960, p. 238-239. Very full bibliography in Ulrich WILCKENS, *Die Missionsreden der Apostelgeschichte*, Neukirchen Kreis Moers, 1961, p. 219-226. — J. DUPONT, *Les problèmes du Livre des Actes*, d'après les travaux récents, Louvain, 1950. — An immense wealth of detail on the literature on this subject published in recent years is provided by Erich GRÄSSER, in *Die Apostelgeschichte in der Forschung der Gegenwart*, in *Theologische Rundschau*, Neue Folge, 26 (1960), p. 93-167.

3. *Foi au Christ et Mission*, p. 9.

4. *Ibid.*, p. 32.

5. *Ibid.*, p. 31.

6. *Ibid.*, p. 140-141. Notice, however, what he says in a footnote, p. 32. "The discourse at Lystra, quite occasional, is *pre-kerygma*, or introduction to a kerygma," — in other words, pre-evangelization.

7. J. WARNECK, *Paulus im Lichte der heutigen Heidenmission*, Berlin, 1922, 4th. edit., p. 61-69 (1st. edit., 1913).

8. A. OEPKE, *Die Missionspredigt des Apostels Paulus*, Leipzig, 1920, p. 178-190; specially p. 190-197.

9. Cf. Martin DIBELIUS, *Paulus auf dem Areopag* (published 1939), in *Aufsätze*

a missionary significance. [1] In other words, if I understand Schrenk's thought correctly, missiology must here open the way to hermeneutics. [2]

Should we not turn the phrase round and say that hermeneutics must here open new horizons to missiology ? On this point, Nauck's [3] remark seems very apposite :

On this subject, how far must we refer to modern missionary preaching ? To my mind, this can only be decided when the character of the discourse in the Areopagus has been brought out. To do this, it must be compared with ancient, Judaeo-Christian especially, missionary practice. Except for the first attempts of Ed. Norden [4] and G. Gärtner, [5] practically nothing has been done towards this. [6]

While waiting for fresh studies to bring us new lights, it is useful to sum up the points which are sufficiently clear — always in the perspective of the subject which interests us : pre-evangelization — without allowing ourselves to get lost in the labyrinth of problems raised by it.

The famous discussion begun in the last century by Ferdinand Christian Baur, revived by Edward Norden and Martin Dibelius, over the historical foundation of the renowned discourse in *Acts* XVII, [7] has led to a few certain points :

1) Its pretended dependence upen Apollonius of Tyana's writing, which Norden upheld, has been proved untenable. [8]

2) On the other hand, the thesis of Dibelius, that the discourse in the Areopagus is « a Greek discourse on the true knowledge of

---

zur Apostelgeschichte (H. GREEVEN), Berlin, 1953, p. 27-70 and *Paulus in Athen* (published 1939), *ibid.*, p. 71-75.

1. G. SCHRENK, *Urchristliche Missionspredigt im ersten Jahrhundert*, (1948), in *Studien zu Paulus*, Zurich, 1954, p. 131-148; cf. p. 145.

2. Cf. Final sentence of the article : « Die Interpretation der Bibel bleibt ständig auch auf die Hilfe der Missionswissenschaft angewiesen. » *L.c.*, p. 148.

3. Wolfgang NAUCK, *Die Tradition und Komposition der Areopagrede. Eine Motivgeschichtliche Untersuchung*, in *Z.Th.K.*, 53 (1956), p. 11-52; cf. p. 26, note 1.

4. Ed. NORDEN, *Agnostos Theos*, Leipzig-Berlin, 1913.

5. G. GÄRTNER, *The Areopagus Speech and Natural Revelation*, Uppsala, 1955.

6. Schrenk, however, admits this (*l.c.*, p. 145) while regretting that Dibelius did not follow up by exegesis, the work done by the studies of Warneck and Oepke.

7. See NAUCK, *Die Tradition und Komposition der Areopagrede*, n. 5, p. 11-12.

8. Cf. A. WIKENHAUSER, *Die Apostelgeschichte* (Regensburger Neues Testament, 5), Regensburg, 1956, p. 199-200.

God » which, « to judge by its style and development of ideas, seems like an element foreign to the New Testament, » [1] demands closer examination :

a) If you mean by that, as Dibelius claimed, that in the discourse in the Areopagus the principal ideas are Stoic [2] with a few harmonics from the Old Testament — the thesis is unacceptable.

Norden's was exactly the opposite ; according to him, the fundamental idea (Grundmotif) is Judaeo-Christian, [3] with a stoic context (Begleit-motif). [4] He also would direct research differently : « if we knew more precisely this Jewish argument which is developed in a rich and abundant literature, we would be able to prove that the discourse in the Areopagus has not only borrowed from it the principle of argumentation, but also its ideological material. » [5] Later research has proved the soundness of this suggestion. Monsignor Cerfaux has written : « The general trend of a discourse of propaganda such as that has nothing new. Prepared in the Greek world after the classical period, the discourse was adopted by Alexandrine judaism. It must not be thought that Paul was the only one to acclimatize this scheme into Christian propaganda. Barnabas, Silas, Luke and many others have used it, with the inevitable variations and adapta-tions of real life. » [6]

For his part, B. Gärtner, in his recent study on the subject, writes : « The Stoic terms can be considered as an integral part of a common basis, proper to the special style of preaching, and explained as an approach of ideas and phraseology expressing the object of the mission ; in short, as an expedient, known and accepted by both Jewish and Christian missionaries. » [7]

Nauck has the credit of exploring the track opened by Norden. Having reviewed the copious material — studied intently for the first time — the author concludes : « The discourse in the Areopagus is a typical example of the missionary preaching which found its model in Judaeo-Greek missionary literature. Luke is one of the best witnesses to a great tradition. » [8] Further on, after briefly setting down the characteristic elements of this missionary literature, he sums it up thus : These com-parisons prove once more that the discourse in the Areopagus is a per-fect summary of the « topics » used in primitive Jewish and Christian

---

1. *Aufsätze zur Apostelgeschichte*, p. 54; also p. 44. Cf. E. GRÄSSER, *Die Apostelgeschichte in der Forschung der Gegenwart*, p. 140.

2. *L.c.*, p. 59.

3. *Agnostos Theos*, p. 3-12.

4. *Ibid.*, p. 13-29.

5. *Ibid.*, p. 29.

6. L. CERFAUX, *Le Christ dans la Théologie de Saint Paul*, Paris, 1954, 2nd edit., p. 18 and references.

7. *The Areopagus Speech and Natural Revelation*, p. 72.

8. *L.c.*, p. 36; cf. also p. 18, 24, 31, 33, 34, 35.

preaching ; it contains nothing which the author would not have known through missionary preaching. »[1]

b) From this we can go forward one step and ask whether the discourse in the Areopagus is an « element foreign to the New Testament » as Dibelius claims. What relation is there between *Acts* XVII and the preaching of Saint Paul, as we know it through other texts ? Having shown how, in *I Thess.* I, 9-10, St. Paul sums up the circumstances of the conversion of his correspondents,[2] Mgr. Cerfaux concludes : « We have before us the outlines of the discourse of Pauline propaganda, which we can reconstruct with the aid of the two discourses to the Gentiles in the *Acts* (XIV, 15-17 ; XVII, 22-31), and thanks to the beginning of the letter to the Romans (I, 14-32 ; III, 21-26) and the First to the Corinthians (I, 21). The passage quoted above from the Epistle to the Thessalonians has a parallel in the closing of the discourse in the Areopagus : *Acts* XVII, 30-31. »[3]

The same trend of thought occurs in the recent thesis by Wilckens ; internal harmony shows that the discourse at Lystra (*Acts* XIV, 15-17) and the one at Athens (XVII, 22-31), are only clear echoes of the plan in *I Thess.* I, 9-10 and *Heb.* V, 11 - VI, 2.[4] For this same reason Nauck can conclude that « one cannot doubt the *historical* co-incidence between the discourse in the Areopagus and Paul's missionary preaching. The Apostle has followed the same tradition of Judaeo-Christian missionary practice which has also crystallized in the discourse in the Areopagus. »[5] Nauck has underlined the word *historical* in contrast to what he calls the *theological* aspect of the question. This affords us a bridge over to our next point.

c) How can we explain the differences between *Acts* XVII and the other texts of St. Paul which we possess ? Nauck's remark seems to us justified[6] : it is true that the greater part of the ideas in *Acts* XVII are found in St. Paul. But those who insist on the connection do not take the difference of accent sufficiently into account ; and on the contrary, those who stress the differences do not appreciate the similarities.[7] How

---

1. *Ibid.*, p. 40.
2. *L.c.*, p. 17.
3. *Ibid.*, p. 18. Cf. also p. 192 : " Ernst Curtius has picked out all the similaries between the Pauline Epistles and the discourse in the Areopagus. " See note 1 with references from LIECHTENHAN and W. SCHMID who maintain a like thesis.
4. *Die Missionsrede der Apostelgeschichte*, p. 86-91.
5. *L.c.*, p. 40. J. R. GEISELMANN insists on the fact that the Pauline preaching to the gentiles is only a development of his preaching to the Jews. *Jesus der Christus*. Die Urform der apostolischen Kerygmas als Norm unserer Verkündigung und Theologie von Jesus Christus, Stuttgart, 1951, pp. 161-162.
6. *L.c.*, p. 41.
7. An exception : the well-balanced discussion by OEPKE, *Die Missionspredigt des Apostels Paulus*, p. 178-197. Cf. Nauck, *l.c.*, note 1. And WILCKENS himself agrees, *o.c.*, p. 88. « ... der Unterchied zwischen dieser Gruppe juden-

can we explain the differences ? One answer is that given by Schrenk[1] :
« Faced with this problem, we always return to the supposition that the
St. Paul of missionary preaching must speak exactly like the St. Paul
preaching to the faithful... Yet in his Epistles we do not find his missionary
preaching. When he exhorts the faithful in the *Acts* (XX, 17...) he is
familiar to us, and speaks as in his letters. Concerning his missionary
preaching, however, his letters only permit secondary deductions, though not
without value.[2]

For Nauck, however, this view over-simplifies matters. This position
only seems obvious to him if you consider the passage *Acts* XVII and
the other Pauline texts alone. He thinks to find the solution by widening
the horizon further and comparing these texts once more with their
parallels in later Jewish missionary literature.[3] In fact, asserts Nauck,
while the St. Paul of the Letter to the Romans is ideologically related
to the Sibylline Fragments, the discourse in the Areopagus resembles more
closely the missionary preaching of Aristobulus.[4] In a word : « In the
discourse in the Areopagus and in the affirmations of the Apostle Paul,
we have two different expressions (Ausprägungen) of one common tradition of primitive Judaeo-Christian missionary preaching. The two types
are remarkable — if we may use the phrase — by a ‘ liberal ’ attitude
and an ‘ orthodox ’ attitude towards the knowledge and worship of God
among pagans. »[5] *Acts* XVII and Aristobulus belong to this first attitude,
Romans and the Sibylline Fragments to the second.[6]

---

christlicher Predigten und jener Gruppe heidenchristlicher Predigten nicht nur
im Staff, sondern vor allen, auch in der Anlage und im Duktus ist ganz augen-
fällig. »

1. *Urchristliche Missionspredigt im ersten Jahrhundert,* p. 144.
2. Cf. also WIKENHAUSER, *Die Apostelgeschichte,* p. 211.
3. *O.c.,* p. 42-46.
4. The differences are notable : 1) On the worship of God, "while the discourse in the Areopagus intends to impress that the one thing necessary for the
pagan worship of God is to be consistent with itself and accept certain
corrections to make adorers of the unknown God adore the Living God (Nauck,
l.c., p. 42) the Sibylline Fragments are a strong attack on idolatry. 2) About
the knowlegde of God, Dibelius (*l.c.,* p. 56) showed that Acts XVII gives two
proofs of man's ability to know God naturally : a) through creation. While *Acts*
XVII (and Aristobulus still more) stress forcibly "pagans can...," St. Paul
and the Sibylline Fragments insist on the pagans' unpardonable sin of not
knowing God. b) through man's relation to God. This aspect is not only missing
in St. Paul, but is even unthinkable, given his conviction that man left God
(*Rom.,* I-III) (Dibelius, *o.c.,* p. 57; cf. Nauck, p. 43-44). This is not in the
Sibylline Fragments either. *Acts* XVII gives it and Aristobulus still more strongly if possible. 3) The idea of ignorance occurs in *Acts* XVII and Aristobulus,
but not in St. Paul, or in the Sibylline Fragments.
5. NAUCK, *l.c.,* p. 44.
6. Cf. E. HAENCHEN, *Die Apostelgeschichte* (Krit.-Exeget. Komm. über das
N.T. begründet v. H. A. W. MEYER, 3), Göttingen, 1959, 12th edit., p. 466, who
speaks of a « milden Richtung » and a « strengen Richtung. »

By way of conclusion, the author answers the fundamental question of the relations between the discourse in the Areopagus and St. Paul. There is, he says, similarity and divergence.

The *similarity* lies in that « Luke, in the order of ideas which he makes Paul follow in the Areopagus faithfully reflects the framework of the first missionary preaching and, of course, St. Paul's method. To my mind, there is little reason to doubt that the discourse in the Areopagus is based upon a sermon really preached by St. Paul at Athens. The only thing is that this discourse was accentuated differently. » The *divergence* lies in the theological perspective. Like any good Greek, Luke welcomes the Hellenic process in Christian preaching, and encourages it positively, by swimming resolutely with the stream. [1]

It would be unjust not to recognize the merits of Nauck's very rich study. Nevertheless, Mgr. Cerfaux's detailed and careful page retains all its value. It must be quoted in full to get a complete view of the whole problem in a truer perspective : « It is not enough to say that the definitive judgment of Paul on the Greek philosophy is directed differently in the epistles ; it is not so definitive as to let pass other more favourable notes. From the beginning of his mission in the Greek world, did the Apostle take up a clear position against philosophy ? The first letter to the Thessalonians, I, 9, retains an echo of propaganda discourse. Later, Paul has severe words for philosophy, Nevertheless in *I Corinthians* and in *Romans*, he recognizes its mission to lead men towards the knowledge of God. If he can say in *I Corinthians* : « in the wisdom of God, the world, by wisdom, knew not God » (*I Cor.* I, 21), he means that philosophy, all the same, following its own powers and nature, should normally have led to this knowledge. In *Romans*, the *theologia naturalis* of the Stoics appears : the aspect of God which can be known (το γνωστὸν τοῦ Θεοῦ) is visible among men, God is manifested to them. For His invisibleness since the creation of the world, His eternal Power and His divinity, are intelligible in His works and can be seen (*Rom.* I). It is not enough to say that this proof, brought forward by the Stoics is only recalled in passing, and has no value for Saint Paul, since in actual fact, the knowledge of God has not led to worshipping Him. Its philosophy could have, and should have, following out its own nature, led men to God, and thus prepared souls to receive the Gospel of Christ

Saint Paul conceives of philosophy as directed toward religion. Without doubt, his religious temperament inclines him to see things from this angle, but in reality, the Greek philosophy of his time, surviving or re-budding Platonism, Neopythagorism, Stoicism, — they threw stones at the Epicureans — turned towards natural theology, theurgy and oracles, even towards revelations of the past, turning the old philosophers and poets into prophets. Philosophy could soon be defined as « knowledge » of God. Never, all the same, had Greek philosophy, except perhaps at rare moments,

---

1. NAUCK, *l.c.*, p. 45-46.

ceased to be a search after real identity with the divinity. The Apostle, therefore, takes it for what it is and wishes to be, in assigning as its end the knowledge of the true God. » [1]

This is not the place to pronounce an opinion on the divers points in Nauck's thesis. While leaving this to the exegesists by profession, we may, however, before closing our parenthesis, heavily underline one point : even in the light of Nauck's conclusions, *the discourse in the Areopagus certainly represents a traditional current in the method of putting the Message before pagans.* [2] That is enough for our purpose here. We can reap the fruit of our laborious journey ; what are the characteristics of the first pre-evangelization, judging from Paul's discourse at Athens ? (*Acts* XVII, 22-31).

Characteristics of the First Pre-evangelization.

Wilckens qualities this very first phase, very significantly, as *apologetics of approach* (vorbereitend-apologetisch [3]) and Schrenk

---

1. L. CERFAUX, *Le Christ dans la théologie de Saint Paul*, pp. 192-193. Cf. WIKENHAUSER, *Die Apostelgeschichte*, p. 211. GÄRTNER, on his side, writes : " The speech depiction of God has no traits that can be called not-Pauline " (*o.c.*, p. 250). Cf. however GRÄSSER's criticism, *l.c.*, p. 142.

2. Current which will prevail more and more in the ancient Church, if we judge by what Nauck says at the end of his article (*l.c.*, p. 46) : " Luke takes part, unwittingly, in the transformation of the idea of God which discussion with Greek theology brought into the Church. The historical value of the discourse in the Areopagus lies in the fact that it is one of the few great witnesses to the meeting of Biblical thought with the Greek spirit in the missionary domain. " HAENCHEN, *o.c.*, p. 467, is full of this idea : " This extraordinary vestige leaves us thoughtful. Christian preaching could no longer count upon certain pre-suppositions among its pagan hearers (which it had found among pagans influenced by Judaism) to make the Message accepted. That is why the discourse in the Areopagus — as at Lystra — presents a new way of preaching (different from preaching to the Jews) to meet a completely different situation. Luke gives a specimen of a missionary programme for pagans uninfluenced by Judaism. " For Haenchen, as for Nauck, the *Acts* is « eine selbständige Theologie... die — mag sie uns lieb oder leid sein — ernst genommen werden muss. » Cf. GRÄSSER, *l.c.*, p. 102. Käsemann, on his side, says of this theology that « sich von der urchristlichen wesentlich unterscheidet und im ihrem Zentrum wie in vielen ihrer Einzeläussberungen als frühkatholisch bezeichnet werden muss » ; E. KÄSEMANN, *Neutestamentliche Fragen von heute*, Z.Th.K., 54 (1957), 21. Cfr also G. KLEIN, who ends his detailed criticism of Haenchen's commentary thus : " If the *Acts* show themselves to be an insufficient source for the very earliest epoch of the Church, they are, instead, first-class witness for the spiritual history of christianity after the Apostles. " (*Z.K.G.*, 68 [1957], 371.

3. *O.c.*, p. 87.

calls it « *threshold missionary preaching* » (anbahnende Missions-predigt [1]). Let us examine its characteristics briefly.

Commenting on the tactics of preparing a way for the Message, as the *Acts* has preserved them for us in St. Paul's discourse at Lystra and Athens, Schrenk states : « The objective aim is the same at both places. We are shown how Paul, when faced with pagans ignorant of Revelation, whether simple or highly cultured, takes the actual situation of his listeners very carefully into account. »

What strikes immediately is this « *captatio benevolentiae* » [2] *which makes him begin from his hearers' standpoint*, a simple process of psychology, happening spontaneously. From the psychological point of view again, there is something more than a mere « captatio » : « he catches the listeners' attention *by some reality in their own sphere of culture*. Starting from a point of mutual understanding, showing respect for their poets, the missionary merits a hearing. » [3] It is obvious, as Wikenhauser observes, that Paul, « like every missionary, had to start from the ideas and convictions of his listeners. » [4] But there is something deeper still. St. Paul « *recognizes the amount of truth which his listeners possess, so as to go ahead on common ground, then giving them the full truth of Christianism*. That is why the Stoic-sounding phrases in the discourse in the Areopagus have a theist, not a pantheist meaning, in the context of the *Acts*. For it was an axiom in the Judaism of the Diaspora, that the *one* God of the Greek philosophy (or the *one* Divine Being) was the God of Old Testament Revelation, » [5] Schrenk says this vigorously : « The objective aspect of this threshold missionary preaching (die sachliche Methode anbahnender Missionspredigt) is that it *seeks to create an atmosphere of understanding, and does not fear to start from the taking-off field of his hearers*, by treating with respect the elements of truth they retain (Achten auf die Trummer seiner Wahrheitsahnung [6]).

How long did this pre-evangelization phase *last* ? We cannot say. One thing is certain : according to his custom, Luke only gives us a plan of the ideas in the discourse and its trend of thought. [7] The

---

1. *L.c.*, p. 145.
2. WILCHENS, *o.c.*, p. 87. Cf. also HAENCHEN, *o.c.*, p. 458.
3. SCHRENK, *l.c.*, p. 146.
4. *Die Apostelgeschichte*, p. 211.
5. WIKENHAUSER, *Ibidem*. Cf. ID., *Introducción al Nuevo Testamento*, p. 250.
6. *L.c.*, p. 146.
7. Cf. A. WIKENHAUSER, *Die Apostelgeschichte und ihr Geschichtswert* (Ntl. Abh. VIII, 3-5), Münster, 1921, p. 147 ; ID., *Introducción al N.T.*, p. 250. — H. J. CADBURY speaks of "an illustrative excerpt" ; K. LAKE-CADBURY, *The*

question does not seem to us of capital importance, if we keep to the principles above stated : Start from the listener and carefully respect his spiritual situation [1] Now we understand better the justice of P. Liégé's view, when he explains the third characteristic of the Word of God in the work of evangelization — « it must be adapted to the groups of people to whom it is addressed » — he goes to the heart of the matter. After the paragraph just quoted, [2] he writes : « The first preachers of the Gospel proclaimed one and the same Christ spontaneously, under different expressions and lights. The New Testament, at once so united and so varied, bears witness to this . The missionary must translate the Eternal Christ into a language which renders Him present in time and space. He must also try to refer to actual events as the prophets did. This adaptation, careful to portray without disfiguring, has nothing to do with « opportunist » apologetics ; *it simply corresponds to the duty of respecting, without doctrinal concession, the lives to be evangelized.* [3]

Conclusion.

In this perspective we can understand the good reasons for the question asked by P. Grasso in his article quoted above, and which has served as starting-point for our research : « Are we sure that the apostles presented Christianism in the kerygmatic manner which a superficial reading of the *Acts* might suggest ? » [4] At present, then, we realize that the necessity of pre-evangelization applies, *à fortiori* to the missionary preaching of our epoch. [5] For there is an interesting

---

Acts of the Apostles, 2 vols, London, 1933, in *Beginnings of Christianity,* I, 4-5; cf. 5, p. 407. Cf. NAUCK, *o.c.,* pp. 18, 36. — Cf. also GEISELMANN, *o.c.,* p. 19.

1. It will be well to note, with Schrenk, the dangers besetting this first stage : danger of remaining at this propedeutic stage, thinking of this first step as quite independent from Christ. This would be taking the means for the end, and forgetting that for St. Paul, there is no preparation possible outside Christ (*l.c.,* p. 145). — Danger of becoming subservient to the listener's spiritual world, instead of being dependent on God's Word alone — Danger of forgetting that the missionary's motive-centre can only be, in the final instance, Redemption through the Cross (*l.c.,* p. 146). — Lastly, dangers of all sorts of confusion and misunderstandings (cf. p. 147). I have tried to reproduce faithfully the clair-obscur in Schrenk's thesis. Far be it from me to declare that the work of pre-evangelization is without risk ! The theologian, like the missionary must use discernment, and see if their efforts really serve their end. Excess of shades of meaning and exaggerated scruples over kerygma, not to mention those influenced by the Barthian School, are equally harmful. Preaching can never be like a theology course.

2. Cf. above, p. ... note ... and the corresponding text in the article.

3. *Evangélisation,* col. 759-760, with the bibliography. The italics are ours.

4. See above, p. ... note...

5. Cf. GRASSO, *o.c.,* p. 427, ss.

aspect which we have purposely left to the end ; which is, that in the famous intervention of Paul at Athens — as at Lystra — there is no attempt at all to prove the existence of God. For Paul, as for his listeners, that was taken for granted (selbstverständlich, says Wikenhauser); his intention is to show them the true nature of God, Who reveals Himself through His works, in nature (XVII, 24, 25) and in history (XVII, 26). [1]

The ideas of P. Desqueyrat and Mgr. Ancel, which launched us into this work, like those of P. Grasso in his article, show clearly that the situation confronting preachers of the Gospel in our own day is radically different. « How can anyone who has no idea of sin understand the doctrine of Salvation ? The pagan whom Saint Paul met in Athens, or in Rome, was sighing for liberation. But what liberation does the pagan of today sigh after ? Therefore, on what should we base our preaching ? » [2]

This is the first point for consideration, so it seems to us, from which to settle clearly the real avenue of approach, the movement and demands of modern pre-evangelization.

1. Cf. WIKENHAUSER, *Die Apostelgeschichte*, p. 201.
2. GRASSO, *Ibidem*, p. 434.

The Catechetical Task
of Disposing the Pagan for the Faith

by Martin RAMSAUER

For the preaching of the mysteries of salvation — as it is done in the catechumenate — an attitude of faith in the catechumen is pre-supposed : an attitude by which he believes that the message communicated to him is the word and the invitation of God, towards whom he therefore takes an attitude of ready obedience.

This attitude of faith is not « in-born » in man. Since the truths to be accepted in faith go frequently beyond the power of his intellect, it is necessary to show that it is *reasonable* to accept this communication with an attitude of faith, (thus we speak of the « credibility » of our faith) and furthermore that there is an *obligation* to embrace God's word by an « obedience of faith » (and thus we speak of the « credendity » of faith). Based on this understanding, faith is realized as « rationabile obsequium » (*Rom.*, XII, 1). Thus we are faced with the task of laying the foundation of the faith, a work which, if successful, will determine the progress of the catechumenate and will leave its mark on later post-baptismal life.

The questions pertaining to the foundations of our faith are treated at great length and with scientific accuracy in « fundamental theology. » These same reflections and proofs — although in more simplified form — can be found in various religion books and especially in so-called Correspondence Courses which are offered to the missionary as an aid for this particular catechetical work also called « apologetics. »

But here we have to ask : Is the customary approach for this particular catechetical work of « apologetics » — as found in these

---

1. Address : *East Asian Pastoral Institute,* P.O. Box 1815, Manila, PHILIPPINES.

books arranged according to the pattern of scientific fundamental theology and intended to serve its purpose of laying the foundations of the Catholic faith — a form suitable to dispose the (adult) pagan for the faith ?

The answer given by pastoral experience is rather « reserved. » But what is the reason for this meager result ? Why are the considerations and conclusions of fundamental theology which give to the missionary again and again that joyful and confident conviction : « I know whom I have believed » (*II Tim.*, I, 12), not also followed by a similar experience in the pagan ? Why, on the contrary, do these same reflections sometimes cause difficulties which disturb and hinder the progress of catechetical instruction ?

This problem touches on another problem closely connected with it. It is a fact, and today perhaps more noticeable than before, that the missionary does not find attention and agreement because he happens to be « white » or a priest. It needs much patience, and also skill to establish contact with the pagan population, to make them « listen, » to arouse in them an interest in religious questions and to dispose them gradually to accept the teaching of the missionary. All this shows the need for an activity that aims at and prepares for the proclamation of our faith (to be done in the catechumenate proper), an activity called « pre-catechesis. »

This pre-catechesis is frequently carried out by a series of « apologetical » talks. Thus the question arises : What is the relation between pre-catechesis and the work of laying the foundation for the faith, which we have just mentioned ? Do both have the same aim and the same suppositions ? Because only then would it seem possible to pursue the aim of the pre-catechesis by way of apologetics.

To understand the peculiarities of the process by which the pagan can be disposed for the faith, it will first be necessary to see more clearly the aim and the actual suppositions of the traditional apologetical argument as presented by scientific « fundamental theology. » Against this background we shall be able to determine more precisely the advisability and use of apologetics in the catechetical instruction of the pagan which will finally determine the character of the pre-catechesis.

THE PECULIARITIES
OF THE APOLOGETICAL ARGUMENT

The peculiarities of the apologetical argument as presented by the « fundamental theology, » are determined by the aim it pursues and the suppositions it rests on.

Fundamental theology gives the scientific-reflex argument for the Catholic faith. It demonstrates its credibility and credendity. The argumentation of fundamental theology precedes logically the actual, revealed content of our faith, makes abstraction from this content, and proceeds independently of it. Through fundamental theology we learn of « the many wonderful external signs God has given, which are sufficient to prove with certitude by the natural light of reason alone the divine origin of the Christian religion » (Pius XII, *Humani Generis*, Denz. 2305).

Although they do not strictly affect the validity of the argument there are signs that the argument of fundamental theology has been developed « on Catholic grounds » — for the defense and justification of our faith in God's revelation — and not, so to say, « at the threshold » to the Catholic faith. This fact is evident from the structure of the argument itself : The presentation of the proof (as found in the treatises of fundamental theology) admits and even stresses the necessity of the will's co-operation for the act of faith, but it does not furnish the motives necessary for the will to accomplish its task.

This may be done (legitimately) only if the motives for the will can be supposed as sufficiently known. And this is the case only with the faithful : they know of the treasures of salvation which they will gain through their faith ; and therefore there is no need of presenting them in detail.

But what the apologetical argument aims at is to show that the act of faith (and in consequence also our hope which rests on faith : cf. *Heb.*, XI, 1) is reasonable, and furthermore that adherence to the Catholic faith is not a matter of one's arbitrary choice but obligatory. Even this last point can be shown with sufficient evidence from the general obligation to practice religion along with the fact that the Christian religion, as revealed religion, deserves foremost consideration. It is not necessary to have recourse to the content of revelation, i.e. to Christ's explicit command and the sanction he added, stressing the severity of the obligation rather than constituting a motivation for the will (cf. Mt., XXVIII, 18 ff and Mk., XVI, 16).

This indicates sufficiently the characteristics of the apologetical approach to which we are accustomed from fundamental theology. And since the argument makes abstraction from the content of revelation, it has necessarily the same validity for any man whether he has the faith already or not. The classical argumentation, however, springs from a self-reflexion and is intended for the believer (as we have seen above). It will give him clarity, certitude and joyful consciousness that : I know whom I have believed ! At the

end of the apologetical argument the believer finds awaiting him
a sense of joyful security which inspires him to serve God readily
— and not the feeling of a heavy, unavoidable obligation. In the
« obedience of faith » the disciple of Christ sees the expression of
his service to God which he renders gratefully and joyfully ; and
he knows that through this his obedience of faith he gains the
treasures of salvation promised for the present and the future life.

THE ADVISABILITY OF APOLOGETICS
IN THE INSTRUCTION OF PAGANS

Against the background of the preceding chapter we now see more
clearly the quite different condition of the prospective, but still
pagan, « catechumen » (if we may use this term). He is still outside the Catholic faith. In order to come to the faith, i.e. to accept
a certain teaching as a binding message from God, and to submit
himself by a life according to this teaching, a proper justification
and motivation is needed. How this is done will depend largely
on the education and the character of the catechumen. But still
more will the missionary have to pay attention to God's action
upon man's soul by which He calls and disposes him to enter the
way of salvation. Although there is a great variety of conditions,
we will now consider some more characteristic cases in order to
find a suitable and effective approach to lead the pagan to the
faith.

1. The « Spontaneous » Conversion.

There are a fair number of cases in which the life of persons
baptized (of the missionary as well as of the Christians), their love
and patience, their joy and confidence, the peace prevailing in
their life and the deep religious devotion they show are in themselves *the* simple fact which arouses attention, esteem, interest and
desire, and which becomes at the same time *the* motive which convinces men spontaneously of the genuineness and superiority of the
Christian religion. From that moment the missionary is for them
God's messenger and his word is accepted and believed as God's
word and obeyed in their life.

Because of God's sovereign providence, almost any incident and
experience may gain a similar importance and become decisive for
the acceptance of the Catholic faith. So, v.g., a word of the Holy
Scripture heard or read « accidentally » may illuminate the life of

the pagan in surprising clearness, giving his life new and fuller meaning and lifting it to a higher sphere.

The « law » underlying such « spontaneous » conversions of persons who in readiness to believe resemble prompt and docile children is this : A « good » which is perceived in its inner relationship to the Catholic faith arouses, under God's grace, spontaneous attention and attraction. At the same time, this impression is so strong and convincing that the « good » becomes the motive for the credibility of the Catholic faith. In such a case, man does not need any further reasoning ; he is frequently not even « disposed » or able to follow a special argumentation. And if it should be forced upon him, it would mean for him a useless detour and perhaps even turn out to be a dangerous stop, since it prevents the catechumen, now so evidently under God's impulse, from receiving God's word without delay and from giving himself with growing love to God. In such cases the missionary has to adapt himself prudently and to be a thoroughly dependable instrument in God's work of salvation : The ways of God are manifold.

This does not mean that such men do not need any further foundation for their faith. What might be unnecessary at this moment is a formal and separate apologetical argumentation. But it might still be possible to give the necessary foundation for their faith by short reflections here and there, on suitable occasions, more in the way of « immanent apologetics. » In such cases more is generally not necessary, especially if our catechumens belong to those who trust more in the sincerity of the missionary than in long arguments. We should avoid in our catechumenate a too « school-like » fashion, as if the value and efficacy of our instruction depended mainly on the amount of matter and details. What really matters — and all our catechetical and apologetical work is only a means to it — is the full and personal surrender of man to God, of the child to the Father. An opportunity to strengthen the foundations of faith by making them more reflex may come at the time of a review of the Christian teaching after baptism, comparable to the apologetical instruction of someone who has grown up in the faith from his childhood.

2. The « Ordinary » Way.

But we cannot always count on such convincing experiences ; this we know from experience. The motives leading the individual to the missionary are of great variety. One seeks peace for his soul ; another, meaning for his life. One is pressed by problems, another attracted by curiosity, and still another comes out of courtesy.

It is usually hard to say what motive was decisive for the individual or what influenced him most. But in all of them there is a certain inclination, expectancy, and also curiosity. They come with a sincere intention — but, as is to be expected, without any inner, personal relationship to the Catholic faith. This is the reason why it would generally be too early to start immediately with the catechetical instruction proper, explaining the content of revelation, which is accessible in faith only. It is therefore necessary to develop first an attitude which is favorable to the faith ; otherwise the ground is not prepared to receive the word of God (cf. *Lk*, VIII, 11-15).

Now, how can this attitude be developed ? Is this not perhaps the purpose of a preparatory apologetical instruction ? Yes — and No ! Yes : A preparation is needed in order to lay the « foundations » for the faith. But : The traditional apologetical approach, as we know it from fundamental theology, this approach alone, will not be able to fulfil expectations in the most satisfactory way.

We have seen above that the apologetical argumentation makes abstraction from the actual content of our faith , that in consequence it is equally valid for both the baptized and the non-baptized, since its reasoning logically precedes the act of faith. But at the same time we have seen that the traditional argument is directed to him who already believes and that for this reason it omits a special motivation for the will whose co-operation is needed in the act of faith. Here now we come to the problem of using the traditional apologetical argument (or simply « apologetics ») in the catechumenate of the (adult) pagan.

Sometimes we may find ourselves trying to « prove » the faith. But we must rid ourselves of this usually unconscious tendency. Aside from the fact that the Christian faith is a free gift of God's grace, we have to remember that faith is never just the final conclusion in a chain of logical arguments. It is more than a rational statement : It is man's answer to God's call ; it is the surrender of the « whole » man to the living God. This goal which calls for the whole man has to be kept in view constantly lest we omit some of the human factors which are instrumental in producing the faith and lest we stress one element to the disadvantage of another. This should be remembered in any apologetical instruction, but it is particularly important when it comes to guide and to dispose pagans towards the faith.

This means that we have to pay attention also to the will , since « it is impossible for man to believe, unless he is willing » (credere non potest nisi volens — S. Augustinus, P.L., 35, 1607). The same point is stressed by Saint Thomas : « Faith is in the intellect only in as far as it is commanded by the will» (*De Verit.*, q. 14, a. 3, ad 10).

How shall motivation for the will be produced? As we have seen above, the motive for the faithful is given by the fact that they already know the treasures they possess and hope for through faith. Thus the will is already disposed to co-operate when in a reflex consideration the intellect recognizes the credibility and credendity of the Catholic faith. But the « catechumen » whom we want to win for the faith does not (yet) know these treasures. What motivation can be used?

Could perhaps the obligation to give the assent of faith be shown with such forceful evidence that the act of faith follows with necessity? No; this would mean to say « that the assent of Christian faith is not free, but necessarily results from arguments of human reason » (Vat., Denz. 1814), an opinion rejected by the Church.

But, after a sufficient demonstration of its credibility, could not the assent of faith be obtained by referring to the consequences of a refusal (fear of punishment)? However, these motives, too, are not « infallible ; » and even if they have « success » — as the result of the emphasis which these motives of fear receive if stressed at the very beginning of the instruction in Catholic faith — we may develop in our converts a religious attitude which has little to do with the spirit of the Glad Tidings and instill in them a disposition that is more concerned about God's punishment than about His love which should impell us (cf. *I John*, IV, 18).

Perhaps we can ask this question : How does the catechumen feel about the instructions which are intended to lead him to the faith?

One thing is certain : Whatever we are going to say about the Catholic faith, the catechumen will very soon find himself faced with the necessity of making a decision . This cannot be avoided, since any instruction on our faith contains a challenge : there is no such thing as an « objective information without obligation. »

And even if such an information should be attempted, for the very sake of its « objectivity » it would have to make clear the obligatory character of the faith for all men. To keep silent about this point would mean to keep silent about Christ, or what is just the same — to deprive Him of the key-position which He holds in the order of our salvation. This our order of salvation knows only one goal which is at the same time supernatural and in consequence obligatory on all men ; to this goal — our salvation — there is but ONE way : CHRIST ; and this Christ we meet in His CHURCH.

If the exposition conceals this point, or does not show clearly the consequences involved in it, it is incomplete in a very essential point — and therefore worthless. Moreover, such an exposition is unworthy of Christ's messenger of whom it is required that he be found « trustworthy » (*I Cor.*, IV, 2).

Thus the catechumen cannot escape being faced with a decision. Relying on what he has heard so far about the Christian religion, and still more relying on what he has seen and observed, he will consider his submission (in consequence to the obligatory character of the church) in one case : as something he is « allowed » to do ; in the other : as something he is « obliged » to do. If he has discovered in the faith the « treasure » and the « pearl » (*Mt.*, XIII, 44-46) he will desire it ; if this understanding is missing, he is faced with a « must. »

Perhaps only now the catechumen realizes with real clarity what the conversion to the Catholic faith involves : Understanding the exclusiveness of the Catholic religion as it is claimed by the Catholic church against the rather syncretistic attitude of his pagan religion, he finds himself faced with the necessity of abandoning his native religion. This he will feel as a « loss, » if he has no other balancing motives ; as a giving-up of his own culture, since he considers the various religions as the expressions of respective cultures. In addition to this he not seldom has to fear unpleasant social consequences of his conversion ; and, perhaps, he also encounters intellectual and emotional difficulties of all sorts and feels the difficulty of meeting the standards of a Christian life.

These difficulties accumulate. And since they touch on some old customs to which men are attached with their feelings, the necessity or obligation of a detachment is felt to be doubly heavy, as a loss and burden. What can be put into the other scale as « compensation » ?

Unless the burden is balanced by a « good » which repays the bearing of the burden, man is reluctant to accept the burden and seeks for reasons to avoid or decline its demands. And the more the missionary argues and tries to prove the necessity of accepting the faith without proposing suitable motives for the will (as is the characteristic of the apologetical approach, which we saw and tried to understand above), the stronger will be the resistance of the will remarked. The man under instruction will especially question those arguments by which his obligation to accept the faith is intended to be proved ; and since they do not give evidence so forceful that he must submit to it of necessity, he will seek reasons against the proposed arguments, or simply deny their cogency. Thus an apologetical discussion starts which has little value and which will not be settled by even more extensive and profound apologetics :

because the reason for the resistance is in its ultimate cause — not lack of evidence, but the lack of suitable motives for the will, of motives by which he would approach the Christian religion as something he « may » embrace rather than « must » accept.

No doubt, in some cases there might be also a resistance because of insufficient knowledge or a misunderstanding : this has to be eliminated by proper instruction. But this kind of « resistance » is not our problem here; rather that which has, according to the encyclical letter « Humani Generis, » its roots in « evil passions » (pravae cupiditates) which hinder the intellect even in the natural cognition of God, so that « men easily persuade themselves in such matters that what they do not wish to believe is false or at least doubtful » (Denz. 2305). Still more justified is this solicitude of the same encyclical when speaking of man's attitude towards divine revelation : « For man can, whether from prejudice or passion or bad faith, refuse and resist not only the evidence of external proofs that are available, but also the impulses of actual grace » (Denz. 2305).

But such resistance of the will cannot be fought with arguments of the intellectual order, which the apologetical arguments are. What is needed are motives for the will. And as long as man does not recognize the Christian faith as valuable and therefore desirable, he is bound to feel only difficulties and burdens, and consequently to resist against accepting the faith. Only with the greatest discretion is the motive of eternal condemnation to be employed. Whenever men submit themselves chiefly because of this reason (whether at the outset, or later in their Christian life) we have the case of Christians (and certainly not only in the missions !) who drag on wearily under the yoke of the commandments of God and the Church, and constantly ask why God couldn't or wouldn't make the life of man less burdensome.

Thus the inadequacy of the traditional apologetical argument and its insufficiency for the catechumenate of pagans becomes apparent : It is not that the argumentation itself is faulty or deficient. The inconvenience lies rather in the limitation of the apologetical argument itself. This argument shows the credibility and credendity by an exclusive process of reasoning directed at the intellect. It gives too little attention to the will which has an essential part in the act of faith and which besides has to carry the « burden. » Therefore effort has to be made to change the obligatory « must » which results from the traditional apologetical argument into a voluntary « may. » But since the apologetical argument of fundamental theology — based on its own supposition (of speaking to the faithful) and aiming at its own specific goal (to give rational justification) — does not do this, and since more-

40

over the attitude expressed by the « may » already presupposes some definite « understanding, » we have to obtain this understanding and by it the desired attitude towards the Catholic faith through a special endeavor antecedent to apologetical considerations : through the so-called « pre-catechesis. »

PRE-CATECHESIS

1. *First Catechetical Contact.*

Since it is psychologically rather difficult to correct an already formed impression of a « must, » prudence demands that we prevent (as much as we can) even the beginning of such an impression.

Before entering therefore into « apologetics » (if it should be considered necessary to treat them separately) we have to show and explain those facts and consequences of the Christian religion which are likely to give satisfaction, to arouse desire and to make men realize that belonging to the community of the faithful and sharing in their « riches » is something desirable.

In line with this demand are the various reasons which in our observation lead the pagan to the missionary. These are usually facts and impressions which he notices with some surprise in his contact with Christians (seeing their life, or reading about their religion) and which instill in him a certain esteem, arouse curiosity, and perhaps even some desire. Now he wants to find out the « secret » which caused his wonder and curiosity, and promises to « enrich » him in one way or another. This is the question on his mind with which he approaches the missionary. It matters very little what « words » he uses.

If therefore the catechumen establishes contact with the missionary by a question which resembles an apologetical problem, it is not to be taken in the literal sense. Generally it is simply an attempt to establish the desired contact or a « pretext » covering more personal questions. Hence what he expects is not so much the answer to the question he asked but « attention, » the feeling of being understood and the opportunity to speak. If we do not realize this condition, it may easily happen that the man who came in a seeking attitude does not feel understood because of the complicated answer he gets to his « apologetical » introduction, that he feels disappointed, loses interest — and stays away. Usually it is not an apologetical problem which prompts the pagan to seek the missionary and to ask questions. But aside from this, it has to be admitted that an apologetical explanation (as the answer to a proposed question) is for most of our listeners too abstract and therefore of hardly any value unless a more personal interest in the Catholic faith is developed by some kind of « preparatory » work.

There are certainly exceptions in which a genuine apologetical question exists, especially in the case of more educated pagans. (Of converts from other Christian religions to the Catholic faith we do not speak here.) But even in the case of a more educated man it would seem advisable to give first, in a simple manner, a preliminary answer till the problem can be treated more thoroughly and in the proper context with other facts of the apologetical argument which will have to be developed properly for this class of catechumens. But at the very beginning the interest should rather be directed towards the « good » to be gained by the faith, especially towards that good which is so to say « responsible » for the individual's interest in the Catholic faith — whatever the particular object may be.

In one case this might be a new and unexpected light and deep understanding of some questions which have long been puzzling him ; in another case it might be unrest which comes over him very suddenly, a desire to obtain forgiveness of his guilt, or a longing for something that would « fill » his life and make it worth living, etc. Thus even in the case of « intellectuals » we should not imitate the course of scientific scholastic theology but deepen first the knowledge of the « treasures » they can expect, and stir up a desire to gain possession of them — before the « price » or the obligations involved, are discussed. More concretely this means that before we start discussing in detail the rather abstract and demanding arguments of apologetics we should lead our catechumens — whoever they are — to CHRIST, « in whom are hidden all the treasures of wisdom and knowledge » (Col., II, 3), as we shall explain in a moment.

All the reflections we have made stress the necessity of a « preparatory » work which has to be done before apologetics can be discussed fruitfully (if it should be advisable to treat apologetics separately) and which in any case has to precede the systematic catechetical instruction.

For this purpose a number of informative talks on the Catholic faith may be given in which the treasures of our faith are explained as far as the pagans can understand them in their present condition. This is done by the pre-catechesis which begins with our first effort to find an audience, to gain attention, and to establish contact with those who are still far from the faith.

2. *Topics of the Pre-catechesis.*

Whatever might be the precise matter discussed in the talks of the pre-catechesis the topics chosen must fulfill two conditions in order to serve the purpose of the pre-catechesis.

The *first* condition is this : These talks have to treat topics in which the people are already interested or can be made interested. We must therefore discuss questions which are taken from the life of the people whom we desire to win for the faith, topics which are the object of their thinking, their wishes (and also of their fears), and which at the same time (as much as possible) contain a religious aspect or can be linked to an underlying religious problem, so that they will realize that a satisfactory solution without consideration of the connected religious point is quite impossible.

The selection of topics may vary from occasion to occasion. But frequently we may find it useful to discuss these or similar subjects : The Purpose of Life (What gives Meaning and Value to our Life ?) — Life after Death ? — Ancestor Worship — Justice and Reward — Conscience and Sin — Catholic Social Doctrine — etc.

Evidently we must also discuss the question of God — but not in the form of a « philosophical argument for the existence of God. » Many of our pagans do not show any doubt in their practical life about the existence of a supreme being. Rather they clearly show some beliefs in their sacrifices and religious customs, even if these are performed in a routine manner without much reflection. The question therefore « Does God Exist ? » may easily cause more harm than good. The question in this form may instill doubts, especially if the « proof » is given in a rather technical philosophical form. Furthermore, our listeners are generally not able to distinguish between a « dubium practicum » and — as is the case here ! — a « dubium methodicum. » Thus someone might come to the conclusion that he is not « obliged » to any religious practice as long as the existence of God is not « proved » to him. Such a result would be definitely harmful.

It is therefore much better to ask « What do we know about God ? » In the answer we can show clearly and convincingly God's power, wisdom, providence, justice, and love. Such an exposition demonstrates strikingly the existence of God and at the same time establishes a closer personal relationship to God, the real basis for any religion. In this point as in so many others we may learn from God's own method : His « Proof for the existence of God » is developed in the first part of the thirteenth chapter of the Book of Wisdom.

It is evident that in discussing these various topics we cannot (yet) give a full answer or a comprehensive proof. We are still in the pre-catechesis. A deeper and more complete understanding will come with the catechumenate when God's own word will teach us. But even now it can be shown — and this precisely is our aim in selecting and discussing these various topics — that the Catholic religion takes an interest in the questions and problems which pre-occupy our audience ; and furthermore, that the Catholic religion gives an answer which is deeper and fuller than the answer given by other religions, an answer which gives light and satisfaction, which opens new horizons in our life, which makes our life truly worth living.

With this, we have already come to our *second* condition which the topics of the pre-catechesis should fulfill. The answer to the question, the solution to the problem, the fulfilment of the desire, it must be shown is CHRIST, He who could say of Himself : « I am the light of the world » (John, VIII, 12), « I am the way, and the truth, and the life » (John, XIV, 6), « Come to me all you who labor and are burdened » (Matth., XI, 28).

Beginning with the instruction of the pre-catechesis our listeners, enlightened by His grace, « may know what is the hope of His calling, what the riches of the glory of His inheritance... and what the exceeding greatness of His power towards us who believe » (*Eph.*, I, 18 f). By this we have certainly set a goal for our teaching which will never in our whole life be surpassed, since it permits an ever deeper realization. But because there is no salvation in any one else but Christ (*Act*, IV, 12), the core of our message of salvation must be Christ (*I Cor.*, II, 2), and for that reason also our proclamation has to point from the beginning, even from the pre-catechesis, to Christ ! To Him each man must gain an intimate, personal relationship which is based on and is the result of high esteem and sincere love for Him. It should be an attitude such as will one day prompt the man to surrender in faith : « Lord, to whom shall we go ? THOU hast the words of everlasting life, and we have come to believe and to know that thou art the Holy One of God ! » (John, VI, 68 f).

3. *The Testimony of Christian Life.*

There is one element in the pre-catechesis (we mentioned it above in the text quoted from *Eph.*, I, 19) whose importance in the work of disposing man for the faith must not be overlooked : the testimony of Christian life.

Our religious instruction, and the teaching of the apologetics in particular, has frequently taken a very « scholastic » form. But the faith from which we expect our salvation is more than mere knowledge. Faith has to manifest itself in life (see   James, II, 14-26) and not only for the sake of one's own salvation. This need has also an apostolic aspect, and it enters the field of our own responsibility.

The outsiders whom we invite to the Catholic faith want to « see » the values of our religion and not only to « hear » of them. To comply with this demand we are perhaps more obliged today than ever on account of the prevailing « materialistic » spirit, although the Christian religion was always judged by the fruits which people looked for in the life of the baptized.

To this end were given Christ's earnest admonition (Matt ., V, 13-16) culminating in the words : « Let your light shine before men, in order that they may see your good works and give glory to the Father in heaven » and the admonition repeated by the first Pope : « Beloved, I exhort you... behave yourselves honorably among the pagans ; that whereas they slander you as evildoers, they may, through observing you by reason of your good works glorify God in the day of visitation » (I Pet., II, 11 f).

In the proclamation of the Good Tidings of our faith the testimony of Christian life, whose importance can hardly be overemphasized, has to support the testimony of our word. « Be imitators of me as I am of Christ » (I Cor., XI, 1) every Christian community should be able to say to those who see its life. If our life is truly « Christian, » we stimulate real interest and arouse esteem and desire, as is required for a fruitful catechesis on our faith. By the contact with a life that is marked by irresistible sincerity, deep religiosity and great cordiality the catechumen receives an impression which often is for him simply *the* proof for the genuineness of the Catholic religion. Anyone familiar with work in the missions knows missionaries who have charismatic gift of leading their catechumens, and even those with more than average education, right from the first instruction towards the center of the Catholic faith. In such cases the motivation to believe is given by the personality of Christ's messenger whose character reveals deep religious devotion and great familiarity with God.

This makes us realize that the instruction of the catechumenate need not necessarily contain a formal apologetical part ; that apologetics may be replaced by the testimony of Christian life (since it contains immanently the apologetical argument); but also that apologetics without the testimony of Christian life will not be very effective. There is only too much truth in what Father A. Liégé, O.P. writes : « It is always the Church that produces the Church. Surely, we speak here of the Church in its entirety ;

but also, and even more is this true of the local Church which continually has to represent Christ in the midst of a world that is tempted to return in signs and words to paganism. The place of the signs is here essential : The Christian communities have to astonish the world, have to raise a question by the manner of their life. Otherwise the preaching will remain abstract, and an empty word, like a human system. The inner life constantly conditions its exterior life : The expansion of the Gospel is a desperate work if the Church is not able to manifest the fact that Christ's spirit is living within her. » (Translated from « Die Katholische Glaubenswelt », Freiburg, 1961 (Herder), vol. III, 331).

Under the influence of the testimony of Christian life, it will probably be not too difficult to encourage the (pre-)catechumen to give the Christian life a try, to pray, and to practise the love of his neighbour. In this resolution the catechumen will be helped greatly if he finds in the community of the baptized his new « home. » The hundredfold reward (Matt ., XIX, 29) may rightfully be expected also by the catechumen since he leaves behind so much for the sake of Christ. But this should not exclusively be seen in the inner peace and joy of his heart ; it should be felt also in the exterior welcome given him by the Christian community.

The effort of the catechumen to live a Christian life constitutes according to Christ's promise a great help on his way to faith : « If anyone desires to do His (God's) will, he will know of the teaching whether it is from God, or whether I speak on my own authority » (John, VII, 17); and « He who does the truth comes to the light » (John, III, 21).

This new insight, promised by Christ, will strengthen the resolve to live a Christian life. God who does not let Himself be surpassed in generosity and love will make the catechumens realize that the afflictions of the present life produce « an eternal weight of glory that is beyond all measure » (II Cor., IV, 17) and that the promise of Saint Peter's first letter (I, 8 f) is given also to them : « ... believing in him, though at present you do not see him, you will exult with unspeakable and heavenly joy when you attain the reward of your faith, the salvation of your souls. »

As a result the catechumenate will be marked by the deep joyfulness (« hilaritas ») which Saint Augustine wanted to see in catechumens as the proof of a fruitful instruction and the guarantee of a joyful Christian life.

CONCLUSION

Thus we come to the conclusion of all our reflections : that the beginning of the instruction of pagans should not be made by an abstract explanation of the « truth » which the Christian faith contains, but by a demonstration of the « good » which the missionary offers; a demonstration which is given by word and also by example : this is the only means to arouse the interest, esteem and desire necessary before a fruitful development of the apologetical argument can be started and further instruction in the Catholic faith can be given.

Acting according to this conclusion we shall also probably better correspond to a much emphasized characteristic of the oriental (and perhaps not only of the oriental) who gains the truth by way of seeking the « good » (which objectively is not to be separated from the truth). If he renders worship to God, he does so because he realizes it as something good.

Perhaps this also offers an « explanation » for the syncretistic character of oriental religions which not seldom puzzles the European. There contradictory elements in this religious beliefs and practices. But is this not a sign of our slow understanding, which especially in religious and immaterial things is rather fragmentary (see *I Cor.*, XIII, 12) ? And is it not at the same time proof for the Church's teaching that the help of revelation was necessary so that « even in the present condition of the human race those religious truths which are by their nature accessible to human reason can easily be known by all men with solid certitude and with no trace of error » ? (Vat., Denz. 1786).

In present conditions it is difficult for man to reach the truth. Likewise the good, inherent in the truth, is scattered as it were in fragments. But this good attracts the attention of man and arouses his desire ; and he reaches for it without separating, through long reflections, the gold from the less valuable material with which it is found, and without always discerning the genuine part from what is specious : he simply longs for the good. And in some kind of intuitive perception he takes the « good » as the proof for the « truth. »

The Ministry of the Word :
from Kerygma to Catechesis

by André Liégé, O.P.

An *a priori* principle of the ministry of transmitting the Word in the Church will inspire these pages : *this ministry must reproduce, as far as possible, the very forms in which God revealed Himself.* Insistence is usually laid, quite rightly, on the faithfulness of the Church's testimony to Revelation. Less care seems to be taken over fidelity to the means used by God. The Church is prophetical ; that is, God continues to reveal His Word in Her and through Her, in continuity with the History of Revelation.

Before justifying theologically the classic distinction between the two principal periods of the prophetical ministry of the Church : kerygma and catechesis, we must first consider a few fundamental elements of a theology of the mystery of God's Word. Then we will be able to see the continuity in the Church's ministry of the Word. From this reflection on the Church's prophetical ministry, the distinction we intend to explain will emerge. Such is the plan of what the reader will find here.

A. THE MYSTERY OF GOD'S WORD

1. The Word, an Act of God.

Theological reflection on God's Word as outlined in the Second part of Isaias, St. John and St. Paul, leads to the assertion that God's Word is fundamentally a *revealing act of God*.

a) Dominating all the manifestations of the Word immanent

---

1. Lecture given at the 6th Doctrinal Symposium organized by the Dominican Fathers of La Sarte College (Belgium), in 1960, and printed in *La parole de Dieu en Jésus-Christ* (volume 15 of « Cahiers de l'Actualité religieuse »), Casterman, Paris and Tournai, 1961, pp. 170-184. — Address of Father A. Liégé : 22 rue du Faubourg Saint Honoré, Paris VIIIᵉ, FRANCE.

to history, summing them up, there is one Act by which God decided to become present to history for His own glory. This is what St. Paul will call the pre-existence of the mystery hidden in God even before the creation (*Eph.*, I). When we say that the formal motive of faith is God Himself making Himself known, we mean that by grace the believer finds himself placed in communion with the transcendent act of the Word of God, by means of the historical manifestations of this Word. Thus only the Word *of* God will be such in the fullest sense, not merely words *about* God authenticated by Him.

b) This act of the Word engages the entire personality of the living God in His intention of revelation. According to the realism of the term « *Dabar* » it is God Himself coming forward to be present in history, to make it question Him. Our anthropological distinctions between the heart, the mind and action, cannot be applied to the Act of God's Word without depriving Him of totality. That is why God's Word is both noetic and dynamic ; revealing awareness and creating principle : love, light, power and judgment. The classic definition of Revelation : « *locutio Dei ad homines per modum magisterii,* » shows clearly the poverty with which the idea of God's Word has sometimes been clad. Isaias expresses it much better : « As the rain and the snow come down from heaven and return no more thither, but soak the earth and water it, and make it to spring and give seed to the sower and bread to the eater, so shall my word be, which shall go forth from my mouth. It shall not return to me void, but it shall do whatsoever I please, and shall prosper in the things for which I sent it. » (*Is.*, LV, 10-12).

c) That is why the Act of God's Word will reveal both the plan of God's glory and the personality of the living God ; God at the heart of His Will's plan and of His action in human history, becoming thus sacred History and His Kingdom. With the same intensity with which the Divine plan is revealed will the countenance of God be revealed.

2. *Manifestations of God's Word.*

The transcendent Act of the Word is only accessible to us through its immanence in the various historical manifestations which constitute revealed History.

a) God's Word, entire and perfect in its Divine source, has made use of many and progressive interventions in the course of time, unified, however, by His revealing intention.

b) The manifestations of God's Word take the form of events

and conscious contact : *God speaks by acting ; He acts in speaking.*
He expresses Himself as a Person using concrete communion, not
confining Himself to the mediation of explicit ideas. He unveils
Himself to the historical consciousness of a community and by
means of events, of which the content of actual revelation the
prophets were charged to deliver.

c) Revelation progresses in the measure that the Act of God's
Word is more involved in the Divine manifestations, making clear
the meaning of sacred History. For being God's Word, however,
each manifestation does not imply fresh affirmation and more
explicit contact. God speaks, even when He repeats Himself !

3. *Jesus Christ, Plenitude of God's Word.*

It is through and in Jesus Christ that the full Act of God's Word
identifies itself in sacred History. God's revealing interventions in
the Old Testament did not equal the revealing intention itself.
The prophets were not identified either with the holy events nor
with the Holy Spirit Who inspired them. In the revealing event
of Christ the manifestation of God's Word attains its plenitude,
summing up and surpassing all the prophetical revelations of the
Old Testament. The Prologue to the Epistle to the Hebrews declares as much : « God, who at sundry times and in divers manners,
spoke in times past to the fathers by the prophets, last of all in
these days, has spoken to us by his Son, whom he has appointed
heir of all things, by whom also he made the world » (*Heb.*, I, 1-3).

Jesus Christ, plenitude of God's Word, what do we mean more
precisely ?

a) By His preaching and works, Jesus Christ brought to an end
the prophetical signs of God's appearance in history. The synoptic
Gospels show Him to us taking up, to explain their full and universal
significance, all the manifestations of God to the Jewish people,
and proclaiming the imminence of God's definitive coming. « The
time is accomplished, » said He, « and the kingdom of God is at
hand. Repent and believe the Gospel » (*Mark*, I, 15).

b) By His resurrection, Jesus Christ manifested fully and definitely
the intention of God's glory. By this event, God's Word showed
human history its final destination, and the Divine power which
would set it en route for eternal life. As in the Old Testament,
God manifested Himself in an Event teaming with revelation. It
was a personal event, concerning Christ Himself, the divine meaning
of which He proclaimed. No wonder that Paul placed Christ's
Resurrection at the heart of kerygma, and that he wrote to the

Colossians : « I am made a minister according to the dispensation of God, which is given me towards you, that I may fulfil the word of God, the mystery which has been hidden from ages and generations, but now is manifested to his saints, to whom God would make known the riches of the glory of this mystery among the gentiles, which is Christ, in you the hope of glory » (*Col.*, I, 25-28). To the elders at Ephesus also he said : « I have not spared to declare unto you all the counsel of God » (*Acts*, XX, 27).

c) God's Word which is Jesus Christ in His Paschal humanity, has a universal bearing, the beginning of accomplishment in humanity. It calls for expansion, not to be surpassed nor a fuller revelation in history. Pentecost is included in this Event, Word of Jesus Christ. The eternal Gospel (*Apoc.*, XIV, 6) will proclaim this accomplishment, and the blessed will sing « the canticle of Moses, the servant of God, and the canticle of the Lamb » (*Apoc.*, XV, 3).

d) Finally, in Jesus Christ, through His manifestations of glory, His Person, His works, His words, His Pasch, God revealed, as far as human minds can receive it on earth, the mystery of God in Himself. He is the Word, substantial and no longer intermediary Prophet, eternal Witness of God's plan and of the Godhead. As St. John puts it : « He that comes from above, is above all. He that is of the earth, of the earth he is, and of the earth speaks. He that comes from heaven is above all, and what he has seen and heard he testifies... he that has received his testimony has set to his seal that God is true. For he whom God has sent speaks the words of God, for God does not give the Spirit by measure » (*John*, III, 31-35).

That Jesus Christ is the Logos, there is the radical principle of the identity of His historical manifestation with the plenary Act of God's Word.

That He is Judge of the living and dead, constituted by the Father, there is the consequence of this personal identification with God's Word, Which present in history, judges it while calling it and casting it forward.

B. THE PROPHETICAL MINISTRY OF THE CHURCH

1. God's Word in the Church.

If Jesus Christ is the plenitude of God's Word, God has nothing other to reveal to His Church than what He has manifested in Jesus Christ. Revelation has been closed since the Apostolic age, the Apostles being the last of the prophets in the strictest sense of the word ; it fell to them to bring out the full meaning of God's Word of the coming of Christ, in the light of Our Lord's own words and the charism of the Holy Spirit at Pentecost. Just as the words of prophecy made one with the deeds of the prophets in the Old Testament, Christ's Word continued by the Apostles makes one with the Event of the Resurrection.

God still speaks in and through the apostolic Church. *Revelation has become Tradition.* That is to say, the Holy Spirit makes God's Word actual in the period of the Church's existence, by preserving the memory, living, accurate and active of all that Christ is in His personal mystery and His communication to men. Living Tradition constitutes a continued prophetism in the Church , not only an objective memory and magisterium, but the entire presence and power of God's Word, realized fully in Jesus Christ and extension of salvation in humanity.

God's revealing Act, then, continues to express itself adequately in the Event Jesus Christ. But what are the expressions of this Event in the daily life of the Church and in the world ? Maintaining the full significance of the term « word » which we have seen, it can be said that *everything which expresses the presence of God in Jesus Christ within the Church is the derived Word of God* : proclamation of the message, signs of grace, celebration of Sacraments, reading of Scripture. The whole Church is God's word, having nothing else to express than what Jesus Christ is for Her and what He does in Her.

2. The Ministry of the Word.

« We will give ourselves continually to prayer and to the *ministry of the word* » (*Acts*, VI, 4).

If it is right to see every Church ministry as an expression of God's Word in Jesus Christ, it is also permitted to mean by the ministry of the word what the Twelve meant in the Acts, the expression of the *Proclaimed Word.* Let us not forget, however, that understood in this sense, the ministry is placed in a context of signs, without which it would be too noetic and purely verbal. It is in this sense that we are going to speak of the ministry of the word in the Church : the Church's preaching, in continuity with the transcendent Act of God's Word, which gives it authority and power in grace, according to the plenitude of historical revelation given in Jesus Christ. As St. Paul asserts : « Faith then comes by hearing, and hearing by the word of Christ » (Rom., X, 17), and again : « The word is nigh thee, even in thy mouth and in thy heart. This is the word of faith which we preach. For if thou confess with thy mouth the Lord Jesus, and believe in thy heart that God has raised him up from the dead thou shalt be saved. For with the heart we believe unto justice, but with the mouth confession is made unto salvation » (Rom., X, 8-11).

3. An Acting Word.

What has been said allows us to allot its true place to the mystery of the word in the mass of Church Action. One would lessen it by reducing its efficacity to being merely occasional ; on occasions when the word is proclaimed, God will act for man's salvation. The only function of the word, then, would be to evoke Jesus Christ and His significance in grace. No, it is in the message, human in form, of prophetical testimony, that God makes the interior testimony of the Holy Spirit reside, in continuity with the transcendent Act of the Word. That is why the word of the Church declares and realizes truth, salvation, reconciliation, resurrection in Jesus Christ. It is a noetic and dynamic word in the message composed in human terms. Otherwise the prophetical ministry would be reduced to a professorship in religion. « The word of the Lord increased and multiplied, » we read in the Acts (XII, 24). And St. Paul again writes : « It (the proclaimed gospel) is the power of God unto salvation to every one that believes » (Rom., I, 16). « In Christ Jesus, by the gospel, I have begotten you » (I Cor., IV, 15).

We seem not to have retained the same conviction of the power of the word in the Holy Spirit which the Apostles had, but to reserve this efficacity to the sacraments exclusively. A typical example. of this is François Mauriac's answer to the question : « What do you expect from the priest ? » His answer : « Dare I admit that I am mistaken enough to expect nothing ? I only ask him to give me God, not to talk to me about Him. I do not under-estimate the ministry of the Word, but you asked for my personal demands. To my mind, a priest's best preaching is his own life. A good priest has nothing to tell me. I look at him, and that is enough. The liturgy is enough too, it is silent preaching. The religious Order that preaches best is the Benedictine Order, because they do not climb into the pulpit but make us live the drama of the Mass and make us grasp the sublime daily action. How will I understand Kierkegaard who writes that God is Some One we speak to, and not Some One we talk about ? How I pity Protestants whose worship is only words ! The holy liturgy — the only preaching that appeals to me and convinces me... »

To remain among literary appreciations, Bernanos was nearer the mark when he made the curate of Torcy say to a fellow-priest : « Teaching, my little man, is no joke ! I am not talking of those who carry it off too easily ; you will see quite enough of them as life goes on ; you will soon know them and the consoling truths they utter. Truth delivers first and consoles afterwards. Besides, we have no right to call it consolation. Why not condolence ? The Word of God ! It is a red-hot iron. And you who teach want to take it up with tongs for fear of burning yourself, why don't you grasp it with both hands ?... »

St. Paul says the last word when writing to the Thessalonians : « We give thanks to God without ceasing because that when you had received of us the word of the hearing of God, you received it not as the word of men, but (as it is indeed) the word of God who works in you who have believed » (*I Thess.*, II, 13). The Apostle was in a position, after the incident at Lystra (*Acts*, XIV, 8-19), to distinguish between persuasive discourses and the wisdom of God's Word.

C. KERYGMA AND CATECHESIS

The exercise of the Church's ministry of the word in the earliest days of the Church makes a clear enough distinction between the function of evangelization and those of catechesis (« kerygma » and « didachè »). In his great doctrinal epistles St. Paul gives catechesis to those whom he has already converted by the Gospel. The author of the Epistle to the Hebrews distinguishes between « the *first elements* of the words of God » and « the *doctrine* of justice, » or « the *word of the beginning* of Christ » and « things *more perfect* » (*Heb.*, V, 12-14 ; VI, 1-3). In the sixth century the historian Eusebius mentions the same distinctions, speaking of the preachers of the

Gospel of the first centuries. « To those who had heard nothing of the word of faith, they went eagerly to speak and transmit the Gospel, the book of Divine teaching. They *laid the foundations* among stranger peoples, then appointed pastors and left to them the care of those whom they had brought to believe... » (*H.E.*, III, 37).

It is this distinction which we must now found theologically, that is, starting from what God's Word is, from its transcendent act to its immanence in the heart of the believer, passing through its historical manifestations in the history of salvation. The act of the ministry of the word has its place between the Act of God's Word announcing the mystery of Christ and the act of faith by which the believer gives glory to the Word of the Lord (*Acts*, XIII, 48). It is in relation to these two terms that the mediation of the Church will assign the norms of its exercise and special pedagogy. First let us examine the term act of faith, in order to come back to the term Word of God later.

1. *The Dialectic Periods of Faith.*

Modern theology and pastoral have rightly insisted on the dogmatic character of faith, on the objectivity of its contents and the orthodoxy of its assertions. This is a necessary reaction against subjectivism of religious feeling and philosophies of religion. It is evident, nevertheless, that this reaction, often somewhat unilateral, sometimes resulted in separating our basic catechesis on the faith and Biblical tradition, older in itself than the modern opposition of subjective and objective. In Biblical tradition the faith first appears as a *conversion*.

It is none the less evident, and probably for the same reasons, that basic catechesis on the faith is somewhat separated from its pastoral sources in a Christian situation where there is little question of conversion. The man who becomes a believer is first of all a man who *converts his heart* and his whole life to the living God, Whose coming he has recognized, Whose call he has heard and Whose Word he has received. To be a believer is to imitate those champions who are praised in chapter XI of the Epistle to the Hebrews, of whom Abraham is the father, as St. Paul says (*Rom.*, IV, 17).

a) The faith, then, is first presented as an act of *conversion*. Does that mean that there will be no belief and adherence to a settled revelation, at least in the new-born stages ? We must be careful not to confuse opposition and distinction : in this case to oppose two types of faith, one of which will be the meeting between persons, the other simply accepting as true.

On God's side, the Word which calls to faith is necessarily revelation : « I am the living God, I will give you life if you accept to expect Glory from Me alone and acknowledge your Lord Jesus Christ. » On the believer's side, changing life and deciding to welcome God, which is conversion (melanoia), imply of necessity a fixed recognition of the identity and intention of the God Who has called him : « I surrender my life into Your hands because You are the Lord of Life. You shall rule my life and I will work for Your Glory. » Concretely, conversion is fixed upon the identity and significance of Christ. This recognition of Christ by the believer will find itself caught up in a free act of complete donation, of one person to Another, much richer than a mere accepting as true the Divine teaching concerning Christ. This is the beginning of the life of faith for one passing from unbelief to the Christian faith.

b) Faith must ripen. It will pass from the stage of conversion to *communion*. It is just the same as in human meetings when the first encounter only gives a global and indistinct intuition of the person met ; intuition which will develop into deeper and deeper intimacy, into a sort of divination with the Beloved and union with His life.

To one who has been converted to God in Christ, it is given to enter gradually into all the aspects of Christ's mystery into which he has been introduced. It is not so much a religious science as a knowledge of concrete communion, giving realism to all the elements which translate into human terms the riches of God's Word in the Tradition of the Church, the continuation of Pentecost.

c) If we chose for our heading : *dialectic* periods of the faith, it was to point out that from conversion to communion there is more than mere chronology in the life of faith, more than passing from what the Council of Orange called *initium fidei* to *augmentum fidei* (cf. *Denz.*, 178).

Chronology changes into a really organic structure of faith. It is like an extension of conversion to communion and back again. Conversion develops into communion, but on condition that communion is ceaselessly animated by fuller conversion. In return, what finds itself intensified in the faith of communion was already included in the global act of conversion , which had nothing of an act without doctrine, in spite of certain appearances. Conversion surpasses itself in communion, but there is no faith of communion which has not first been and continues to be faith of conversion. It is like a crypt which runs the whole length of the nave and not like a porch which is left behind when entering the nave.

There are not two kinds of faith , nor two successive stages of faith — stage of conversion, stage of doctrinal belief — but two dialectic elements of Christian faith, one living reality. The Post-communion for the Sunday before the Epiphany seems to illustrate this analysis : « Enlighten, O Lord, Thy people, and inflame their hearts with the splendour of Thy grace, so that they may ceaselessly recognize their Saviour (faith of conversion ?) and their desires may be fulfilled » (faith of communion ?).

2. Dialectic Periods of God's Word.

Faith ever refers us back to God's Word, its basis. We said above that God's Word is indissociably dynamic and noetic.

Were there only question of accepting beliefs, God's Word could be reduced to a Word that teaches. If there is question of stirring up continual conversion and introducing conscious communion, we can see the correspondence which must exist between the Act of the Divine Word and the believer's act of faith in all its fulness.

That is why one could, with a delicate sense of shades, since we mean dialectic extension and not opposition, compare the periods of faith and the fundamental attributes of the Act of God's Word. This would lead us to say :

a) that it is *chiefly the dynamic aspect of God's Word which stirs faith as conversion* , bringing forward man's life, the Divine assault, judgment. As the *Epistle to the Hebrews* expresses it : « Keener than a two-edged sword, it separates even soul and spirit, joints and marrow, it discerns the intentions and thoughts of the heart » (*Heb.*, IV, 12) — not that the noetic attribute of the Act of the Word is absent or inactive ;

b) that it is *chiefly the noetic aspect of God's Word which nourishes the faith as communion* : enlightenment, wisdom. According to the wish of St. Paul to the Ephesians : « May the God of Our Lord Jesus Christ, the Father of Glory, give you a spirit of wisdom to reveal and make you understand... » (*Eph.*, I, 17) — without out-dating the converting action of God's Word.

3. Dialectic Periods of the Prophetical Ministry in the Church.

If the act of prophetical ministry must model itself on the revealing Act of God, cause of the act of faith, we see at once that certain consequences impose themselves on this ministry :

a) *The primordial function of the ministry of the Word in the Church will be to stir up the faith of conversion, basis of all life of faith, without ever being able to suppose it acquired*, even from baptism for a child born into the Church by this sacrament.

Baptism is the sacrament of faith. In the case of baptism of infants, the Church receives them as participating members of a community adult in faith, capable of taking charge of these neophytes to lead them to the adult age of faith, when they can ratify personally their public profession of faith — conversion to Christ — and the obligations of a holy life which result from it. If it takes about twenty years to form an adult socially and psychologically, why should it take less — outside exceptional cases — to reach the adult Christian state ? Baptismal ratification continues, then, for some twenty years, until the child, born prematurely into the Church, by the maturity of his conversion, has come up with the convert baptized as an adult, thus becoming a fully responsible baptized soul. Now, it is by evangelization, the exact meaning of which we will define later, continued right through adolescence, that the infant members of a baptized community will be brought up to the full exercise of their membership of the same community — for the Church is a community of adults. This does not mean that an adolescent cannot have already set out on the path of Christian conversion but that this conversion only acquires its dynamism and stability after passing through the first experiences of human existence. *Adherence to beliefs is not enough, although it must always determine and express conversion better, in the personal ratification of the baptismal promises.*

b) *In its doctrinal function, the ministry of preaching must always have missionary energy*, so as to sustain and deepen conversion, to assist the interior strengthening of belief. This applies specially to Lenten preaching and missions in the home country.

c) It will be sterile to pass on the details of belief before having at least roused conversion ; we know the danger of confusing faith with a mere formal orthodoxy, but it would be infidelity to the Word to neglect deepening the faith of communion inaugurated at conversion.

From our foregoing reflexions, two types of prophetical ministry in the Church prove themselves necessary :

A primordial word (call it : missionary preaching, kerygma, evangelization) ;

Subsequent preaching (call it : doctrinal preaching, catechesis) in which several forms should be distinguished. St. Thomas Aquinas, for example, distinguishes four kinds of ministry of the Word ; the first is evangelization (*conversiva ad fidem*) ; the second is catechesis — catechism preparatory for sacramental practice ; the third regards spiritual life (*de conversatione christianae vitae*); the fourth concerns the deepening of the more profound mysteries of faith (IIIa, 71, 4, ad 3m). It seems essential to us, as our preceding analyses suggest, to stress the two basic accents of the prophetical ministry. Even if the practical exercise of this ministry unites the two, which is quite normal, it is useful to consider them separately, especially concerning kerygma.

It remains, therefore, to examine the two essential functions of the ministry of the Word — Evangelization and Catechesis.

4. *Evangelization.*

Properly speaking this is : *the first impact with the Good News, of God's coming in Christ to found His Kingdom in the power of the Holy Spirit, to rouse personal conversion and lead to entrance into the Church by Baptism.* The dynamic Word, usually accompanied by signs : God has come ; He comes today ; He will come to judge the world, but the Judgment is already taking place because of the Gospel.

In the New Testament, the verb *to evangelize,* used in an active sense, means « to proclaim the Event of the Good News of Jesus Christ » (Cf. *Luke,* IX, 6 ; XX, 1 ; *Acts,* XIV, 7 ; *Rom.,* XV, 20 ; *I Cor.,* I, 17 ; IX, 16). It is the first mission received by the Apostles : « Go, teach the Gospel to every creature » (*Mark,* XVI, 15).

The *Gospel* is the absolutely Good News, which comes from God and concerns His Kingdom among men, expression of the plan of His love (*Mark,* I, 14 ; *Rom.,* I, 1 ; XV, 16 ; *II Cor.,* XI, 7 ; *I Thess.,* II, 8-9 ; *I Peter,* IV, 17). It is a Gospel of peace (*Eph.,* VI, 15), of salvation (*Eph.,* I, 13), of grace (*Acts,* XX, 24).

Christ proclaimed *the Gospel of the Kingdom of God* (*Mark,* I, 15).

After Pentecost, the Apostles proclaimed the *Gospel of the Reign of Christ,* made king by His Resurrection and definitely fulfilling the preceding promises of the Kingdom. As St. Paul says : « *My Gospel, the message of Jesus Christ, the revelation of the mystery which was kept secret from eternity, which now is made manifest...* » (*Rom.,* XVI, 25).

After the period of historical Evangelization, will come the *Eternal Gospel* proclaiming, with the end of history, the Good News of the Kingdom and the Judgment in glory (*Apoc.,* XIV, 6).

He who announces the Gospel is compared to the heralds (*kerux*) of felicitous royal proclamations in the ancient civilizations. For the Gospel must be proclaimed publicly and universally.

The kerygmatical Word, then (from « kerygma, » the contents of a proclamation entrusted to a herald), does not go into the details of the *Credo* , not through doctrinal minimism, but because the Revelation is globally and dynamically contained in the proclamation of Jesus Christ, as within a personal synthesis. It certainly intends to make souls attentive to God revealing Himself in Christ but by causing a break in former existence and a passionate attachment, a decision for life. Looked at from close range nothing is as doctrinal as kerygma but under the form of a *message.*

Under the occasional manner of testimony rendered to Christ by the dedication of daily life, or in the more determined manner of a missionary announcement, we have found the specific place of the ministry of the missionary word in the Church of today as in the Church of the first centuries. This is not the place to examine its demands, it has sufficed to give the character of its principles.

5. *Catechesis.*

We are not going to consider the different types of catechesis but to reflect on the whole ministry of the Word which deepens the primordial work of evangelization. Catechesis exposes the totality of contents in Revelation — Tradition in the unity of the Christian mystery. We mention a few of the essential laws of this transmission of the Word.

a) CATECHESIS FLOWS FROM THE GOSPEL.

The Gospel is taken here in its meaning defined above : announcement of the Good News of the coming of the reign of God in Christ, made King of mankind by His death and resurrection. It is the contents of the apostolic proclamation (or « kerygma »), to which man has been enabled to convert his whole life. All revelation is a development of the dynamic message, all catechesis is a continuation of evangelization. There is no growth in faith without previous conversion which remains active.

Two consequences can be drawn from this :

All catechesis should be Christocentric. It is by Jesus Christ that God manifested and still manifests His glory in history. If conversion means to recognize Christ's exact identity, Christ becomes the subject of attribution of the whole revealed mystery. Whatever aspect of this mystery is studied, there will always be question of Christ, plenitude of God's Word.

All catechesis must bring man back to the initial act of his conversion, act which, in one way, he never gets beyond. In the measure that conversion has not been chronologically distinct from catechesis, as for baptized infants, catechesis will always have a dialectic period of evangelization, without which it would be mere religious instruction.

b) CATECHESIS MUST UNIFY THE DIFFERENT ASPECTS OF THE CHRISTIAN MYSTERY AND PRESERVE THE ORGANIC BALANCE OF REVELATION.

This results from the kerygmatical origin of the Christian *Credo*. Living faith first feeds on synthesis. Catechesis which did not continually bring out the unity of Christianism as one organic whole flowing from one kernel and being resumed in it would not bring to birth in men's hearts the reality of the Christian mystery. It would stop at committing to memory a collection of articles of faith. Three consequences follow : — Development of the different aspects of the mystery should be made according to the *concrete logic of revelation* , not according to an à priori logic or personal system, but according to the logic of the events of salvation, through which God proved His Will to save and His presence in history. God's Wisdom inscribed itself through events ; Sacred History is, therefore, the bearer of a Divine intention which unifies it and manifests the analogy of faith.

Does that mean that one plan imposes itself on all Christian catechesis ? No, of course not. But it seems to me that both personal choice and adaptation to individuals, should arrange to follow this development :

— *Jesus Christ, the Revealer of God's plan and mystery* : proclamation of the Kingdom by the coming of the King.

— *Jesus Christ, the Personal Realization of God's Plan* : Pasch of the triumphant Christ.

— *Jesus Christ, perfecting His Kingship, in the Church* : the Spirit and the Church, extension of Christ's Pasch till His Parousia.

— Each aspect of the Christian mystery must be given the importance belonging to it from its proximity with the centre of Revelation. This means, *first of all*, the avoidance of pseudo-speculative fantasies, empty of religious sap, and subtle developments on points where God's Word is reticent. It *also* means resisting the want of balance which subjective spirituality, peripheric devotions and theological variance of opinion fatally introduce into presentation of the faith. While the official magisterium protects the deposit of faith against unorthodox deviations, the catechesis of ordinary magisterium must be careful not to stress unduly the latest dogma defined or elucidated as the most important. The faith of the Church on one aspect of the Christian mystery is usually expressed in several dogmatic or disciplinary regulations which must be taken together and not isolated. Every Council has a limited aim according to the contestations which have rendered it necessary. Catechesis could not be chiefly anti-heretical, although it must meet the needs and problems of the modern mentality.

— Within the contents of the faith, different plans could be arranged ; some aspects of the mystery are the already positive anticipation of the glorious life of intimacy with Christ ; others are less susceptible to interiorization, like the dogmas concerning the significance of evil ; others again form the object of adherence to the will of Christ for the historical period of the Kingdom, everything touching sacrament or salvation except the sacred humanity of Our Saviour and the communion of saints. The two last plans obviously draw their light from the first, which dictates an order of catechesis on the Church, for example, in which the reality of the Holy Spirit completely dominates the reality of the Church's institution.

c) CATECHESIS CREATES A CHRISTIAN COMMUNITY.

It is addressed to a people, not to a collection of individuals. A people destined to become more and more such as their faith increases.

Catechesis for one person treats him as a member of a people.

The duty of catechesis, therefore, is clear ; it must bring out the ecclesial nature of the whole Christian mystery. As Christ is the centre, the Kingdom is present everywhere. This is not one particular aspect which can be taken among others, but an aspect which must influence all the others.

d) CHRISTIAN CATECHESIS IS INDISSOCIABLY DOGMATIC, MORAL AND LITURGICAL.

This is so because it is the same living Christ in whom we believe, Who, in immediate dependence of faith, gives a new meaning to the whole life of the believer and calls for new behaviour from him. It is the living Christ too Who comes sacramentally to consecrate with His presence human situations, to make them a definite part of the Mystery.

Here, the catechist's task will be to bring out the aspects of the Christian Mystery by their *significance* as much and more than by their explanation. The significance concerns the whole man and affects his behaviour as much as his convictions, while the explanation chiefly appeals to his intelligence. This will lead to proposing vital and personal analogies, taken from human experience, rather than purely conceptional ones, in order to penetrate Christ's Mystery. God's behaviour through Christ reveals human experience in itself and dictates its laws, while thoughtful human experience can discover in faith the meaning of the mystery of love. This gives back to anthropomorphisms a place given them by the Bible often denied them by learned theology. For human spirituals and intellectuals, wishing to be pure, often become abstract, while concrete spirituality is lived by the whole person.

In practice, catechesis naturally has doctrinal, moral or sacramental emphasis. To prevent emphasis becoming separation, catechetical thought must bring out the unity of faith in Christ and of the moral and cultural acts involved by it.

e) IN ITS EXPRESSION CATECHESIS MUST RETAIN TRADITIONAL CHRISTIAN LANGUAGE, WHILE CREATING A MODERN CHRISTIAN VOCABULARY.

A certain vocabulary is the inheritance of Judaeo-Christian tradition. We know the importance of language for creating a community and transmitting a spiritual tradition. When this has, besides, the guarantee of Biblical inspiration, we realize that Christian catechesis must pass it on as a living heritage. More than of dogmatic formulae, we are thinking of revelation's grand expressions : *Kingdom, Life, Glory, Grace, Parousia, Testimony, World, Mission, Mystery*, etc., which must fix Christian attention. But a needed complement to this effort is the creation of modern equivalents which will convey God's Word clearly to the mentality and sensibility of today.

We said, at the outset, that the whole ministry of the word in the Church should be faithful, not only to the contents of Revelation, but also to the forms of pedagogy used by God in manifesting Himself in the History of salvation. The distinction, in unity, of the two functions of evangelization and catechesis in the ministry of the word is one of the most important applications of this principle. We only hope we have proved it in a sufficiently convincing manner.

Mentalities and Milieus

The mentality of a person to whom God's message is
addressed and the milieu in which he lives have a
profound influence on the way he receives and thinks about
God's Word. The religion teacher should be keenly aware
of these two factors, and he should carefully take them into
account in the way he presents and explains God's message.

Man in Presence of the Word of God

by Marcel VAN CASTER, S. J.

Catechesis is transmission of the word of God to men. It requires above all fidelity to this word of God in all its authenticity; it is very fortunate that this first requirement is emphasized again nowadays. Instead of spending most of our time describing what men think about God, we ought to pay more attention to proclaiming what God has said about God. Hence our first aim will be to know ever better the word of God.

We must not be satisfied to proclaim it merely to men, but at the same time we must help them to welcome it fully in faith. It is therefore most important for us to know the man to whom we speak. When Jesus announced the message of His Father, « He knew what was in man » (John 2, 25). By following His example, we try to realize the attitude of man in presence of the word of God.

In this respect the strong and weak points of man towards the word of God, are to be found on three levels :

1. The Christian anthropological level : What is the real position of man in respect of God's call ? Grace and sin ; knowledge by faith, in more perfect light but still veiled ; liberty awakens and develops, while it cannot yet in this world victoriously overcome various obstacles.

2. The psychological level : According to age and temperament, which abilities are first of all observed ?

3. The sociological level : Which influences derive from modern mentality and social structures ?

The study of Religious psychology and sociology has already been the subject of numerous articles in this Revue. [1] But an accurate

---

[1] Address : 184 rue Washington, Brussels, BELGIUM.

[2] Volume XI (1956), Decennial Tables, pp. 111-128, and special number on Religious Psychology, Vol. XII (1957), pp. 198-396.

appreciation of psychological and sociological facts presupposes a sufficiently clear view of the existential situation of man. For this reason we will endeavour to determine that which in Christian anthropology best characterizes the attitude of men in presence of the word of God.

Such as we present it here, this situation is directly destined for those who are baptized. [1] Subject to certain shades of meaning, it applies also to the non-baptized ; because it concerns the status of man, called in fact to be united to God in Christ. [2]

1. *Living According to the Spirit and Fighting in the Flesh : Growing Towards the Stature Accomplished in Christ.*

Man is « *called.* » God comes to meet him by His inward grace and outward revelation. By granting ability to do so, God calls man to live according to charity, which is the accomplishment of the mystery of Salvation. Therefore Christian anthropology does not consider man outside his relationship with God, or the true divine plan of Salvation, nor as dominating by his own power the natural forces put at his disposal, nor as plunged into an absurd whirlpool, in which he finally sinks ; but called and supported by the living God.

We may describe the situation into which the man must live his Christian vocation as a tension between a thesis and an antithesis, tension which develops into a superior synthesis up to total life.

a) By His death and resurrection Christ has entered as « First born » in the complete Salvation to which God calls all men. He still continues today His work of Salvation by sending His spirit to us. From the present moment, we can and must « live according to the Spirit » which means recognize and accept the revelation of God, live in conformity to our union with Christ. We must trust God to keep us free enough from purely earthly things to consecrate and give ourselves in joyful submission to union with God.

b) But the grace, conferred to us by God, is still challenged by worldly antichristian influences or by anything insufficiently impregnated with Christian life. We are fighting in the « flesh, » which

---

[1] MOUROUX, « Baptism and Christian existence, » in *Du baptême à l'acte de foi,* Paris, L'Ecole, 1932.

[2] FRANSEN, P., « Towards a Psychology of Divine Grace, » in *Lumen Vitae,* XII (1957), No. 2.

means that we suffer from numerous weaknesses in which God's strength has not yet penetrated, and we are not completely liberated from sin, into which we often fall again. By reason of our condition of life « in the flesh » we are also exposed to be led into temptation, to persecution by the unconverted world and to attacks of the devil.

This tension between Spirit and flesh has its reaction as well on our own comprehension of the word of God, as upon our liberty to live in accordance with our Christian vocation. The word of God is transmitted to us in a veiled light. The human spokesmen of the Christian message, are awkward servants ; the audience very often lacks the required aptitudes to understand this message sufficiently well. But the grace of Christ acts through these awkward messengers and amidst these imperfect disciples. *Liberty* is not an unalterable possession of man upon earth ; it is accompanied by all the oscillations of the « spiritual » in the material-spiritual unity of the human being. It must awaken from a sleepy state and continuously make appeal to the grace of God, in order to react with Christian liberty against the changing influences to which it is submitted. [1]

c) The synthesis of Christian anthropology is based on the eschatological character of man's position. Our condition of life is directed towards the accomplishment of the divine plan of Salvation. We are « going » and the kingdom of God « comes » in its plenitude.

This abundance of the Christian life is a gift from God. It was already granted to Jesus Himself, and one day it will be granted to all those « who live in Christ. » The « expectation » is therefore a fundamental characteristic of the proper attitude to be taken by man in his earthly condition.

But this future has already begun. The final gift of God, works in advance mostly in the sacraments. Thus the Eucharist is an experience of love, whose plenitude belongs to future life, and already upon earth, it is offered to us in the seed. The multiple display of human forces amidst all worldly facts, what according to Christian terminology is called « Christian humanism » is therefore eschatological in the sense we have defined it here. This display with all the efforts it entails to reach more human conditions of life, struggle against sufferings, experience of values of life for each one and more real common life among men : this building of a better world is but a transitory preparation to a

---

[1] See : Nuttin, Psychoanalysis and spiritualist conception of man, p. 128, 147, 167 ; and Schoonberg, *Streven*, nov. 1951, p. 108.

definite transformation. All aspects of human life on earth are only temporary. For each man, they terminate at his death and for all humanity at the end of time. But this end of the temporal is transition from temporal to the eternal, under aspects we shall know but later on, when God will bring them into effect.

On our side, this preparation is after all nothing else than our *co-operation* with God, who by Christ continuously grants us more abundant gifts in order that we may always be ready to give active welcome to His complete final gift.

Our condition of existence is a participation in the pascal condition of Christ. Already born to the new life, but still imperfect and affected by sin, we grow through strife and death up to the point where we reach the « accomplished stature of Christ » risen again. [1]

This condition of man has important consequences for catechesis. We shall now point out a few among them.

2. *The seed and the field.*

Being attached to the service of God, who comes to meet men, the apostle of faith will also go to meet men, which means that he will go to find them where they are and such as they are with the true disposition of their soul. He usually finds them much absorbed by their daily occupations, performed without a clear conscience of their dependence to God. For many, the struggle for life is an exacting concern ; pupils have so many school subjects to learn ; children like to play and their exuberant young vitality scatters their interest. [2] Therefore, we must first help them to find a certain silence in which the word of God may be heard, in which they can gather their strength to answer the word of God.

When they are ready to listen, they take various attitudes. Jesus referred to them in His parable of the seed and the field (Luke 8, 11-15). Some seed fell « by the wayside. » Men may retrench themselves against the word of God and remain « *distant.* » Like the Pharisees, they remain closed to a divine revelation which does not agree with their own opinion ; then the devil comes and immediately takes the seed away. « And again some fell on stony ground. » They who when they hear receive the word with joy but do not let it take root ; *superficial,* they risk losing the word as soon as

---

[1] In a manual we are now preparing *Man in Presence of God,* this theme is developed, based on texts from the New Testament.

[2] GRUBER notes this in *Lumen Vitae,* XII (1957), 2, and quotes testimonies in his work : *Jugend im Ringen und Reifen,* 1956, pp. 282-283.

they hear another voice. And that which fell « among thorns » is choked with the cares and pleasures of this life : overwelmed by human concerns, they oppose God's action and yield no fruit. But that which fell on good ground brought forth riches. Those who listen « *ready to give themselves* » grow in faith, put into action in charity.

Generally, these various attitudes are not neatly separated from each other. They are rather to be found in varying proportion in the heart of any man who hears the word of God. For each shade of such varied mentalities, specific remedies, useful for catechesis, may be determined. But here we are giving a few suggestions relative to the overall condition of man.

The dynamic character of the action of God in His revelation and the co-operation of man in his answer requires *much patience and confidence* in catechesis.

In its present stage, revelation is in fact authentic but still incomplete. It will only be at the parousia, i.e. at the moment of final intervention of Christ, that it will be absolutely clear in which way God will communicate Himself to us and what our quality of Christian means. In the meantime, the word of God is very mysterious, it is a revelation in a veiled light of faith. We have always to preach mysteries and our audience has to welcome mysteries. However, the mysteries revealed by God do not enclose our knowledge into narrow limits, but may be compared to horizons which allow us to perceive already the beginning of a path whose end is not yet clearly profiled.

Therefore, we may not confine ourselves in a too human light : we must on the contrary *open ourselves for the reception of an increasing faith*. This applies as much to the teacher as to the pupil. Religious teaching consisting solely of a material transmission of immutable truth expressed by invariable formulas would cause sclerosis. The religious teacher will try to improve continuously his own penetration of revelation and always adapt and renew his methods of presentation.

He must always consider his pupils as non-adult Christians going towards a more complete faith. All education must take advantage of the increasing strength of the pupil who develops through many repeated trials, errors, corrected attempts, towards a full accomplishment of what is provisionally a dynamic but rough outline.

The formation of faith must take into account the state of the forces acting amongst Christians : the grace of God in an awkward and sinful man, who while progressing in Christ, prepares himself for the plenitude of Salvation. The development of Christian faith is related to judgment as well as to liberty. Therefore, it is a mistake to go too quickly and demand adult knowledge and will from those who are not yet fully adult.[1] On the other hand, no man is competent to determine that one or another point of the Christian message nor the appeal to perfection of Christian life « do not mean anything » to certain pupils, by reason of their age or their milieu. We must not forget that the Holy Ghost addresses the soul interiorly in a way that we ignore.

Man's incapacity to express what happens on the level of the faith, and the absence of sincerity, consciously or unconsciously introduced in the expression of this faith, renders mostly impossible the control of the results obtained by this teaching. The pupil cannot express adequately what he really grasps in his knowledge of faith. Man's behaviour never corresponds entirely to his deep faith.[2]

An important conclusion appears to us to derive from the parable of the seed and ground. The one who proclaims the word of God is a sower and he must fulfil his task with patience and confidence. The sower knows that God has placed in the seed a wonderful force of germination ; he ploughs the ground to make it ready, and he sows the seed generously ; he does not indiscreetly pull the young shoots but relies upon God who will let him, or others after him, bring in the harvest in due time.

Catechesis requires patient and confident workers at the service of Christ, who is the Sower of the word of God. They try first and above all to understand and show the word of God in all its strength, they also look for the difficulties and possibilities to be found in man and make every effort to prepare the field to receive the seed. They avoid too mechanical or too human methods, because their proclamation is the supple and generous gesture of the sower who trusts the Lord of Life to grant a prosperous harvest.

---

[1] FORTMAN. Zij die geloven, haasten niet (p. 37-51), in Buytendijk and « a Problematiek van de middelbare schooljeugd, » Spectrum, 1957.

[2] Concerning the limit case by GRAHAM GREENE, in *The potting Shed*, see MONDEN, *Streven*, XI (1957), pp. 272-277.

The Christian Message and Apologetics and the Modern Mentality

by Bernard HAERING, C.ss.R.

It is most damaging to the Christian cause for too great an emphasis to be placed on apologetics, and for the defensive to be selected as the principal role. The Christian, and in particular, the theologian is not an apologist in his relationship with non-Christians, but a messenger of joy, proud of his faith. He sees in the « still unbelieving » and even in the adept of a hostile ideology to Christianity, a seeker rather than an enemy against whom he must defend himself. His kind look, through which shines a living faith, will be able to discern the desires for truth hidden behind the behaviour pattern.

I. GOD'S ACTION THROUGHOUT HISTORY AND THE MODERN MENTALITY

God engaged humanity in an intimate conversation by revealing himself in Jesus. He has sought man wherever he could be found so as to guide him along the right paths. The eternal Word become man at such a moment of history, in such a civilization and in such a context of ideological struggle. The revelation then, is not only a word from heaven, but an appropriate and understanding word addressed to man in his own sphere. Qumran's manuscripts provide a new and convincing proof of this, and the preaching of faith and apologetics must remain loyal to this rule.

---

1. See biographical note in *Lumen Vitae*, XIII (1958), p. 416. — Address: Alfonsiana Academy, via Merulana, 31, Rome, ITALY.

Every epoch has its own standards, its own way of expressing its longings and desires. In accordance with the conception of life certain values and truths will become more accessible than others.

An epoch yields to truth in a certain measure only, in its own particular style and no other. It has above all the capacity to expand in goodness or degenerate into error and nihilism. These phenomena are often referred to vaguely as « the spirit of the age » or « modern mentality. » « Spirit of the age » can refer either to the way of life of an epoch — a way recognized by men of varying intellectual accomplishment — or to the « ideals and spiritual currents » dominating it.

The defenders of tradition, the obstinate representatives of a past age, have a tendency to condemn outright the new mentality. This is not a Christian function, since God is present in every epoch. Hope expressed in « the spirit of the age » is sustained by God's action, who throughout history has, and is, preparing man to receive the good news. Each epoch, each civilization, each mentality carries within it the seeds of the Logos. Our task is to separate them from what is false and discover them in their inadequate wrapping with a passionate love of truth.

Every epoch casts a shadow of the future. It aspires to a liberating truth and to values that will satisfy its most ardent desires. To ignore these facts is to invite the modern mentality to glory in its errors and nihilism. The lack of understanding is not only a grave peril to the mind open to good and evil, but a serious menace to the representatives of the Christian truth.

On the one hand then, we have the errors of the age absorbing the energies of the modern mentality, and on the other, a crowd of apologists, weary of life and crouching behind the screen of eternal truth. Inwardly and unconsciously they are obsessed with the past, and have been caught in the whirlpool of yesterday and today.

Immutable truth is ever young and vigorous. It can only be conveyed to the modern mentality if outworn formulas are discarded and bold action undertaken. The Christian who does not cleave to unintelligible forms and customs but has a deep and living love of truth will discover that he is capable of holding a friendly dialogue even with the modern mentality. He can perceive what is good in it.

By drawing on his treasures of inherited and assimilated truths, and presenting them in a new form, he will develop an awareness of the arduous currents flowing through the modern mentality, and will be stimulated afresh.

The salvation of man is accomplished even in contemporary

244

history, and the present and the future belong only to those willing to acknowledge truth and the march of time. Those however who insist upon the methods of the past will find nothing but dross in the modern mentality, and the lifeless figure of former truths.

The church's function today is to *separate*. It is part of its eschatological role. And the grace accorded by Christ and His message will finally seep into the minds of many and a decision will have to be taken. Separation and decision presuppose that good dwells in the heart of man, that he is capable of purification and perfection. The modern mentality IS man, and the Christian who regards it as something to be taken by the horns will only succeed in strengthening what is evil in it. It is like the workers in the parable who were determined to tear up the weeds even if it meant trampling on the good corn.

An apologetic inspired by a deep faith and charity towards men will be far more effective in its attempts to spread the truth than the noisy shouts of self-defence. Truth must be revealed in the language of the times and by the use of values that the modern mentality understands. Only thus can the real operation of separation and salvation be performed.

II. THE PAULINIAN APOLOGETIC AS AN EXAMPLE

By virtue of the Charism received, Saint Paul had to wage a fierce battle against the ethics of the law. His fight was anything but negative.

In the Paulinian message concerning the law of faith, law of grace and law of Christ, we learn that they were purified and completed, and all that was false was removed. Yet in performing this he was able to respect the Jews' passionate love for the alliance with God in the Old Testament.

In his message to the Greeks, he preached the « folly-wisdom » theme of the cross, thus paying deference to the Greeks' special love of wisdom. And he was able to communicate the richness of law and wisdom, the ineffable joy that could be found in truth — the truth that leads to the path of knowledge and virtue, the one and only source of happiness.

St. Paul's example should be followed if an effective separation is to be made.

In the light of Paulinian theology, we shall attempt to show — by an example of a confrontation with collectivism and existentialism — that conversation with the modern mentality must be positive if it is to participate in the final mystery of separation.

III. A POSITIVE CONFRONTATION WITH COLLECTIVISM

The sufferings derived from the deadly results of an individualism without end, human concentration in towns and industries and various other causes, produced in the latter half of the XIXth century a conception of life that expressed a new community spirit. this phenomenon found little response from Christians, and was at times brutally rejected. The Modern mentality, overflowing with vitality, turned to Marxism and its various forms of collectivism.

Christians should deal with Marxism, first by pointing out with impunity the great danger to religion and civilization, and then asking themselves why this doctrine was able to arouse the dynamism of the contemporary mind. Was there not at the root of this Marxist collectivism the grave neglect on the part of Christians to realize what is true solidarity and to grasp the misery around them ? A worrying thought indeed, but one that might show at last where the effort of Christians should be directed.

Karl Marx offered no immediate rewards ; on the contrary, he promised suffering that must increase and become total in the struggle for a classless society. He demanded unremitting selflessness and solidarity. It was the idea of solidarity that stirred the imagination of the workers, and they responded to the call to unite and suffer that a new paradise might be formed for future generations.

Communism resorted to trickery and terror ; yet it must be conceded that the pioneers who played a decisive role in its development could have been saints had they been enrolled in the fight for the kingdom of God.

The workers then resenting the many injustices perpetrated on them revolted against individualist preaching. They were disgusted with the egoism of Christians who thought of saving their souls as cheaply as possible. Not for them the sacrifices demanded for the world redeemed by Christ !

Marx, and many of those who embraced his doctrine with a religious fervour judged Christianity by those Christians who were clinging to an epoch that was both individualist and obsolete. The word « Christian » was not only dishonoured by the anti-social behaviour of Christians but by the negative attitude of those who professed belief towards the spirit of the age, spirit of solidarity.

Christianity that flourishes on truth cannot remain anchored to a meaningless individualism. While conserving the truths of the past, it must accept the driving impulses of the epoch with its fresh yearnings, for deeper solidarity and a common culture. It must also recognize the natural evolution of social and economic structures.

These values might have remained obscure because the previous epoch had been contaminated with the bad « spirit of the age ». But Christians should have been the first to feel the warm breath of this new spirit reviving old Christian truths, especially the solidarity of those called to be the « salt of the earth » in their striving towards a new heaven and a new earth. In this way they could separate the truths of the old and new mentality from their errors.

Marxism offered a new conception of life, and especially a means of achieving social progress. Its first recruits were certainly not drawn from Christian circles, for at that time so many Christians were not only individualists but were very satisfied with themselves and tenacious of their rights. They were easily provoked into the defensive, and a new type of apologetic became symptomatic.

Marxism sailed on the winds of the modern mentality and fed upon forces that sprang from Christianity. Thanks to the millennium, the Christian of the West learnt that salvation cannot be accomplished without common responsibility, that our meeting with Christ will be all the more personal if we work together for the salvation of all and bear testimony in social circles of the saving power of God. Was it not the Almighty Saviour of God who began this great social experiment ?

Karl Marx could never have exercised such a powerful influence on the masses had Christians given an authentic realization to all that was best in the modern mentality. Also, the promise of suffering and an earthly paradise could not have won the proletariat if Christianity in the XIXth century had kept pace with the times and interpreted afresh the real Christian hope of a *final fulfilment in all things and the redemption of mankind and all world structures.*

We can stoutly affirm that we have no need of Karl Marx and his theories of class hatred and a purely earthly paradise. Truth can be found without him. But the pernicious results of his teaching must be accepted as a judgment for our lack of vigilance, and a call to examine our own deficiencies.

It is not by mere accusations or scientific refutation, but by a loving affirmation of the Christian truths, values and virtues for which the world hungers, that we can save the modern mentality from the cold grasp of Marxism. We must proclaim aloud and with all our strength the real truths, the real values and the real virtues that can bring peace to this troubled era.

If Marxism is not to absorb the entire energies of the modern mentality in its struggle for a new community, the words and actions of Christians must clearly indicate that hope has nothing in common with an assertive egoism. It is useless placing hope in the beyond if our earthly mission is unfulfilled. Salvation in Christ concerns not only the soul but also the body, social life, and the whole atmosphere in which men work out their salvation.

The Christian must not heed a modern mentality that is contaminated either with individualism or collectivism. *He must live on his own truth.* But to give this truth vitality, we must talk to the modern mentality in terms it will understand, and before contamination takes place.

When encountering the 'open mind' in a modern mentality, care must be exercised both by theologians and preachers, not to fall into the common error of giving preeminence to certain values. The principal danger in the modern mentality imbued with Marxism is materialism and the belief that human progress is automatic. This danger is all the more threatening since what is only promised by Karl Marx is already attained by many anti-Marxists and Christians. They in turn boast about the non-Marxist world and its productivity. But communism has only to perform an interplanetary feat for their confidence to evaporate like smoke.

A Christian discussion with Marxism and with the modern mentality must find a deeper purpose if it is to be fruitful.

IV. THE CHRISTIAN ACCOMPLISHMENT OF EXISTENTIALISM

In spite of all disorders, human nature tends to its true end, to the accomplishment of its being ; that is why in the spirit of the time, in an epoch's idea of life, protestation always arises against every attempt to empty or falsify the sense of human existence. Such a protest seems to arise in the sense of life in existentialism. It is a spontaneous attempt of human nature to escape the foolish boredom, the impersonality of the masses, the mechanism of a merely external organization. The existentialist of every shade wishes above all to be master of his own existence ; he defends himself from the world of things. Put forward as a new means of fighting false collectivism and the herd spirit, this idea of life can also become an enemy of authentic community civilization.

Existentialism is an instinctive human revolt against excessive planning, considered absurd, against meaningless, soul-less formulae, against law merely imposed from without and resented as fetters on the liberty of invention. The existentialist loves risk, liberty's adventures. He sees and seeks in it the strengthening of his personality, the realization of his existential possibilities. As a person, he wants to show he is never satisfied, never at rest. The impulse to realize himself, to fill the interior void, is found in atheistic, as well as in Christian, existentialism although the world of values is totality different in the two. The sense of life proposed by existentialism is indifferent in itself from the ideological standpoint, for in this current of modern thought, we can find the energy for a Christianism eager for risk and authenticity ; but it can also lead man to make self-will an absolute end to the detriment of his own existence.

Nevertheless it would be following a false trail to consider Sartre's atheistic existentialism as the archtype of this very living modern thought and simply to ask : How are we to treat this wrong idea ? The Christian existentialism as in the philosophy of Gabriel Marcel, is no less at the origin of the new sense of life than the different forms of non-Christian and anti-Christian existentialism. In the light of God, the Master of history, we must admit that this reasonable protest of modern thought against routine seeks its realization much more in the practice of a courageous Christian life than in Sartre's foolishness and the nausea with existence which follows it.

We should not, therefore, have in mind principally or exclusively, when confronted with modern thought, atheistic existentialism alone, and concentrate all our forces on rejecting this degenerate modern growth. The Christian must have his eyes open, of course, and beware of false attitudes and errors in an intellectual current which finds so powerful an echo, and makes so deep an impression on speech, costumes, actions, the theatre, cinema, daancing and music. Non-Christian existentialism spreads its ideas much further than its admitted circle of adepts. Several times in a few years, the Holy See has been obliged to warn us against the existentialism which is the enemy of all law, and against the resulting *moral situation*, and we must take this warning very seriously. But Christian life must not degenerate into a kind of spiritual hypochondria, a sickly fear of bacteria. A Christian must not spend all his energy on the one preoccupation : not to be contaminated. The danger of contamination will be so much the less as the Christian life is the more intense and as we meet modern thought more positively, with active faith.

In this way we will purify the atmosphere and reduce the danger of contamination even for others.

If existentialism protests violently against the herd spirit, traditional settings, soul-less formulae and inadapted human laws, the true Christian will not lament the dangers threatening law and order, but will raise aloft the *will of authenticity in life and the care to act in all sincerity*. The man who comes up against a too narrow exterior order is not an enemy of the law for all that. Perhaps he is seeking sincerely to find the true sense of law and order, which abuses and formulae hide from him. Professors and teachers who praise exterior order unceasingly to their young people, and burden them with countless regulations, may possibly succeed in training sluggish and docile natures to be honest, obedient men exteriorly. But you will look in vain among them for spontaneity and imagination in doing good, or power to influence others. The more unruly types, on the contrary, the most sensitive to the influence of today's existentialism, will finally go so far in their revolt against narrowmindedness and hatred of formalism that they will challenge even the general value of moral rules.

Without being hostile to the existing order of life, the Christian, from the basis of the very nature of Christianism, must struggle relentlessly against slipping into formalism and routine. The great Doctors of the Church, like St. Augustine and St. Thomas Aquinas, have explained insistently in the New Law « the law of Christ » (*Gal.*, VI, 2), its constant openness to the work of the Holy Spirit through grace, to the call of the moment and our neighbour's needs. Today we understand better this aspect of Christian morality than the Christians of the eighteenth century, obliged to live under absolutism that multiplied ordinances and directions.

If you put before a young man, particularly incined to the existential view of life, real Christians, the saints, as the tough pioneers that they are and always will be, as the real explorers of new ways to practise the great commandment of charity, he will easily learn that the profound order and intelligent observance of laws in general, in no way make a man a machine, but rather provide him with means of using his own possibilities in setting out boldly in the path of right and service of others.

The existentialism of Sartre, chiefly occupied in producing fresh proofs of its liberty — not to say caprice — can think itself mighty and original compared with a merchant attached to the letter of the law ; but all its adventures, inspired by the arbitrary, appear miserably small and insignificant compared with a Christian who, awake to the needs of the moment, undertakes and bravely continues ever new inventions inspired by brotherly love.

Whatever its form, existentialism gives the basic tone of a period of transition. Many traditional forms are resented as an unbearable restraint by a young generation living in the greatest social changes the world has seen up to now. The danger certainly exists of hurling essential and indispensable moral standards into the whirlwind of progress. But this danger will only increase if, in the name of Christianism, we seek to defend not only the essentials, but also the multiplicity of laws of a gregarious society tending towards collectivism, and other worn-out structures, with the same ardour and obstinacy. By so doing, we would not only discredit Christianism, but provoke revolt against soul-less formulae, quite natural in itself, in an atmosphere of absolute hostility to law.

If the young man of today has a taste for risk and wants to prove his freedom, let us not overload him with rules, warnings and prohibitions, which will either paralyze his energy, or more probably, make him revolt violently against law and order. Let us rather give him big jobs to do, calling upon his enthusiasm and love of liberty, and giving him full scope for his freedom of invention.

Christian life does not mean clinging to the strings of the law, but valiantly scaling the heights. The more we are drawn to the summits of the Sermon on the Mount and the great commandment of love for others, the further we get from legal limits. At any epoch, it is a fatal injustice against « the law of the spirit which life in Christ Jesus gives » (*Rom.*, VIII, 2) to rivet the Christian's attention exclusively on the prohibitions or limits of the commandments. A limit has a fascination which either cramps enthusiasm or psychologically provokes its violation.

When the existentialist morality wishes to overcome this legal limits attitude by getting underneath it — in matters of the flesh : pride, infidelity, impurity — the Christian answer can only be to multiply the bars of the barrier or to fix attention on them.

As St. Paul says, the Christian is not under an exterior law ; if he allows himself to be led by the Spirit he will not strain all his forces to reach the limit imposed by the law. The fruits of the Spirit: « charity, joy, mildness, helpfulness, goodness, confidence in others, gentleness, self-control, » (*Gal.*, V, 22) have no law against them, as the Epistle to the Galatians says : « If the Spirit animate you, you are not under the law » (*Gal.*, V, 18).

Routine and the herd spirit are avoided, not by giving way to selfish unrestrained desires, but in yielding to the urge of grace and the needs of the hour ; not by despising Nature's law coward-fashion, but by being ready to do big things and be faithful in little ones, even to heroism.

Before God we are not mere numbers ; to each one of us He gives an individual name. Each one has received individual gifts, as well as those of human beings generally. Therefore, each one must discover the mission God has chosen for him, not only in the world in general, but in his own talents and capabilities.

The law of Christ, according to the Apostle of the nations, is a law written in minds and hearts. Whoever lives by this law escapes the narrowness of self, shares the freedom of God already, and finds in his very « existence » the deep meaning of his life.

These truths cannot fail to influence the sense of life in an existentialistic epoch ; moreover, this very conception of life will help us to understand essentially Christian truths, and to practise them in a more intense and authentic manner. If Christians give the true answer to this modern mentality, anyone who is not completely immersed in atheistic and pretentious existentialism, will realize where he can find real authenticity and healthy liberty.

The Art of Dialogue
With « Those Who Think Differently »
from Ourselves

by Dr Klemens TILMANN

> « ... Be always ready to answer with
> kindness, respect and a clear con-
> science, anyone who may ask you the
> reason of the hope that abides in
> you » I Peter III, 15.

> « ... You must make known the
> marvels of Him who has called you
> out of the darkness into His admirable
> light » I Peter II, 2.

I. THE PRESENT SITUATION

We have catechetics and homiletics, but we do not teach how to
talk about religion and the conception of the world with those who
do not share our beliefs. In this field, we have neither a profound
theoretical knowledge nor the practice which would enable us to
show others how to discuss religious topics. We see our young people :
workers, artisans, students pass into a world where the prevalent
ideas are different from ours. We know that they are exposed to
numerous, violent and well-organized attacks. What happens ? We
teach them the Truth, but often only for themselves, so that they
can repeat it at religious examinations. Perhaps we say to them
« Defend your faith ! », but we do not prepare them for the struggle
nor give them the arms they need. We even say : « Be an apostle
at your place of work » but we leave them alone to fulfil this task.

---

1. See biographical notice in *Lumen Vitae*, XI (1956), p. 605. Address : Klug-
str., 91, München 19, GERMANY.

Perhaps they find themselves face to face with experienced enemies of Christianity who expose their ideas with arrogance and assurance, and who come out the winners ; or they may have to do with Jehovah's Witnesses to whom they are an easy prey ; or again, they may come in contact with a member of a Protestant sect, and in spite of their 8 to 12 years of religious instruction, our young people do not know how to put him on the road which will lead him to the Catholic Church. Let us take for example the girl whose boyfriend does not go to Church. All she can say is : « Why don't you go to Church ? » Finally he does go, but nothing has been gained by that.

For the most part, our young people find themselves helpless and unprepared to discuss religion ; still less are they formed and equipped to arouse enthusiasm.

If we are not equal to the situation, and never have the upper hand in conversation with those who think differently, grave consequences will result. We are afraid of a conversation about religion, we hide our faith, we are embarrassed, we do not want to be known as Catholics. The Church is thus deprived of the immense advantage of having missionaries everywhere and is ridiculed because of her members, and the field of action is left free to the enemies of the faith. In this way the well-known atmosphere comes into being, in which a word on religion is never heard, in which the « others » set the tone, and in which God and His cause are lost. The good will of a young man cannot assert itself ; he lacks the necessary skill and technique for this « explanation. » He himself becomes subject to error as he experiences how feebly he can defend his cause ; the « others » win. Thus the name and the cause of God are dishonoured.

There exists the need for instruction bearing on how to treat of religion with those who do not share our beliefs, and this need is not confined to the laity. In addition to Homiletics and catechetics, the priest himself needs to learn, as part of his pastoral duty, to talk familiarly to those of other creeds ; he needs to be instructed in the art of discussion.

II. DIFFICULTIES AND PROBLEMS
IN THE ART OF DISCUSSION

Without doubt, instruction in the art of discussion meets with many difficulties. First of all, this instruction must vary considerably according to the age, the maturity and the temperament of the speaker. The apprentice of 14, the young girl of 16, the scholar, the student, the peasant and the priest have different possibilities of speaking of the faith. No one can lay down a definite rule therefore. Moreover, the method will vary according to the interlocutor and to whether he is a protestant or a believer, one who is seeking the truth or one who is indifferent, one who is ignorant, hardened, contemptuous and aggressive, or even an experienced and fanatical enemy of the Church. Furthermore, in a veritable dialogue, it is not the method alone which counts ; other factors play a more important part : an exact knowledge of the vision of the world which is proper to each of the speakers, the personality, the attitude of mind, each one's possibilities and capacity for reflecting, and for expressing his thoughts. Both can direct the discussion as they wish.

III. RULES

Let us now try to lay down some practical rules, without, however, claiming to be systematic or complete. These rules are dictated by the subject which is broached, or imposed by conversational tactics or suggested by psychological considerations. Some demand a high degree of disinterestedness and of goodness. Others are more suited to the young, others again to the priest who has the care of souls ; many are applicable in all cases and situations.

Try to realize exactly what your interlocutor wants. — Is he seeking the truth, or more light ? Does he want to combat so-called errors ? Is he really interested ? Has he only a superficial curiosity ? Does he simply want information ? Does he want to lead you on ? Is he looking for an outlet for his bad temper ? Does he want to attack the faith itself, either because of his own interior uncertainty, or through ill-will, anger or hatred ? You will act quite differently according to each case.

Try, above all, to change the false interior attitude of the other party. — Often, the object of his question or his attack is not the essential. His question is often only the expression of a false interior attitude. If we manage to raise the conversation above the level of anger, superficial views, prejudices, passions, want of respect, etc., we have then created the atmosphere in which we can treat of a religious truth calmly, seriously, respectfully and without quarrelling. Only thus will the other be able to perceive a sacred reality. From thence flow other rules.

4

Never make aggression your principle. — A fundamental rule, the most important in the majority of cases : « Treat your enemies as friends » says Ghandi ; thus one makes them one's friends. You must neither dispute, nor want to show that you are right, become agitated, nor ridicule your interlocutor. You must want to help him. You must approach him just as he is, with his problems, preoccupations and deceptions ; you must bear them with him, share them with him, understand them. This liberates one. Do not feel offended (« it is not a question of me, but of you and of the Truth) nor allow yourself to be turned aside in any way from the charitable attitude which helps, saves and sympathizes with others ; triumph by kindness. Remain friendly, cordial, sometimes even full of good humour. Hearts are often opened to the Truth far better in this way than by arguments. We must strive with all our might, not to combat and win by force, but to walk unarmed beside the other, and help him. Certainly this attitude is the most fruitful in an exchange of ideas as to the meaning of life and of the world.

Bring out the truthful elements in your interlocutor's ideas. — He considers something to be true and wants to see it approved ; try to find this element in his ideas. Every way of seeing things has some exact elements in it. We should never contradict immediately, for then we only pay attention to the negative aspect of our neighbour's ideas. But if you bring out what is true in what the other says, if you insist on it even more than he does, then he feels that he is understood and appreciated ; he is calm and well-disposed to hear something disagreeable, that is to say, whatever will show him where he is wrong and lead him nearer to the Truth. Learn to distinguish the true from the false in every statement. But the Truth is your business.

Make the desires and the intentions of the other your own. — You are already doing this in approving whatever is true in his ideas. But he wants something more. Every man thirsts to be esteemed, and wants to be taken seriously ; he has no desire to appear a fool and to be in the wrong. Never hurt him in his honour. Furious attacks often come from a heart which is tormented ; proofs are useless in a case like this, but questions asked in a kindly way are not. For example : « You must have lived through some hard times to speak in that way ; what has disappointed you so much ? » Try to find out in this way the motive behind his feelings, his bitterness, or his contempt, and make his intimate desires your own.

The discussion must not leave a man irritated by his defeat, but one who is beginning to see the Truth and charity, one who is comforted, on the way to recovery, grateful, perhaps even a friend of the Church. This is absolutely necessary, even in cases where we must speak with force. Finish on a reconciliatory, kindly note : « Perhaps this will help you. I hope I have been of some service to you. »

Be satisfied when the other is ready to show respect for part of the truth. — Madeleine Sémer used to say to her sons who wanted to remove the crucifix from their home : « If you cannot yet believe what is true, consider it as the symbol of disinterested love, which sacrifices itself for others. In this way you can respect it and it can have some meaning for you. » In this way we do not ask too much from the other party, but we show him the nearest approach to the Truth.

Encourage the other on the road of Truth. — One day I said to a protestant lady : « You are rich in many things : you know about God and about Christ ; you have the Word of God, and much else besides. But you do not yet possess the whole Christ, you do not yet know what He does during Holy Mass, and what He wants to do for you as well. *You are on the way. Do not stay half-way, nor stop just before you reach the goal.* » Confirm the other in the Truth and in his efforts, encourage him to follow more and more closely the call of God ; this interpretation of his ideas will perhaps make him appear better than he really is, and make him wish to live up to his reputation (perhaps it will be our words which will put him on the right path). This is the real way to draw men nearer to God and His Church.

Ask the other party questions. — This is certainly one of the most important rules. Young people should be initiated into the art, and we should give them the correct formulae, beginning with : « Whoever made you believe such a thing ? » and ending with : « Do you know exactly from where you drew your concept of life and of the world ? » We could ask a protestant : « Why are you a protestant, anyway ? » « What could the Catholic Church do to prepare the way for protestants to enter ? What do you expect from the Catholic Church ? » « What ought we to change, according to your ideas ? Wouldn't you help us to do it ? » When you are visiting a lapsed Catholic, you could ask first of all : « Are you satisfied with the services in your parish ? Are the hours convenient ? Have you any desires to express ? » — But then go on to ask : « Would you like to see something more in the Church than there is at present ? Don't you want to help us to fulfil these desires ? Wouldn't there be cause to worry, if the Church were no longer there ? » — Another question : « Isn't it cowardice not to face up to the most important questions ? » You can also ask : « Wouldn't you like to consult an expert in religious matters ? You aren't afraid ? I'll come with you ! » If you are faced with a scoffer, words such as the following, said very calmly, will often produce the right effect : « Allow me to ask you one question : Is there anything you respect ? » If he says yes, ask him : « What is it ? » Then say : « Do you like it when others make fun of it ? » If he says he has no respect for anything, say : « I can have no respect for someone who respects nothing. » Certlainly, many other questions can reduce a person to silence. From the defence, you must pass to the attack. For example : « Why do you work ? » « To earn my living » « And why do you live ? You ought to reflect on that ! » One day St Philip Neri was questioning a young man about his plans for the future and kept on asking : « And after that ? » until they came to talk of death.

Instruction in the art of such discussion should include a whole collection of these questions which would serve to open people's eyes to the Truth and bring about the required interior attitude.

Leave it to your interlocutor to prove his charges. — Most of the time the others make their assertions and you despair of being able to refute them. Do the opposite. Say to them : « There is no God ? How very interesting ! How do you know that ? Can you prove it ? No ? Then you ought to be more careful before making such statements. »

Do not prove, but show, first of all the possibility of the truth in question, then show that it is reasonable, and finally show that it is the reality. — Proving anything does not produce faith. Arguments have a very negative effect, because the interlocutor bristles up against accepting the Truth. Moreover, he believes most of the time, that he has the right to expect a mathematical or scientific proof, a false presumption which can never be realized. Therefore, as often as not, he will be disappointed by the proof.

But if he concedes the possibility (if God is a Person and has created the world, He must also have the possibility of communicating with us), he will begin to see its reasonable aspect (it is easy to understand that God, who created us, wants to communicate with us) and he will even feel its probability (it would be astonishing that God should have created the world and men with so much care and wisdom, only to retire after that into an eternal silence). He will thus arrive on the threshold of the Truth, and from then on, he will be disposed to examine the reality.

Let us proceed in the same way in the question of the existence of God. Do not prove, but ask questions : « Do you think it is foolish to believe in God ? » « It is certainly possible that God exists, or can you prove perhaps that there is no God ? » If the other speaker admits the possibility of the existence of God, then we can continue : « We must get ourselves accustomed to this possibility that God does exist and that He knows and loves us, as Christians say. Perhaps it is true ! » Then the interlocutor will feel how important it is for him to face the problem one day. « Otherwise it could happen that our entire life could be wasted. »

Show how much importance you attach to real facts. The interlocutor is less convinced by the Truth itself than by deeds, especially by worthwhile deeds. Then our words do indeed become a witness. One day, in a train, as I heard some sectaries making fun of Catholics, I told them how some young Catholics whom I knew devoted themselves to the cause of Christ, really living the Bible, and how highly I esteemed their conduct. Immediately the tone changed. I had introduced the reality into the conversation, instead of the Truth in general. The result was that we found that there was common ground between us, where our views and aspirations met.

Whoever can speak enthusiastically of what pleases him in the Catholic Church, has an advantage if he speaks of practical examples of charity, of the devotedness of missionaries, for example. No one is offended by hearing of another's personal experience. In this way, everyone can bear witness to the Cause : all that is necessary is that he himself should be convinced. One can speak quite simply, with faith and conviction, of Confession ; acknowledge the existence of the fault and the importance of the mercy of God.

There is always a good reply which can be given. — It can happen to anyone not to know the real answer to a problem. But even a young person can reply in a case like this : « There is certainly an answer and probably an excellent answer . I don't know it, but I will try to find it out.

Direct the conversation. — Talks often have no result because they deal with points which are not interesting. You should not be afraid to change the subject and get on to another where you are more at home. For those who have had little instruction, it is an easy way of bringing a complex conversation to an end. When a young girl tells how profitable she finds her work in a Catholic Youth Movement, no one is astonished that she is, and wishes to remain, a Catholic. If someone else speaks enthusiastically of a great saint or a contemporary co-religionist, the interlocutor can hardly contradict. Moreover it is necessary in every discussion, not only to reply and defend oneself, but also to bring the conversation round to a theme with which one feels at home and where one has the upper hand ; then especially, one will be able to make the Truth and Love of God apparent.

Show Christianity as a liberating Truth and a redeeming Love.
— Certain people have shabby or false images of God, of Christ, of the Church and of their life in us ; in the same way, their ideas about human existence, happiness and the meaning of life are mean and false. Therefore, Christianity appears to them as a dogmatic constraint and a burden. Show them the good tidings of joy, salvation and love which Christianity contains, as well as its invitation, its being a free gift, a treasure and a source of immense possibilities. Show how it contains the truth which makes us free by giving us the true meaning of life : how it is a light and a solution for all vital problems : show how we find in it the victory over selfishness and the corruption of the world, over disorder and sin ; show that it is the way we must follow in order to become what our intimate aspirations would have us to be.

We must give our young people slogans and ready-made answers.
— At the time of the national-socialist ideology, a particularly efficacious slogan was : « The Catholic concept of life and of the world is the only one which admits all positive values. Other concepts have only partial views. » Catholic life can radiate affirmations like these.

Another example : To anyone who claims that Buddha is more ancient than Christ, answer : « Buddha, Lao-tse, and Confucius prepare the way for Christ. » In this way, their value is recognized, while at the same time their limitations are clearly expressed. Again we could answer : « Our faith dates from a thousand years before Buddha. Abraham believed in the Christ to come. » If anyone asks you : « Why are you a Catholic ? » answer : « I am a Catholic because the Catholic Church is the only one which gives a clear, enlightening and liberating answer to all the decisive problems which life brings » (Chesterton).

Do not forget the spiritual dispositions necessary before the Truth of Christianity can be accepted. — Religious truths are on a higher plane than the facts of natural science. They demand certain exigencies before they can be grasped interiorly. The road is closed to those who are selfish, presumptuous, superficial and the slaves of their passions. God does not reveal Himself to the insolent, and the great truths are only shown to those who pray. Thus an exposition of the Truth must often be accompanied by the call for a realization of the dispositions required. For example : « The truth of Christianity will only be understood by one who, during his life, has one day performed a really disinterested action. » Or : « These truths are only revealed when one takes God and prayer seriously. » Whoever does not keep these dispositions in mind conducts the discussion in vain. He even makes himself and the Cause he is defending ridiculous.

Pray for « the others. » — Prayer alone will put you in the right attitude and inspire you with the right sentiments towards your neighbour. Then only do you dispose of the means of opening his heart to God and to the Truth : the grace of God.

These rules can be completed by many others.

The special rules for priests who discuss religion with those of other creeds would fill a section on its own. In this case the discussion has already begun silently by the very fact that a man wears an ecclesiastical habit. How can one set about making a lapsed Catholic understand the obligation he has to baptize his child ? What dispositions are necessary in order that an exhortation to go to Church may prove fruitful ? So many problems open a new field of action.

IV. CONDITIONS FOR A RELIGIOUS DISCUSSION

Many of the rules indicated cannot be punctually followed by everyone. They are linked with certain conditions. The better these are fulfilled, the better the discussion will bear fruit. The instruction and religious formation must conform to them as to a pedagogical principle.

The first condition is *to be convinced personally.*

Another condition is *the will to persevere and to progress.* Lenin said : « Whoever is not ready to crawl in the mud for the revolution, is a boaster, not a revolutionary. » In Christian language, this means : « Whoever is not ready to crawl in the mud for Christ is a boaster, and not a Christian. »

Third condition or recommendation : *do not let us seek to combat, but to help and to liberate.*

Finally, *the appropriate religious knowledge is necessary.*

261

The image which the early catechists gave of the faith certainly made discussion about religion difficult. The Catholic Faith was presented as a « religion of duties, » for it was stated from the beginning : « In order to get to heaven, we *must* believe, keep the commandments, receive the sacraments and pray. » Such a triple obligation, so heavy to all appearances, is not easy to defend or promote. It has no radiating force. Another difficulty lay in the transmitting of the message because of the abstract and purely objective way of thinking and speaking. In order to assure the other easy transmission and welcome of religious truths, we must bring out, when speaking of religion, its worthwhile and saving character, its elements of redemption, of ennobling, of transfiguration, of happiness, as well as its aspects of real and actual happenings.

You must know the language appropriate to each truth in particular.

The best method is to employ the interrogative form.

a) *Christ* : « Do you know the most celebrated personality in the history of religion ? He is invoked thousands of times every day. Millions of men are happy in His service, because His teaching alone means salvation. It is Christ. You ought to think about that seriously.»

b) *The Church* : « Do you know which is the most astonishing society in the world ? The Catholic Church, without any doubt. It is the biggest religious society. In it are found men of all classes and nations : devoted men, heroes of brotherly love ; former communists, workers, politicians... How is it possible ? You should think it over, calmly and deeply. Have you ever heard of Damian de Veuster ? You ought to read something about this apostle of the lepers. Hundreds of people have followed his example. We have people who dedicate themselves by the thousands to the service of their neighbour, through love. Is not this force of charity overwhelming ? Where does it come from ? »

c) *The Bible* : « Do you know which is the most widely read book in the world ? It is a remarkable thing, it is neither a success story nor a love story. It is the Bible. It is by far the « best seller » not only of our own time but of all times and it is also the book which has done most to regulate, raise, transfigure and make human life happy. Read the New Testament, veritable source of our vision of the world and of life. »

The young girl whose friend does not go to Church must also be able to give an effective relpy. When she says to him : « Come back to the Church, » her words are often only the manifestation of her helpless good will. She ought rather to say : « You don't take God seriously. Your life is a lie, you act as if God were not your Lord and your Creator. He who says that he will not give one hour out of the 168 hours in the week to hear Sunday Mass has already given God the last place in his life. It is already apostasy and atheism. » If her friend replies that he does not know what to do in church, she should answer : « Well, take your missal and sit at the back of church. It is worth it. It won't come without an effort. » Or perhaps, she could say in a conciliatory way : « We can read and prepare our Mass together. »

V. PRACTICAL CONCLUSION

Without any doubt, we need « dialogetics » beside the homiletics, catechetics and general pastoral training. For the making known of the Word of God to lead men to Christ and to the Church is not done only by preaching, catechetical instruction and the administration of the Sacraments but also, and in large part, by conversation. The art of religious discussion is necessary for the priest in his pastoral ministry, as well as for the religious formation of the laity. To these also the words of Christ apply : « Whoever does not gather with me, scatters abroad » (Matth., XIII, 30).

Christianity must be *a movement* and the Church must be spread by all her members and not only by her official ministers. Confirmation, in particular, demands this from all.

1. *Insertions to Be Made in the Teaching of Religion and in Youth Movements.*

Exercises in discussing constitute the best means of forming the young for religious discussion with those who do not share our beliefs. For this end, we must make use of the teaching of religion, of the different youth movements (youth clubs, students' circles, apostolic societies, etc.) and of appropriate courses and organized days. It is above all necessary to make this formation an essential element in the programme of religious instruction. It is an essential part of the end of this instruction if one assigns to it as a task, according to Pflieger, « to enable catechumens to dominate life as Christians and to face the world as believers. » There is still time if one looks at it from the social and not merely the individual point of view ; that is to say, if one wishes to instruct the Christian in his duties towards his neighbour and the Kingdom of God.

The teaching of religion, we repeat, must not only transmit knowledge, but have an influence on the children's lives in order to make
them apostolically-minded. Moreover, it must initiate and lead the
Christian to speak up for his Faith, to be ready to fight for it in
public, to defend it in conversation, to procure its diffusion, to work
for the salvation of his neighbour. It is not therefore, merely a
question of knowledge and of Truth, nor of living personally according to the Truth, but of passing on this Truth, of serving it,
and of helping and serving others in their journey towards it.

This will lead us to think the Truth over again, and deeply,
considering it from a new aspect. We must search in every Truth
the (comprehensible) value it has in life for each one, its richness,
its meaning for us humans, its power of transformation, of action
and of progress. We must not put in the first place the idea of
duty ; we must not exaggerate it. But we shall begin by the saving,
liberating, enriching and comforting aspect of religious truth.
Beside its intellectual aspect, which was the only one in the foreground formerly, we will seek out whatever in it encourages and
touches man, makes him enthusiastic and directs his life towards
God. We shall not only ask : « What is true » but we shall also ask,
and sometimes insistently : « What does our life demand » or
« What does that mean for us ? » Our faith is not a science but a
doctrine of salvation ; what has been revealed for the salvation of
man is a revelation of love which must lead to salvation and eternal
life.

The teaching of religion must have new ends in view : « You must
know this » does not suffice ; nor does : « You must live in such or
such a way. » One should also say : « You must be able to answer
questions, to advise others, to dissipate errors, to make the Truth
shine out, to fight for your cause, and win, so that you gain souls
for Christ. » Each theme thereby acquires a new actuality, a new
seriousness, a fresh urgency. Thus one equips oneself for the duties
of life.

2. Begin Right Away.

Before catechetics explore this domain thoroughly, we *can and
must begin in a practical way.*

The writer of this article has often taken as an exercise, during
a course of religious instruction to children of 10 years, a dialogue
with « a man in the train. » He sits in front of you during the
journey, asks you what school you go to, and hearing the word
« Catholic, » he begins to ask : « You are baptized ? But why ? »
The writer would ask questions just like a man who knew nothing

at all about the Faith but who was interested in it and so got the children to explain everything to him. All formal knowledge disappeared and the children learnt in this way how to show a stranger in what true religion consists and what it means to them. Every rhetorician ought to be able to set forth his faith in the same solid, attractive and convincing way to an Asiatic student.

3. *Team Work.*

Several catechists have worked as a team. We now have to extend this initiative as far as possible, find out the best methods, gather together all the experience which has been gained here and there in instruction or in students' circles, and thence perhaps, have sessions. These teams must work out apologetics adapted to our times, which will not only give proofs, but will help and keep in mind the values of life, of the attitude to be adopted, of the means of gaining access to people, of points of contact etc. They must work out formulae ready made for question and answer, give typical examples, giving exactly : the religious idea, the sentiments of the speaker, the tactics of discussion, the psychological processes ; they must prepare true-to-life examples radiating love, warmth, joy, and the happiness of possessing a treasure superior to every other.

VI. A POSSIBILITY FOR THE CHURCH

The Church, which now propagates the Faith only by means of those of her members who have received an official mission, possesses immense reserve forces, which she can set in motion. Her army of « professionals » can be transformed more and more into an army of ordinary people. Why should the proselyte of error be more adept at pleading his cause than one who works for the real Truth ? The Truth, too, can be proposed in simple formulae. All that is required is that its defender should be given the arms and the training which he cannot procure by himself. Our aim must be to make every young Catholic able to tell others, without the slightest embarrassment, what the Catholic Faith means to him. It is not very difficult. A living testimony to Christ, which is much more valuable than a mere knowledge of the Catholic Faith, will then become possible. Naturally, much will depend on human limitations, on the lack of ability, the indifference and the shyness of both parties concerned. Nonetheless, we have here an immense possibility.

Our Lord said : « You are the light of the world, » « You are

265

the salt of the earth. » This is true of every Christian who has been confirmed. God does not want His Spirit to become silent. « It is yours to proclaim the exploits of the God who has called you out of darkness into his marvellous light » (I Peter, II, 9). These words, which St. Peter addressed formerly to all Christians without distinction, apply even more to the Catholics of our time, when the world is inundated with whole armies bent on propagating falsehood. God, however, will give us the gift of eloquence and all the necessary force to bear Him witness before all the world.

Institutional Environment
and Religious Life

by Joseph H. Fichter, S.J.

There are many types of " environment "and the investigation
of environment as a factor in the pursuit of religious activities
may take many forms. As Gabriel Le Bras has stated, " Each
one of us is deeply influenced by his environment and his liberty
suffers pressure from many different factors. . . From infancy
we are subject to our *physical, geographical* or *ethnical* environment. " [2]

Influences are reciprocal in all phases of social life.

Institutions affect people as well as other institutions. People
change mores and are changed by them. Because of this dynamic
reciprocity in society, it is practically impossible to hold any of the
variables constant long enough to make *precise* conclusions concerning the *degree* of influence of one or another. In other words,
we are dealing with elements and factors which are not subject
to satisfactory quantitative analysis. In spite of this physical
shortcoming of social science and of the fluid character of social life,
we may make a sociologically valid analysis of mutual influences.

---

[1] The Reverend Joseph H. Fichter took his degrees (B. A. and M. A.) in sociology
at the St. Louis University ; he received the doctorate of philosophy (section of
sociology) at Harvard University. His principal works are : *Francis Suarez, Roots of
Change, St. Cecil Cyprian, Christianity, James Laynez, Textbook in Apologetics.*
This last book, published by The Bruce Publishing Company (Milwaukee, 1951),
contains two parts, the first being taken up with classic apologetic, simplicity,
clearness and conciseness being its chief merits. The second part offers a choice of
quotations taken from the great Catholic authors whose works constitute an important contribution to a sound apologetic. Fr. Fichter's book is an invitation to a
more profound study. — Address : Loyola University, New Orleans, U. S. A. (Editor's note).

[2] Le Bras, Gabriel, ' Influence of Environment on Religious Life '. *Lumen Vitae*'
Vol. III (1948), no. 1, p. 6.

In this paper we are speaking of cultural or institutional environment only. The culture of any community is its sum of patterns of social behavior and thought which are relatively integrated and have some permanence. The expected patterns have become institutionalized in many ways according to the basic needs which they fulfill (e. g., religious, familial, economic, etc.). Thus when we here speak of the *institutional environment* we mean the various customary ways in which people think and act socially when they· pursue their principal roles and attempt to maintain their key status in the social structure.

It is extremely important to note that persons think and act largely as a result of the way in which the expectations of their status influence them. This does not mean that they are mere automatons, but it does mean that their " liberty suffers pressure. " Each status is not only an extrinsically evaluated position in the social structure ; it is also a web of reciprocal relations and a vehicle of function. Thus we may say that a person's social thought and behavior conform largely to institutionalized patterns centering around his key status.

The cultural patterns, which combine in various ways for the social position, relations and functions of people within a community, are also an expression of the values or interests current in the community. Thus statuses are both a result of, and a vehicle for, the culture values. In other words, the moral level of a community can be roughly judged from an analysis of the kind of patterns which have become institutionalized into statuses. In a supernatural environment they will differ greatly from those in a secular and materialistic environment.

The social unit from which the facts and conclusions of this paper are derived is St. Mary's parish in a large southern city of the United States. There are 10,946 baptized white persons living within the parochial territory, but only 6,727 of them can in any true sense be called members of the Catholic parish. Within the limits of a monograph it is impossible to reproduce even a significant portion of the results obtained by a corps of research personnel over a period of two years. It is likewise impossible to include complete evidence for each statement made.

We shall select three statuses among the many which are present in the parish and attempt to dileneate both the values they express and the manner in which they influence religious life. In doing this we shall briefly review the content of the institutional environment of St. Mary's parish as it is displayed in (a) the adolescent status, (b) the occupational status of the adult male worker, (c) the class status of the adult female. In each case we shall note how the peculiar patterns of the status affect different phases of the religious life of the parish : (a) the sacramental activities of the adolescent, (b) the parochial organizational participation of the male, (c) the practice of the social virtues by the female.

(a) The *status of adolescence* is seldom thought of in terms of a value-construct, but it is actually a fruitful source for the interpretation of cultural values. Ideally speaking, the adolescent is preparing himself for his future functions in the various social groups in which he will participate. In this sense, adolescence itself has a function and the adolescent is pursuing a role made up of institutionalized patterns.

In the parish under consideration the young people aged fourteen to seventeen years follow certain conventional patterns of behavior. Both those who are still attending a school and those who are employed generally follow similar ways of acting. For example, companionship within each sex category and between the sexes can be plotted and gives rise to both the " gang " pattern and to the " dating " system.

Boys and girls in this age category seldom cooperate successfully as a bisexual group in the religious or recreational program of a parochial organization. They do not play cards, nor dance nor carry on common recreation with each other. The Girls'Sodality wanted to sponsor a dance in the school auditorium, and the several difficulties encountered indicate the values and behavior of adolescents. The girls wanted the lights turned down low as they are at the commercial dance halls. The Pastor would not permit this. Most of the boys who came to the dance came in a group and after standing around the walls for about an hour decided that the girls were " too young for them. " Other boys came with their " steady girl friends " (from outside the parish) with whom they danced the whole evening. Neither member of the pairs danced with any other partner.

This occasion exemplifies several habit-patterns. When a boy and girl " go steady " they seem to lose interest in all group activities in the parish. This is not a companionship preparatory to the more permanent union of marriage. The individuals tend to be alone a great deal of the time, keep late hours, enmesh themselves in the occasions of sin. On the other hand, the girls form friendship cliques among themselves, and the boys also form gangs. The members of each separate clique spend a great deal of time together, frequently idling in the corner drug stores, and when they have enough money they may attend the movie shows.

In the movies the individual boy or girl may slip away from the group and sit with one of the opposite sex during the performance. This happens when parents have forbidden their children to " have dates. "

The point of this description is that the dating system and the gang system have become institutionalized among the adolescents. They are *expected* by their fellow adolescents to act in this way and to have the values that accompany such behavior. If they do not follow these customs they lose status among their peers. This does not mean that no youth defies the patterns. There are some who do, and they are recognized immediately as exceptions. They lose whatever influence they might have had for changing the mores of the whole youth group. It is these exceptions who are usually the faithful members of parochial youth organizations, and their refusal to conform to the institutionalized patterns is a partial explanation for the failure of the organized parochial groups to attract membership.

But the influence of these institutionalized patterns of adolescence goes further. The individual boys and girls become indifferent to the demands of their religious life. A reputation for piety gives little prestige in the secularized culture of adolescence. Recreation which is acceptable must be enjoyed at night, and the late hours on Saturday night interfere with the reception of Holy Communion on Sunday morning. The habitual companionship of male and female adolescents tends to establish a romantic complex which is precocious and frequently immoral. The interests and values of the young people are diverted away from the apparently unexciting virtues and practices of the religious life in the parish.

(b) The *occupational status* of adult male parishioners is a second source for the interpretation of the cultural environment. The primary function of the occupational role is the provision of material essentials for the individual and his family. But this apparently simple goal is also surrounded by various institutionalized patterns of thought and conduct which the individual is expected to follow. After all, he must " make a living " in the milieu in which he lives and cannot entirely segregate himself from it.

In St. Mary's parish, the majority of employed males are wage earners in the lower middle class. Whether they are white collar workers, transport workers, or semi-skilled workers, they are all subjected to relatively similar " demands of the job. " They are regimented according to hours, place and conditions of work ; they exchange their labor for money wages according to their productive capacity ; they are oriented to think of their working hours as much more important than their leisure hours and their occupation as paramount in comparison to their family role.

The expected patterns of thought and behavior in this sensate materialistic culture tend to exaggerate the importance of an increasing material standard of living. This in turn requires that economic emulation take the place of spiritual or intellectual processes. The " success ideal " current in the American culture does not escape Catholic men, and all of the channels of social control (radio, magazine and newspaper advertisement, even the novels and movies) tend to keep this ideal before him. Anything which goes contrary to this idea — as the fullness of Catholicism certainly does — is not acceptable in the general community.

The values contained in the successful fulfillment of the occupational role account for the kind of example which these male adults provide for their children and other members of their family. The importance of commercial success in the bourgeois milieu influences them to send their children to business colleges rather than liberal arts colleges, to convince their children that they must get into a well-paying occupation, cultivate friends who will be helpful in an economic rather than in a spiritual sense. The mixed marriages of the younger generation, the abandonment of religion by both parents and children, the hard cynical attitude toward the humane virtues — all of these are directly connected with the exaggeration of occupational roles.

The men who are pursuing this ideal by following the expected patterns have neither the time nor the interest to participate in parochial organizations. The only exceptions are found in the Ushers' Society, which has, as its main function, the collection of money, and the special committees which may be occasionally formed by the Pastor to meet some financial crisis in the parish.

Here again, as in the youth groups, only the relatively unsuccessful men are likely to be found among the active members of the parochial organizations. The institutionalized ways of thinking and acting are contrary to voluntary, time-consuming, spiritual activities which carry with them little prestige and no remuneration. " What's in it for me ? " is the question which seems to lurk in the minds of most men of the parish.

The Holy Name Society, the Society of St. Vincent de Paul, even the Parents' Club and the Choir, contain very few active male members. The only men's group with a large active membership was a group formed for the support of athletics in the parish, and this was eventually disbanded by the parish mainly because it was more secular than religious. The fate of this exceptional group is simply further evidence of the fact that the institutional environment of a secular culture influences the adult male workers away from the organized religious groups of the parish.

(c) The *class status* of adult women is a third matrix of institutionalized thought and behaviour which affects the religious life of parishioners. In the class structure of the parish we discover a relatively large segment of the female population who follow the norms of behaviour of the secular community. The class status of these married women is of course the same as that of their husbands, and the women under consideration here are the wives of the male workers mentioned above.

Women, for the most part, are the culture bearers of any society. They express the ethos of a community in ways related to, and in support of, the status which their family enjoys. In general, it may be said in this southern urban parish that the aspiration for a higher standard of living is the most forceful motivation for the conduct of women in this group. The women tend to form social cliques which help them to maintain their class status and which may be a springboard for higher status.

There are certain expectations which are unconsciously followed : there must be a Negro maid or cook at least for part-time work in the home. The woman must have sufficient leisure to demonstrate that she is not of the lowest working class. The family should possess a telephone and radio, and if at all possible an automobile and television set. These are all symbols of a rising standard of living and are not necessarily objects which of themselves give utility and enjoyment.

The cultural environment has been so thoroughly impregnated with the value of upward social mobility that many of these women are not even aware of its impact upon their religious beliefs and practices. This influence may be best demonstrated in the manner in which they fail to practice the virtues of charity, neighbourliness and justice in the community. These are certainly important components of the religious life, but they are not so formalized as church attendance by adolescents and organizational participation by adult males.

In the first place, the presence of a lower caste, the Negroes, makes it possible for these women to exploit their own status. An unreasonably low pay is given to maids and cooks. The cleft in the community between whites and Negroes is widened by the refusal to associate with Negro women or to allow their own children to play with Negro children.

Except in extreme instances, as accident or sudden death, these adult females do not lend assistance to neighbors (nor do they expect any in return). If the neighbours have sickness in the family, they should hire a nurse ; if they need someone to watch the children for a few hours, they should hire a baby-sitter. In fact, the concept of a willing neighbour always ready to assist others is interpreted in one of two ways : either the woman is an inquisitive interferer or she is a foolish person unacquainted with the standardized habits of the community.

This seems a clear example of the manner in which the cultural environment interferes with the practice of the Christian virtues even when an individual Catholic woman may deliberately seek to defy that environment. Here again, only the relatively static woman, who is unwilling or unable to follow the demands of her class position, may be found trying to pursue the Christian virtues to their fullness. Some of these do exist in the parish, but they are exceptions. They are " odd. " They do not appreciate how people ought to act. The general result is that the large majority of women in this class conform to the institutionalized class patterns and neglect the social virtues of religion.

In conclusion a warning must be offered to the effect that the complete analysis of institutional influence on the parochial behavior of Catholics is much more complex than it may seem in the above pages. It involves a conflict between the religious institution and a series of secular institutions, between the perennial Christian value system and the volatile modern value system, as well as between the individual parishioner and the various institutional complexes in which he exists.

The institutional environment has a much greater influence than most Catholics seem willing to admit. On the other hand there is a growing awareness of this influence by many careful social observers. Resistance to the institutional environment is possible on the part of holy individuals who recognize its presence and its power. St. Mary's parish, like almost every other parish, contains such relatively *isolated* individuals.

From our own parochial research it seems clear that the religious patterns of thought and behavior must become reformed and reinstitutionalized by the various statuses in the parish. Personal resistance to the secular environment almost demands the price of idiosyncracy. Status resistance means the development of cultural patterns that are shared in each category by at least a few adolescents, a few male workers, a few adult females. Religious reformers cannot escape this sociological fact.

Structure and Methods

The family, school, and parish are basic structures at our disposal for transmitting God's message. The use of these structures and the methodology employed in them should be scientifically studied, carefully evaluated, and prudently put at the service of God's Word.

The Family's Part in Religious Formation

by Pierre RANWEZ, S. J.

I. IMPORTANCE OF THE FAMILY'S PART IN RELIGIOUS FORMATION

The importance of the family can be examined from three different aspects : 1) the natural and supernatural mission incumbent upon it , 2) the amount of influence it exercises and 3) the present particular urgency of family action.

1. *Natural and Supernatural Mission.*

Paternal and maternal duty does not end with the birth of a child and is not restricted to satisfying solely physical needs. Natural morality demands that fathers and mothers take care of the complete education of their children. Knowledge of God and the disposition of a soul ready to obey Him are, however, the basis of humanly correct behaviour. Parents are therefore bidden by natural morality alone to make God known to their children and help them to serve Him. In the supernatural order in which the family as such is introduced by the sacrament of marriage, the educational mission is more precise, goes deeper and passes from the plane of abstract requirement to that of a very concrete duty.

According to Canon Law (1013), the bearing and education of children is the primary end of marriage. Canon 1113 states : " Parents have the very grave obligation of procuring for their children, by all means in their power, religious and moral education as well as physical and civic education and looking after their temporal well-being. " The mission entrusted to parents by marriage is, therefore, not limited to the sole duty of fecundity of the flesh ; the Church asks them to accept a spiritual fecundity. United to each other as

---

[1] Address : 184, rue Washington, Brussels, BELGIUM.

Christ is to the Church, parents are called upon to give sons to the Church and bring them to the Kingdom of grace firstly by presenting them for baptism, then teaching them and having them taught truths of the faith and preparing them to receive the sacraments.

2. *Family Influence Predominates.*

Leaving the field of law for that of facts, most often we see that family influence outweighs external influences.

The family reaches the personality of the child very intimately and often marks it almost indelibly ! The early years are passed almost exclusively in the family sphere and it is at this time that ineradicable attitudes become fixed deep in the psyche. Through the parent-image the child will presage the face of God ; at this time, too, behaviour is fixed progressively, trusting or fearful, open-hearted or withdrawn into himself.

In the family and through the parents' influence, the child awakens to knowledge and liberty. Now from the religious point of view, this awakening is of capital importance : will the essential object of knowledge be God or transient worldly things ? Will liberty be governed by God's Will or by whims and passion ?

The family is normally the most coherent and most stable educative sphere.

3. *Nowadays the Family's Part Is Capital for Faith.*

In many countries, when institutional and traditional safeguards to faith are overthrown or attacked, the necessity of deepening and spreading faith is more explicitly obvious. From this point of view, the family must play an eminent part by awakening personal religious attitudes and convictions.

II. THE FAMILY'S TASK MUST BE TWO-FOLD : PARTICULAR AND IN COLLABORATION WITH OTHERS

The family is a cell of the Church and when parents form their children for religious life, they do so in the name of the Church, delegated by her and directed by her leaders. In the work of religious formation entrusted to the family, however, one part is given almost exclusively while the responsibility for another part is shared with other educative spheres.

The family's own task concerns one particular age (early childhood) and one aspect of religious formation (the first awakening of faith) and a certain interiorisation of Christian Revelation).

In addition to its own task, the family must also collaborate in other spheres and with other educators ; the convergence of efforts will respect the psychological unity of the child and show him the true face of the Church, which is union and charity of all in Christ.

Effective collaboration implies great attention and wide mutual respect on everyone's part : know what belongs to each one and let him exercise his influence ; efforts should next be truly merged, not merely juxtaposed.

Collaboration will first be between priests and parents. In the first place parents will be fitted for their task : pre-nuptial and post-nuptial preparation, given in a friendly manner. Priests should watch that parents and future parents have an opportunity of expressing their difficulties, cares and way of looking at things. It would be hardly suitable to have fathers' meetings on one side and mothers' on the other ; contact should usually be made with couples gathered together.

The priest's influence in guiding the parents and helping them in their task will be exercised by personal and collective contacts throughout the whole growth of the child and family.

The principal opportunity for meetings between priest and parents will perhaps be in the preparation for the sacraments : baptism, confession, confirmation, Eucharist.

For each of these sacraments, three points should be established between the priest and parents :

— the manner of instructing the children and disposing them for proper reception (except of course for baptism ; instruction will come later in this case).

— the ceremony in church ; how to make parents and children participate therein.

— the family celebration or, better still, family paraliturgy which could serve as an immediate preparation or continuation of the liturgical feast.

Such collaboration implies meetings either between the priest and each couple separately, or between the priest and parents grouped together (for instance, the parents of all the first communicants of one year or same confirmation group). These meetings should be the scene of real discussion and a kind of team work. It would indeed not be enough to give orders. It is desirable that parents should be able to make plans with the priest and see how to prepare the children, how to take part in the liturgical celebration and carry out family liturgy, under his direction and with him.

Collaboration between parents and teachers, between parents and those responsible for children's groups, could be similarly considered.

III. MEANS OF FAMILY RELIGIOUS EDUCATION

Parents' educative ressources are very different from those in other spheres. Parents are requested above all to create an atmosphere, bear witness, be associated with their children in the participation of the same Christian life of prayer and faithfulness and, lastly, to use wisely all available pedagogical means (conversations, reading, prayers, paraliturgical celebrations).

1. *Creation of an ' Atmosphere. '*

External surroundings can encourage, or on the contrary discourage, the action of grace. The two dominant notes of the atmosphere created by the parents should be austerity and joy : a certain poverty, silence and discipline, a certain quality of peace and joy.

2. *Bearing Witness.*

What are the predominant principles of this witness ?

Above all, parents should be a sort of first picture of God for their children, a kind of transparency of His presence. Four characteristics should be apparent above all : love, generous kindness, a certain holiness shown by piety, humility and Christian pride.

3. *Family Scope in Participation.*

Parents will follow the path to God with their children ; they will go together towards the Lord.

This participation will, first of all, be in the realm of prayer. It is not enough for parents to make their children pray, suggesting or imposing children's prayers ; they should often be united together in the same prayer. Apart from that, parents will be helped to come nearer to God by realizing more and more that their own progress influences the spiritual journey of their children.

4. *Principal Means Available.*

The family is neither a school nor a place of worship ; it is a sphere of life, where we work, rest, eat, amuse ourselves, develop physically and spiritually, pray together. Religious formation should in some way be linked to these activities ; the importance of conversations, reading, prayer and eventually paraliturgy, should be particularly noted.

IV. MAIN AIMS OF THE FAMILY IN RELIGIOUS FORMATION

In the three preceding parts we first underlined the importance of the role of the family; then we sought its originality in the unity of the Church ; lastly we considered the ways of exercising it and the means available to the family in its task. In the last part we would like to define the principal aims the family must pursue in the work of religious education.

In this, five principal aims are to be distinguished : the awakening of faith and sense of God, a certain Christian sensitiveness, a certain Christian culture, a certain firmness in Christian practices, the choice of life in accordance with the voice of God.

1. *First Aim: Awakening of Faith and Sense of God.*

Faith lives in the child from the moment of baptism, but has to be expressed in a conscious act of faith. When speaking of God, no allusion should be made to speculative knowledge but to knowledge which is lived rather than expressed in words, a knowledge associated with love. The sense of God has sweet savour, is upheld by love and animated by hope. It is an instinctive and obscure knowledge by which God is felt, not at all like a scientific object but as a living Person in His ineffable mystery. The sense of God is awakened and expressed in prayer ; it is identified with faith inasmuch as the latter merges obscurely but lovingly in consciousness.

The importance of awakening the sense of God cannot be stressed too much. Systematic and abstract teaching, which will come later and is indispensable to the normal development of a well-balanced Christian personality, implies the sense of God as the necessary foundation. But we must admit that systematic and speculative teaching is often given to children who have no such foundation. The result is deep misunderstanding : children manage to get through their catechism lessons, but in fact they do not know what it is all about. The apparent development of religious life in such conditions is inconsistent.

We said that normally it is the parents who awaken the sense of God in their children. This implies stages linked and complementary to each other, briefly as follows :

Firstly, a certain *ambit* or atmosphere should be created around the child. The message about God can only come in gentle, peaceful surroundings ; it will be prepared in an atmosphere of joy and by the presence of uplifting and beautiful realities (take the child into a lovely garden, open the window on the blue sky or a tree in flower) beyond which the child will be able to divine the Creator.

Witness will be developed in such surroundings. Parents will be humble images of God for their children. Through them the child will, in a way, be able to experience love, Providence and the holiness of God. The joy of knowing he is loved by his parents will be a first invitation to welcome a higher love ; the generosity with which parents surround their children will be a representation of the magnanimity of God and their humble and respectful attitude before a mysterious Presence beyond them will direct the soul of the child to the mystery of the Living God.

The message about God will, however, only be received by souls already prepared. *Dispositions of the soul* must be aroused in the child, rendering him capable of welcoming the Divine Guest and recognizing His Presence. Foremost in these dispositions will be a certain self-control by which the child will outstrip his whims and fancies (a selfish and capricious child would never be able to unfold himself to the gift of God). The second disposition will be a certain expansiveness towards others and a certain sense of generosity. In a baby this generosity is still very elementary ; it will be developed by encouraging gestures towards others (smiling and giving things), gently discouraging aggressive or exaggeratedly possessive gestures (grasping a flower, hurting an animal). The third disposition will be the sense of admiration ; to be interested in something not only to eat it or possess it but admire it unselfishly.

When the child is thus disposed, the parents can pass to the next stage : *demonstrate God by expressing Him.* Two paths or means are available : admiration and love.

God is greater and more beauteous than the beautiful and great things the child can admire : a nocturnal sky, the sea, great stretches of mountains or plains.

God knows us and loves us more than a father or mother can ; it is in the love of God that the father and mother love their small child and the latter can call Him " My Father " " Our Father ! "

Prayer and the gift of self must follow immediately upon knowledge. Parents will then unite with their children in a participation of the same praise, the same thanksgiving and same adoration of the Creator.

2. Second Aim: a Christian Sensitiveness.

In the same way that the sense of God must be acquired before passing on to speculative knowledge about Him, so is it desirable that the child be able to establish himself progressively in a certain inner balance and realize the harmony of his sensitive and intellectual faculties with religious necessities. It is also desirable for him to experience what might be called Christian reflexes, react rapidly, easily and flexibly in the sense of Christian requirements. In short, in a way rediscover beyond Original Sin something of the harmony and balance of the earthly paradise.

If the father and mother of mankind have transmitted a certain lack of balance to us, Christian parents can aspire to give something of the lost heritage back to their children.

This refound balance will not only make life brighter and more joyful, but also more open to truth and the call of God.

Parents are really asked, by all their behaviour and the Christian ' training ' they give their children, to dispose them to receive, in a heart well prepared and helped by a well-balanced sensitivity, the gifts of the Holy Spirit. The Spirit of God will be able to act in a ready and peaceful soul ; the house is ready for the coming of the Divine Guest. The soul will heed and obey His Voice.

3. Third Aim: a Christian Culture.

A culture is characterized by the choice of certain values and by an original manner of understanding such values, expressing them according to a popular wisdom or philosophy, in the framework of a language and original artistic forms (poetry, music, singing, dancing, etc.). A culture usually characterizes a human community, a nation, a district ; but each town, village, quarter, group of families, or better still each family can, in varying degrees, give an original and personal mark to culture.

Some cultures are impervious to religious values ; for instance, a culture directed entirely towards material and technical success, rendering them divine as the highest possible value ; culture directed to the deification of the race ; culture directed to pure aestheticism, the pleasure of knowing for the sake of knowing. Other cultures are open to religious values. This is not the place to note their characteristics. In the perspective of Christian culture, one family or group of families, will put more store on one value than another : joy, audacity, faithfulness... another family will give a more important place to art, technical realizations or the splendours of nature ; that will depend on the parents' profession, temperament and that of their children, their studies, etc. They will turn to singing, reading, conversations, embellishment of the home, excursions, travel . In this way a mentality will be created, a turn of mind, a way of interpreting history and acquiring a Christian appreciation of events, men and things, a way of establishing each reality in its place and discovering more consciously from day to day that the earthly universe is the sign, preparation and anticipation of the Eternal Kingdom; that, unless it is deception and imposture, glory in this world can only be the reflection of God's glory.

4. *Fourth Aim: a Firmness in Christian Practice.*

If Christian life is constant invention under the impulsion of the Holy Spirit Who guides each of the faithful, and according to the directives of the Church officially interpreting God's Will, this initiative and liberty must develop in a sound, pliable framework, strong enough to help the Christian to keep to the right path through difficulties and temptations, and sufficiently pliable to allow him to adapt himself to varying and sometimes unpredictable circumstances. The family will therefore be asked to implant strong traditions and habits, first of all in the domain of human and secular behaviour which should be, as it were, governed by the *spirit of duty* and not at all by whim.

Next, the *life of prayer*: the rhythm and style of the life of prayer is doubtless personal to each one, but we know the importance of a framework and habits capable of maintaining willingness in times of weariness and aridity. Once again, it is in the framework of the family and in very early childhood that a certain discipline of prayer will be accepted and developed : morning and evening prayers, prayers before and after meals, etc.

The third sphere is that of *Christian use of the sacraments* : regular attendance at Sunday Mass or perhaps daily Holy Communion, regular confession, traditions about baptism, confirmation, first communion, marriage and — let it be insisted upon — traditions only too rare about Extreme Unction proposed in good time to the sick and received, not at all as a harbinger of great sorrow, but as announcing the Lord and His joy.

5. *Fifth Aim: Sense of Vocation and Choice of Life.*

We underlined how one of the principal tasks of parents is to awaken their children to liberty. We said the important thing was to help them to make their first free act a choice by which they replied affirmatively to God. Day after day this first choice will have

282

to be ratified, thoroughly examined and adapted to new situations; welcome God in joy and sorrow, hear and reply to His multiple calls.

But in the same way that this first free act is important, another free act, engaging the whole life in a given direction, is also primordial. This choice of life, or rather this reply to the Divine Call, should be prepared at length and will be like the first test of another act of liberty which we accomplish at the hour of our death and which will establish our eternity for ever.

One of the signs of success or failure of an education is the choice made by a young man or girl at about 16 or 17 years of age.

The parents and the whole family will progressively be able to arouse the conviction in a young man or girl that life is a service and gift for the good of our neighbour and the glory of God.

Adolescents must find an atmosphere in the family which will help them to become progressively aware of the personal appeal addressed to each one. Without any indiscreet pressure being applied they should feel they are understood, helped and supported in their waverings, uncertainties, deliberations and decisions which are, at the same time, more realistic and generous.

The choice will scarcely be affected by advice but by a certain attitude in the family community towards life and, above all, by the example of the parents : the way the father does his work, how the mother approaches her tasks, trials and joys in life.

CONCLUSION

What we have said about the role of the family might perhaps seem to suggest that this role is indirect and at a tangent. The family usually has no part at all in the collation of the sacraments, nor perhaps the largest part in religious instruction, above all in what is called the teaching of catechism ; it is, however, this teaching of the catechism which is often considered as the main point and vital centre of religious formation.

Beyond this first impression we must recognize that in a less visible way — perhaps because it is deeper — the family joins the child again in an intimacy which others rarely achieve and that, on the other hand, the message it imparts is at the same time the most fundamental and the most complete, the most perfect in its fine shades.

Perhaps we ought to say that what distinguishes family formation from that given in other spheres of life and by other educators is not so much the fact that the family gives another part of the teaching, is isolated in another sector of education, but that it is a different plane : the family has the task of adapting the Christian message to each one, helping each child to assimilate personally the whole of Christian teaching and requirements and insert Christian values in all the manifestations of life and activity. In the family we learn to interpret the Gospel faithfully and penetrate the multitude of secular actions with Christian spirit.

In this role of the family perhaps insistence should be on the influence towards discovering the Christian aspect of love and liberty.

If the family has such an important task to accomplish, it must not fail. But alone the family cannot succeed ; help is needed; parents must be enlightened, supported and a whole effort of collaboration considered.

Help is needed from priests and teachers, together with mutual help between families collected together in small groups.

Here we must insist on the kind of help to be offered.

Obviously, priests, teachers and those running various organizations cannot just ask the family to help them in their own task and then believe they have helped the family to obtain the glory of God.

It would similarly not be enough to wish to help by imposing a behaviour incompatible with its own temperament and unsuited to the family's concrete requirements. The help offered will above all and most often be a collaboration. Perhaps one of the most interesting forms of this collaboration will consist in encouraging families to group together and, stimulated and guided by the priest, form prayer, research and action groups.

A great effort must be made so that priests, parents and religious meet each other, each respecting his own vocation and that of others, each bringing to the others that complementary part without which the efforts of all will be partly unfruitful. Such trusting and generous collaboration will help not only those who receive its support, but will contribute to give each one a greater esteem of his own vocation and feel how the family can do nothing without the help of the priesthood and celibacy consecrated in religious life.

The Catholic Home,
Source of Life and Faith

by Jean GUITTON

Things we have seen done are educational. As we get older we are more and more struck by the strength of early training. It would seem that the period we call youth and even maturity (when a man has a social function, working for his town and fellowmen) were a kind of parenthesis, after which the interrupted flow of early life is resumed : reminiscences of childhood come back in a light, early habits revive, and with them family traditions and new inherited views.

Michelet, who had made a study of great men of history, used to say that at fifty individual maladies give place to hereditary ones ; thus Louis XIV suffered from stone and Napoleon died of kidney trouble like his father. But this is not only true of illness. Good which is inherited becomes visible when life's foliage has been blown away by the first November winds.

I want to apply this truth to the Christian education one receives at home. It will not be profitless in these days of general scepticism when man is rebelling and uprooting himself and likes to call himself ' no one's son ' with neither father nor mother nor ancestry — like Melchisedech.

To many secularized minds it is a sign of inferiority to have been brought up in childhood in an atmosphere of faith. Or at least, the mark of an unshackled mind is the rejection of these early lessons as soon as one grows up. The sort of story that always finds favour in France is the one after the style of Renan in his *Souvenirs :* belief can be forgiven if it has cast a veil of poetry over our earliest

---

[1] M. Jean GUITTON has already contributed articles to *Lumen Vitae* : II (1947) p. 628 ss. ; IV (1949) p. 21 ss. and p. 630 ss. ; V (1950) p. 146 ss. — Address : 1, rue de Fleurus, Paris 6e, FRANCE (Editor's note)

years, if it remains in the adult mind with the vague gentle persistence of a memory. In short, faith is looked upon as a good thing, fruitful and honourable, when it is a homely, artificial atmosphere of childhood days. It will be conceded to be useful in the training of the young. One may admit that a person who has never had a background of faith will show a certain hardness and angularity which is a handicap to intercourse with others or to communing with Nature. That is why your Hegelian will say that it is good to begin with faith, which is truth for infants, in the same way as, in order to become a human being at all, it is necessary to have been born of a mother and surrounded by her warmth and care. Without the mother's tender influence, the tissues will harden too soon ; a sort of child-man will evolve, a monster with no real childhood ; and this is what some geniuses lack, such as Pascal, Leibniz, Kierkegaard, all great minds arising suddenly and without preparation. [1]

But the human being cannot remain a child, and the problem is how to disencumber oneself of these too tender cares, how to cast off this provisional ignorance, without too great a disturbance or crisis, and simply by the process of growing up. Childhood should come to an end for us with an initiation into Existence, respecting the early mystery but abolishing it. This is what the modern unbeliever thinks, knowing that each belief has its *moment* of truth, but it must be annihilated or rather merged into a higher concept. Childhood's faith is, as Léon Brunsvicg says, an ' age of intelligence ' which it is useful to have passed through but which must be left behind at the age of reason. The unbeliever is always asking himself how the mind can become so easily superstitious, how Pascal could jot down notes on bits of paper instead of persevering with his calculations on infinity (Valéry) ; how Pascal in his last days could give a free and intellectual assent to the early certainties of his youth, confirming with all his genius the unjustified conduct of childhood days.

First of all it must be remarked that the kind of certitude which the child possesses is not the same as that of the instructed adult. It is true there must be a transformation and the difficulty of this is constantly increasing in a world where the adult's environment is multiform and sceptical, very different from the calm, sheltered and conventional environment of the child. Yet is the faith of the child or uninstructed irrational and explicable only by the constraints, influences and suggestions of adults ?

---

[1] See my book *Pascal et Leibniz*, Paris, Aubier, 1951, p. 14.

If I look back upon my own experience, if, like Newman, I try to define what my first religious impressions were, I find my earliest notions of Existence. The sense of Being and of the divine awoke together in my soul. I do not know what can be for a child brought up without any belief the discovery of the *Dasein*, the being-here-and-there, as philosophers today call it. It seems to me impossible that the child's *Dasein* could be of the Heidegger sort, that is to say, a *Dasein* ' for death. ' The child is ignorant of death. To know himself here-and-there and to believe in God is one and the same act for him, as it was for Descartes. My first impression of Being was precocious ; I can remember it now as a kind of intoxication, but it sent me to my prayers. I mean by ' impression of Being ' that sense of apartness in the midst of things, even alien to those who love you, having one's private citadel, existing for oneself alone, a solid and indestructible accident. In the family religious setting, this consciousness does not detach itself from the aids of religion and its familiar, transcendent images. Religion does not creep in by means of any *will to believe* : it is absorbed in the home, of which it is the development. It is sucked in with one's mother's milk and is therefore different in character from that of adult years. Even the finest Christian feels the difference between these two worlds : the one visible, the other impalpable, inexplorable, which surrounds and penetrates the visible, but is itself invisible ; which is always object of will, of action, desire, but never of vision. And if faith seeks for signs of the Supreme in the world, it will only discover traces in the sand. It is not the same in childhood. Religion is mixed up with the essential feelings which will form the personality. It is because they know and feel these bonds that mothers make their children take part in the actions of faith at the same time as they learn life's first lessons, so that faith and life shall spring from the same source. The sensation of being, of being loved and of believing thus become one and the same.

Thus later on, when consciousness exercises itself on the problem of Good and Evil, it refers them to a presence which one can please or grieve, to a Mother Being who smiles or weeps at your behaviour, and duty is never looked upon as an obedience to rules as set forth in manuals.

Moreover, as the monuments and images of religion are associated with customary places, religion is linked with topography ; it is present in city churches and still more perhaps in country chapels. The crucifixes and statues of Our Lady contribute to this local presence. This sentiment of quasi-local presence existed in paganism ;

287

its grandeur lies there, insofar as it places the ' numinous ' in Nature, which becomes sacramental. I am here speaking of true paganism, the paganism of Vergil, from which religion rose high, not the false naturalism of the moderns to which religion has descended. As the pagan child brought up in the religion of the Lares and Penates found the gods everywhere and saw them incorporated in his daily life — so the Christian child in the home finds his faith not merely a rite or acquired dogma, but a religion in the Latin sense of the word. That is why those who have been piously brought up, even when they have lost a definite faith, will keep up some ' religion ' as a mystery, a relation to an unknown Eternal Being. [1]

When I was a child, separation introduced by human life and science did not exist for me ; the distinction between morality and religion had no meaning ; everything was more simple and doubtless more like what went on in undeveloped communities (though these are scarcely known to us, because the sociologists like to debase origins). The beginnings of things are always most obscure and confused ; they are the assembly point of the highest and the lowest, but the wisdom of the Church has purified what were impure elements in the natural rites of the home. If there be any traces of superstition among a Christian people, it is purified by grace and is nothing more than an instrument (as when some locality is made holy by pilgrimages) ; likewise, the Catholic child escapes an imprisoned mentality. Father Christmas lives on but as the symbol of a lasting truth, the truth of a bountiful God, friend of simple folk, and more than ever generous on these cold dark days. It is the same with family rites. Father, mother, little brother, the table, bread, bed, the front door, the visitor to the house, the spelling-book — the sign of the cross, hands joined, gaze heavenwards — hymns, priest, Mass, host on the tongue : these things are all one world, not two distinct ones. The distinction between heaven and earth does not exist, still less that between immanence and transcendence. It is poetry and truth, as Goethe would say, who would not dissociate the two. We will need many tears and much genius to recapture it in our old age.

---

[1] Perhaps the absence of feeling for the sacred which is so marked in contemporary thinkers comes from this lack of home training. Formerly, and even in the 19th century, those who ' freed ' themselves from faith preserved this sentiment of sacredness with regard to nature and the history of man. They were neo-pagans. Nowadays the atheist has no roots and that is why he is a rebel. Revolt, which the pagan did not know, is the effect of this disappearance of sacredness.

The Parish in the Teaching of Catechism?

by Father Domenico GRASSO, S. J.

The problem under consideration in the present article is the community aspect of Catechesis. Does this imply creating a consciousness of belonging to the Church at large, or to the Church through membership of a Parish? If this be the case, catechists and teachers of Religion should strive to bring home to their children not only an awareness of their membership of the Church, the Mystical Body of Christ but also that of forming part of a well-defined community, the parish community of the place in which they live. Would not the very teaching of Religion demand this, aiming as it does at the formation of the « total Christian » who realizes that it is only through membership of a parish that he can attain to the full community life of the Church?

The point here is not one of mere facts. It is taken for granted that the faithful are « parish-minded. » No one will deny that. We are stating a question of principle. Does Catechesis demand that we make the Christian realize the vital part he is called upon to play as member of the parish community, complementary though it be to his duty to the Church at large? The problem is very real because the life of the Church cannot be lived in a single

1. Reverend Domenico GRASSO was born at Roccabascerana, Italy. Having completed his Secondary studies, he entered the Society of Jesus in 1934, and was ordained priest in 1946. In 1944 he took his Doctorate in Classics, and became Doctor of Theology in 1950. He has published essays on Modernism, among others Il Cristianesimo di Ernesto Buonaiuti (Brescia, Morcelliana, 1953), La Conversione e l'apostasia di Giorgio Tyrell, (Rome, 1957), a book of Apologetics for the laity: Gesù Cristo et la sua opera (Rome, A.V.E., 2nd ed. 1958), and numerous articles on the problem of religious conversion; five of these have been translated into Spanish under the title: Genesis y psicologia de la conversión (Barcelone, Eler, 1956). He has also collaborated in the Enciclopedia cattolica and the Enciclopedia filosofica. At present he teaches Pastoral Theology at the Gregorian University. — Address: Piazza della Pilotta, 4, Roma, ITALY (Editor's Note).

community. It has to be split up into local communities, not only because of the hierarchical constitution of the Church, but also by the very nature of its community life, created and developed as it is by preaching the Word of God, administering the Sacraments, and particularly by the celebration of the Holy Eucharist.

I. THE THEOLOGY OF THE PARISH

The answer to our question is not to be considered apart from our conception of the nature of a parish.

Since 1925, the parochial institution, especially in Germany, has given theologians food for reflection, with a view to determine the nature and function of the Christian life. Conclusions are now sufficiently clear.

According to some theologians — mainly liturgists — the parish is a Church in miniature, « an image of the Universal Church, » [1] « a spiritual reality, » [2] an auto-realization and a self-realization of the Church, a daughter-Church of the Mother-Church, an « Ecclesiola, » a tangible manifestation, to us and in us, of the plenitude of Christ. [3] Consequently, it is a « mystery, » because it is the place where the mystery of the Church is made visible to the faithful in a concrete and intelligible way. These expressions make of the parish « God's Holy Family, » an « organic cell of the Mystical Body of Christ, containing the life of the whole Christ and the whole Church. » [4] This opinion rests on the function attributed to the parish-priest in Canon Law, [5] in particular to his duty of celebrating Mass for the people. It is in the Eucharistic Sacrifice that the parish priest represents, with his community of the faithful, one sole offering in Christ.

This essentially spiritual conception of the parish makes of it a « sui generis » organism, essentially supernatural, the nature of which is the object of theological study and also, in a subsidiary way, of Canon Law, and religious Sociology.

On the other hand, another theory, held chiefly by Canonists, sees in the parish, an institution created by the Church solely for the spiritual necessities of the faithful. It maintains a distinct attitude of reserve on the definition of « Ecclesiola in Ecclesia, » because

1. A. WINTERSIG, in *The House of God*, Nr 8, p. 16.
2. J. PINSK, in *Liturgical and Parochial Questions*, 18 (1933), p. 202.
3. M. SCHURR, in *Benediktinische Monatschrift*, 19 (1937), pp. 89-90.
4. M. SCHURR, *op. cit.*, p. 90.
5. C.J.C., can. 462.

this definition obscures the distinction between the parish — which is an ecclesiastical institution — and the diocese — which is a divine institution. Moreover, the parish is not a juridical community, but simply a community in the wide sense of the word, by virtue of the relationship created spontaneously among people living in the same area and sharing in the same life. [1] These opinions tend respectively to give greater or lesser importance to the parish in the life of the Christian. To those who see in the parish a spiritual organism, where the life of the Church is realized and made visible, it is the normal place for the Christian to live his spiritual life. From the very fact that he resides in a certain parish, the Christian belongs to it and is under the authority of the parish priest, who, alone, is responsible for his parishioner's spiritual life. In this case, the parish monopolizes the life of the Christian living within its boundaries. The latter cannot possibly disinterest himself from it or break away from it by giving his name to other institutions. Alternatively, those who uphold the second opinion see in the parish nothing more than an institution created by the Church for the care of souls. Though the Christian can be invited to share in its life, he must in no way be forced to do so, say the upholders of this opinion. Only one thing matters, the spiritual advancement of the faithful, which can be brought about wherever the Church exists, that is to say, wherever the Word of God is preached, wherever the life of grace is dispensed by the Sacraments and above all by the Mass, whether in the parish or elsewhere.

Neither of these two opinions goes so far in its conclusions as to assert or deny explicitly the importance of the place to be attributed to the parish in the Teaching of Religion. Strictly speaking, the first opinion upholds this view. If the Christian cannot live his supernatural life outside the limits of his parish, if his parish priest alone is responsible for him before God, then Catechesis must aim at forming a faithful who is « parish-minded. » According to the second opinion, this outlook does not exist. For the Christian, to be « parish-minded » or « Church-minded » is one and the same thing.

---

1. This idea can be found in the article by O. Neil v. Breuning, *Pfarrgemeinde, Pfarrfamilie, Pfarrprinzip,* in *Trier. Theol. Zeitschrift*, 56 (1947), 4, spec. p. 258.

II. PARISH AND DIOCESE

To judge between the two opinions above mentioned, it is first of all necessary to admit that there is some truth in both. It is impossible to consider the parish as a purely administrative organism. If it is « pars dioceseos » (a part of the diocese) according to the definition of Canon Law, it shares necessarily in the properties of the diocese and of the Universal Church. According to St. Paul, the Church is the Mystical Body of Christ, an idea which can be applied equally to local churches, diocesan churches or to the Cathedral Church. [1]

Therefore, if the parish is part of the diocese, i.e. of the « Cathedral » church, it necessarily has a share in the mystical and supernatural qualities of the latter. The part participates in the nature of the whole. On the other hand, it is in the parish that the Church is made tangible, there that the Christian comes into contact with her. It is in the parish that the mystery of Salvation is proclaimed, and that the Christian pays his public debt of homage to God. The aim of the Church, which is to communicate to the faithful the life of grace, is normally realized through the ministry of her priests, above all by her parish priests. Again, it is through the parish that the Christian is integrated by Baptism into the Mystical Body of Christ.

But when all this has been said, it must be acknowledged that the parish shares to a certain extent in the nature of a community. If, according to St. Paul, all those who drink the Lord's cup are made one body, [2] it follows that the faithful centred around the Eucharist together with their pastor form, as it were, a unity and a community. In the same way, the distribution of grace through preaching and dispensing of the Sacraments by the parish-priest, cannot fail to establish between him and his parishioners, links of spiritual relationship, recognized by Canon law itself. [3]

Although these arguments make it possible to go beyond a purely juridical conception of a parish, they are not sufficiently conclusive to justify either a true theology of the parish or the conclusions drawn from it, because the mystical and supernatural properties come to the parish from its relationship with the diocese and the Universal Church. The juridical thesis is right in maintaining that the parish as such is the responsibility, not of theology, but of

---

1. *I Cor.*, X, 17.
2. *1 Cor.*, X, 17; *Rom.*, XII, 5.
3. Can. 768 and 1079.

Canon Law, because the parish as such was not created by Christ, but by ecclesiastical legislation. Historically speaking, the parish institution derives from the needs of the pastoral ministry, when the increase of the episcopal community (the only one required in the hierarchical constitution of the Church and the only one to exist for three centuries) obliged bishops at the head of vast dioceses to found, outside the boundaries of the Episcopal See, various centres of worship where the faithful could participate in the celebration of the Sacred Mysteries. (In Rome, those places were called « tituli »). As Christianity developed in the countryside, the bishops were obliged to appoint resident priests to provide for the spiritual necessities of the faithful in the neighbouring villages. Thus was born the « Parish » as we know it today. The Church could have created new dioceses, instead of parishes, and kept the community constantly gathered round the bishop.

Once they had been set up, the parishes did not become closed units. Their real shepherds were always the bishops, with the parish priests as their collaborators (cooperatores ordinis nostri). In other words, the parish was and remains to this day, even after the decree of the Council of Trent sanctioning their existence, part of the Diocese, just as suburbs are parts of a town. They were, therefore, open and dependent communities.

If such are the conditions, the community outlook in the Teaching of Religion supposes necessarily the outlook of the Church at large and, against this background, a certain « parish awareness. » Baptism incorporates the Christian into the Church, not into the parish. The former of ecclesiastical origin and the latter of divine origin are institutions created respectively by the Church and by Christ, for the faithful, true members of the Mystical Body. Their importance in the Christian life is relative. They are parts, and as such dependent on the whole. Canon Law therefore, while asserting that each one of the faithful has his parish priest to whom is entrusted the care of all those living within the limits of his parish, does not oblige them to turn to him in their needs. It leaves them free to provide for their own spiritual welfare as they think fit. This proves that in the mind of the Church such institutions exist for the benefit of the faithful.

It must be admitted that especially today, when ever wider perspectives are offered to the Christian, insistence on the importance of the parish might be fatal to the ministry of souls.

III. OTHER PRINCIPLES

The parish, like the diocese, is a tangible illustration of the principle of the localization of the Church, itself a visible society by nature, requiring a place where the faithful can assemble to listen to the Word of God, receive the Sacraments and, above all, participate in the celebration of the Mass, in which the Church reveals itself to the full, as continuation of the Incarnation. But if the proclamation of the Word, the administration of the Sacraments and the celebration of Mass require a definite place , it cannot be affirmed that this place must necessarily be the parish church, to the exclusion of any other. The parish, indeed, has priority, founded as it is on the « principe territorial, » the most normal of all principles which bring people together in communities. By creating the parish, the Church has consecrated, at least in practice, this fundamental notion of social life.

However, the « principe territorial » is not the only one : men come together for many other reasons, as for example, the requirements of their profession or their trades. [1]

Now, the Church, ever seeking to implant herself in all human structures, cannot possibly ignore institutions holding out such prospects for the salvation of souls. In other words, in the same way as the Church by creating the parish has sanctified the « principe territorial, » she could likewise sanctify other principles of association among men by using them for the ministry of souls.

In connection with this, mention has been made of the creation of so called « category » parishes, gathering together for example, workers or clerks. The authorities are not in favour of these projects, except as temporary measure for national parishes in emigration areas. But the opposition does not entail a question of principle. The parish according to categories might indeed appear to favour class distinction, a thing which the Church seeks to avoid. However, this does not prevent these associations being used for pastoral work beyond the limits of the parish, in which case they would become extra-parochial.

Here too, the Community outlook in the Teaching of Religion is none other than the outlook of the Church at large. The « principe territorial, » in spite of its pre-eminence, is not the only one. If the evolution of social structures were to impose on the Church

---

1. On this subject there is an interesting article by Karl RAHNER : *Friedliche Erwaegungen über das Pfarrprinzip, in Schrifte zur Theologie*, II. Einsiedln, 1955, 299-339.

new institutions based on other principles, no theoretical reason could prevent it. The Church has herself founded and encouraged extra-parochial and extra-diocesan associations, such as Third Orders, Marial Sodalities, Catholic Action Movements, as they exist today in certain countries.

IV. THE PROBLEM OF DECHRISTIANIZATION

It is of no mean importance to remind people of the difficulties a ministry limited exclusively to the parish would have to face.

Everyone knows the painful situation made public in many countries by inquiries connected with religious sociology. We are referring to the phenomenon of dechristianization. The question does not only concern the mass of lapsed catholics, who, however, still retain faith in the depths of their consciences, but also the masses returning to a pagan outlook. The re-christianization of those masses is the most urgent duty of the Church in our traditionally catholic countries.

To come then to the point : Is the parish, created to uphold the faith, a suitable institution for the re-conquest of these so-called dechristianized masses ? There has been much talk about the missionary parish and the necessity of transforming all the pastoral ministry into a missionary campaign. No doubt this necessity exists. But the real problem is : does the parish dispose of adequate means for this tremendously difficult work ? We have the answer to this question from those who have experienced and faced up to the difficulties in question. Abbé Michonneau, whose competence in parochial questions is universally acknowledged, affirms in his excellent book on « The Parish, Missionary Community » : « The mass of real pagans is not touched by the parish, and the latter, even if it were exclusively consecrated to the work of their conversion, cannot do more than touch the fringe of the problem. » [1] Hence the necessity of extra-parochial movements devoted to work among those masses. Abbé Daniel [2] and yet others [3] are all of the same opinion. It is clear then how dangerous it would be to lay too much stress on the idea of the parish as indispensable.

Inquiries on religious sociology have revealed not only the fact of dechristianization, but also that of a progressive deepening of

---

1. *La Paroisse, Communauté missionnaire*, p. 371.
2. *Paroisses d'hier, Paroisses de demain*, Paris, 1957, pp. 248-49.
3. G. B. Guzzetti, in *La Scuola cattolica*, 1953, spec. pp. 435 ff.

different mentalities according to differing social circles. The workers' mentality differs from that of persons following liberal professions or living in rural areas. Therefore, if specialized parishes are out of question, it is the clergy at work in the parish who must be specialized. But how many parishes could afford — with the increasing problems arising from the crisis in vocations — to have a specialized clergy for the various sectors of their apostolate ? The only solution is in the creation of extra-parochial movements with specialists for the various social milieux.

Let us conclude then by saying that though the parish — founded as we said on the most normal of principles does possess a certain priority, there is no place for a rigorous « parish awareness » in Catechesis. All community-mindedness finds its fulfilment in the wider notion of membership of the Universal Church. There, the secular clergy and Religious both men and women, together with the laity, will all find their meeting place. Every association having its rightful place in the Church will bring the faithful to that Universality which is the characteristic of the Church, Mystical Body of Christ, sole Mediator between God and men. And all the time, these associations will prepare and uphold the part the Christian is called upon to play in the dioceses, parishes, and various ecclesiastical organizations.

This being said, we recognize that, in the parish, Catechesis will keep a special character and will not have in view merely the family, the school, or other apostolic movements, but will be complementary to them. But this will be the subject of another article.

The Catechetical Apostolate
of Lay Teachers

by John Hofinger, S. J.

In the United States in particular, more than in any other country of the world, through the Confraternity of Christian Doctrine, unsalaried lay teachers take a special and most important part in the Church's teaching work.

The CCD apostolate in the United States takes many forms in general, to collaborate with the hierarchy in promoting religious formation, both doctrinal and spiritual, which begins in early infancy and continues all through life. The Parent-Educator Program shows parents how fully to exercise the most important and indispensible general form of the lay catechetical apostolate, the religious teaching and formation of their own children. Within the framework of the diocesan catechetical office, CCD members cooperate in courses for the religious formation of children and of young people, and in activities for the religious education of adults (programs during the school year, Vacation Schools, Discussion Clubs). The CCD also implements Lay Training Courses on all levels for study of the content of the Christian message, of catechetic methods, and of psychology and sociology in relation to the catechetical apostolate. And, finally, the CCD Apostolate of Good Will strives to develop in all Catholics increased love and understanding of their non-Catholic neighbors, to promote truly tactful and enlightened zeal for their conversion.

The Confraternity of Christian Doctrine is primarily a parish society. But it is the special work of the Diocesan Office of the CCD

---

[1] See the biographical note in LUMEN VITAE, X (1955), p. 243. — Address: Institute for Mission Apologetics, P. O. Box 1815, Manila, Philippines (Editor's note).

to train, supervise and guide catechists. This Office draws up the programs for the training of teachers, lays down the conditions for the reception of applicants and the training qualifications for their official appointment as CCD teachers. This Office also has the right and the responsibility to supervise the training of teachers and their actual teaching. The syllabus and textbooks, the method and content of all Confraternity classes in the diocese are to be determined by this Office. The Diocesan director again is to provide all the help needed by teachers in the course of their work and to offer them opportunities for further spiritual and professional guidance. The function of the National Center of the CCD is of an advisory nature, but it has a vital role in the whole organization. Its chief functions are mainly 1) to provide the best available training for CCD Leaders, 2) to inform the Diocesan Offices of the progress of the various forms of the CCD apostolate in the United States and in other countries, 3) to prepare and make available teacher-training manuals and all the other material needed in the various forms of the CCD apostolate.

Such a summary description of the work and the organization of the CCD cannot give any idea of the abundance of catechetical material on various levels published under its auspices, of its detailed program for the selection, training and authorization of lay teachers, or of the number of children, young people and adults actually reached. Suffice it to say in particular that, without the cooperation of CCD lay teachers, the problem of giving an adequate religious formation to the millions of Catholic children attending public schools would be completely unsolvable, as would that of the continuing religious formation of minimally instructed adult Catholics.

The CCD itself is well aware of the many and difficult problems attending all the phases of its many-sided apostolate and is continually studying them and finding new and improved solutions. But it might be useful to point out the special value of the lay catechist, his special needs and difficulties, and also some special aspects of the training and the help that he needs. By so doing, we may, perhaps, suggest to our priest and religious readers some further means of interesting zealous members of the laity in this official lay catechetical apostolate, and of inspiring and assisting those already engaged in it.

I. THE SPECIAL VALUE OF THE CATECHETICAL APOSTOLATE OF THE LAITY

In their daily life in the world, lay catechists personally experience the irreplaceable value of religion for such a life. From their own experience, they know how religion could and should penetrate, transform and ennoble the ' ordinary ' life of people in the world. Thus Our Lord and His Church expect from laymen authorized to proclaim His message a special *vital quality* in their religious teaching, giving their students a formation that is close to life and fully directed to living reality.

Again, the religious formation given by a lay teacher should have a special quality of *naturalness*. It should, that is, really be adapted to the concrete conditions, needs and potentialities of the students, leading them toward Christian living informed by a spirit quite different from the secular spirit of our times and also quite different from that of any Christian ' ghetto. '

Such vitality and naturalness are of special importance in teaching children who do not attend Catholic schools. To a large extent, they come from Catholic families with little Catholic life. Such children are under the constant influence of the secularized education given in the public schools. Even if they are in no way directly influenced against religion, the very lack of any kind of religious teaching gives the impression that religion is of no great importance in human life. Their brief " released-time " or Sunday lessons in religion, then, have at once to convince them of the supreme role of religion in their lives and to give them religious instruction. Who could be expected to carry out this most difficult twofold task more effectively for such an audience — a Religious whom these children cannot help considering as coming from " another world, " or a fervent lay man or woman, who by the very fact of his religious vitality, of his eagerness to teach the truths of the faith, shows the compatibility or religion with " real life " and the importance of religion in life. For innumerable boys and girls in the upper grades and in high schools, an intelligent, tactful and zealous lay teacher can far more easily demonstrate the value of religion in daily living than can an equally gifted priest or sister.

Nevertheless, the lay teacher will stress the role and authority of the priest and bring out continually the *absolute necessity for genuinely Catholic subordination* to and harmonious collaboration with him. Here again the older pupils will readily listen to him.

II. THE SPECIAL DIFFICULTIES AND NEEDS OF LAY CATECHISTS

The religious teaching of children attending public schools obviously presents a far more difficult catechetical situation than does the ordinary instruction given in Catholic schools. A higher quality of religious teaching is needed if these students are to be given true religious formation, and yet this teaching must be carried out under much less favorable circumstances, and often under positively unfavorable ones.

2. The lay CCD teacher is, in the vast majority of cases, a voluntary, unpaid worker. But is there not also a field for qualified lay teachers working as adequately salaried, full-time ' parish assistants ' or catechists (such as already exist in some European countries), who could give their full talents, time and energy to this work ? Such lay people could also assist the priest in many material ways and thus free him for his special priestly work. One does not become less ' apostolic ' from the fact of receiving the means of subsistence in return for one's apostolic work, or no priest or Sister could lay claim to this title !

Let us consider these difficulties and special needs in somewhat greater detail.

1. *Catechetical Concentration.*

Thus these Confraternity classes demand from the teacher, above all, a higher degree of catechetical concentration on the very essentials of Christian doctrine and Christian life. This concentration should never be mistaken for mere simplification or abbreviation. Simplification makes the lessons ' easier ' for both the teacher and the students but only in a very short-range view. Genuine concentration is far more difficult for the teacher to achieve, but it effects true religious formation ; it makes each lesson a living seed of Christian truth that can bear lifelong fruit in Christian learning and living.

2. *Attractive Presentation.*

These classes need to be made more attractive, more interesting to the students than do the classes in religion given in Catholic schools. If children in Catholic schools find some of their religion classes dull, they will still not usually be allowed to leave school, and one can hope that the Catholic environment of the school and the whole atmosphere of the education given in it may compensate for a low quality of religious instruction. But in the classes for public school children will the children continue to come and come regularly if they find the teaching dull ? And if they do come, how will they benefit from a class that gives them no religious inspiration ? But how difficult it is to make classes truly interesting for such children ! Many of them come from families with no religious background. The hour appointed for the class is often, if not generally, not very convenient for them ; the place is frequently not too suitable ; the teacher does not have at hand the technical helps available to a teacher in a regular school class.

Since the apostolate of lay catechists is so important and, at the same time, so difficult, the catechetical movement in the United States must strive in every way to prepare these teachers as well as possible, and to facilitate their arduous task.

3. Training of Teachers.

1. The apostolic spirit of the Catholic laity in the United States makes it relatively easy to secure the required numbers of volunteer catechists : in some places, it seems, more people apply for the preparatory training than are actually needed. Obviously, not every fervent Catholic possessing sufficient knowledge of Christian doctrine also possesses the capacity to be trained for this particular kind of teaching or can successfully conduct such classes. The best training course cannot work miracles ; and this kind of teaching, as it is needless to say, requires the moral qualities not only of a good Catholic but also of a good catechist and educator.

2. Candidates must be provided with the necessary knowledge of *Christian doctrine*. We might say that the lay catechist needs, above all, to acquire a thoroughly ' kerygmatic ' approach in each of his lessons. He needs to see clearly for himself how the fundamentals of Christian doctrine form a wonderful unity, the Mystery of Christ ; he should himself experience the transforming power of the Christian message, rightly proposed. Training should aim at this and the regular retreats recommended for all C. C. D. teachers should be thoroughly ' kerygmatic. '

3. The *course on method* given to future lay catechists should make the students acquainted with a very simple but efficient method of religious formation. Here we intentionally use the singular ' method ' rather than ' methods. ' For the danger in proposing

many methods is that future teachers will not learn to handle even one, and when they go out to teach, after some futile attempts of various kinds, they will return to the obsolete and fruitless but easy method of explaining the text of the catechism word by word, and then asking the students to memorize this ' beautiful ' doctrine. Would we not do well to follow the example of Fr. Jungmann ; in his *Katechetik* which is written for professional teachers of religion in the very homeland of the catechetical movement, he introduces only one method, ' the ' catechetic method which is the fruit of the recent efforts in the field of religious didactics, and then he shows how this one method applies to different kinds of religious instruction, allowing for and even requiring appropriate modifications. [1] When we do so, we can be much more hopeful that the students are really understanding the method we are teaching them, and that they are becoming thoroughly acquainted with it by the necessary catechetical exercises.

4. Everyone connected with the CCD work of training lay catechists realizes, of course, that without *a thorough spiritual formation* they cannot adequately fulfill their apostolic task. If such formation is necessary for priestly and religious teachers, obviously it is needed for laymen also. And this formation must, for them too, be of such a kind as to teach them how to carry it on for themselves, how continually to deepen and grow in their personal participation in the Mystery of Christ all through their lives. Otherwise, there is obviously far greater danger than with those who are living the priestly or religious life that these lay teachers may lose their living interest in the message they are proclaiming and that their catechetical efforts will therefore bear little or no fruit.

5. Every future C. C. D. teacher therefore needs most especially to be brought into close and personal contact with *Sacred Scripture and the Liturgy*. These are the living sources of Christian vitality and the most fruitful means of elementary initiation.

6. The basic training given to lay catechists before their appointment as teachers needs to be continued by careful guidance, both spiritual and professional, all during their time of teaching. In addition they need good text books and even a *catechetical review* which, among other things, will enable them to continue their own educational, kerygmatic and spiritual formation.

---

[1] J. JUNGMANN, *Catéchèse*, 2nd edit. Brussels, Édit. LUMEN VITAE, pp. 129 et seq.

CONCLUSION

We have stressed the work of the lay teacher through the CCD, since this is the special field assigned to them by the Church. But, conditions being what they are, more and more lay teachers of religion will be needed also in Catholic schools themselves. The situation of such teachers is substantially the same as that of religious teachers, and they need, therefore, a similar catechetical training.

There are many other ways in which apostolic-minded laypeople can spread Christ's message, according to their special talents and circumstances. But we are not mentioning them, since we are dealing with the catechetical apostolate properly speaking. But it should always be remembered that the first field for the catechetical apostolate of the married laity is in their own families. The religious teaching and training of their children is the inalienable right and duty of Catholic parents. They are the first messengers of Our Lord to their children before they attend any school ; and no school can make up for the lack of a thoroughly Christian education in the family, an education which the school should need only to complement.

Selected Readings for Busy Teachers

The following bibliography has been limited to readings from: *Bible Today* (BT), *Lumen Vitae* (LV), *Theology Digest* (TD), and *Worship* (W).

1 God Meets Man

Biblical Sign

GENERAL

De La Potterie, Ignace. "The Meaning of the Word of God." LV 10:1, pp. 15-30.

Dheilly, Joseph. "The History of Salvation in the Bible." LV 10:1, pp. 31-44.

Hofinger, Johannes. "Our Message." LV 5:2-3, pp. 264-80.

Levie, Jean. "Jesus' Message in the Thought of the Apostles." TD 12:1, pp. 27-32.

Lobez, Pierre. "Literary Genres in the Bible." TD 4:2, pp. 67-71.

Maly, Eugene. "The Nature of Biblical History." BT, pp. 276-85.

Novak, Vincent. "Teaching Salvation History." BT, pp. 115-19.

―――― "Teaching the Old Testament." BT, pp. 368-77.

O'Doherty, Eamonn. "The Unity of the Bible." BT, pp. 53-57.

O'Keefe, Vincent. "Towards Understanding the Gospels." TD 9:1, pp. 9-13.

Rahner, Karl. "Scripture and Tradition." TD 12:1, pp. 3-7.

Schilling, Othmar. "The Bible and Archeology." TD 6:1, pp. 33-37.

Schokel, Luis Alonzo. "The 'Proof from Scripture' in Theology." TD 9:1, pp. 33-37.

Schoonenberg, Piet. "The Sign. Introduction to the Catechesis of the Word and Sacred Signs." LV 14:1, pp. 9-18.

Seper, Francis. "The Bible and Literary Forms." BT, pp. 392-97.

Sloyan, Gerard. "God's Sacred Design Summed Up in Christ: The Heart of Catechizing." BT, pp. 412-17.

Smyth, Kevin. "The Inspired Writer as God's Instrument." TD 8:1, pp. 15-19.

Stanley, David. "The Concept of Salvation-History in the New Testament." BT, pp. 686-93.

PARTICULAR

Arana, A. "The Age of Man and Biblical Genealogies." TD 8:3, pp. 149-53.

Audet, Jean-Paul. "The Meaning of the Canticle of Canticles." TD 5:2, pp. 88-92.

Brunet, Achille. "The Book of Daniel." TD 5:1, pp. 58-63.

Bushinski, Leonard. "Striking a Covenant." BT, pp. 218-23.

Cantinat, Jean. "The Parables of Mercy." TD 4:2, pp. 120-23.

Cantley, Michael. "Introduction to Apocalyptic." BT, pp. 500-504.

De Fraine, Jean. "Adam and Christ as Corporate Personalities." TD 10:2, pp. 99-102.

Dubarle, A. M. "History and Myth in Genesis." TD 6:2, pp. 95-99.

Eichrodt, W. "The Ten Commandments." TD 6:3, pp. 177-82.

Faley, Roland. "The Message of Judith." BT, pp. 505-10.

Iglesias, Salvador. "Literary Genre in the Infancy Gospel of St. Matthew." TD 9:1, pp. 15-20.

Leal, Juan. "History and Symbolism in St. John's Gospel." TD 11:2, pp. 91-96.

Legrand, Lucien. "Creation as Cosmic Victory of Yahweh." TD 11:3, pp. 154-58.

McKenzie, John. "The Literary Characteristics of Genesis 2-3." TD 6:1, pp. 19-23.

Murphy, Roland. "Where Is the Wise Man?" BT, pp. 31-37.

Rigaux, B. "The Woman and Her Seed in Genesis 3:14-15." TD 6:1, pp. 25-31.

Vawter, Bruce. "The Johannine Sacramentary." TD 6:1, pp. 11-16.

—— "The Prophets: Men for Our Times." BT, pp. 23-29.

Liturgical Sign

Aubert, Roger. "Liturgy and the Teaching Church." TD 1:1, pp. 3-7.

Fischer, Balthasar. "The Risen Christ in the Liturgy." TD 8:2, pp. 123-26.

Godin, André. "The Symbolic Function." LV 10:2-3, pp. 269-76.

Hofinger, Johannes. "Evangelization through Liturgical Feasts." LV 10:2-3, pp. 243-60.

Jungmann, Joseph-André. "The Pastoral Liturgical Idea in the History of the Liturgy." W 30:10, pp. 608-22. Also in TD 5:3, pp. 159-63.

Lechner, Robert. "Liturgical Preaching." W 37:10, pp. 639-50.

Poelman, Roger. "The Pascal Plan of God. The Event and the Institution." LV 7:2, pp. 285-92.

Ranwez, Pierre. "Catechesis and Liturgy." LV 10:2-3, pp. 269-76.

Schillebeeckx, Edward. "The Sacraments: An Encounter with God." TD 8:2, pp. 117-21.

Stenzel, Alois. "Liturgy and Education in Faith." LV 11:4, pp. 617-24.

Doctrinal Sign

Cooke, Bernard. "New Perspectives in Dogmatic Theology." TD 8:2, pp. 69-73.

Hofinger, Johannes. "The Apostles' Creed Is a Real Prayer." LV 9:2, pp. 193-208.

Lyonnet, Stanislaus. "Redemptive Value of the Resurrection." TD 8:2, pp. 89-99.

Vollert, Cyril. "Doctrinal Development: A Basic Theory." TD 6:3, pp. 159-63.

Witness Sign

Gerard-Libois, Jules. "Personal Testimony in the Community." LV 11:4, pp. 639-46.

Gilleman, Gérard. "The Educator, Witness to Charity." LV 9:4, pp. 556-68.

Grasso, Domenico. "The Catechist as Witness." W 38:3, pp. 157-64.

2 Man Meets God

Faith: Communion with God

Arnold, Franz. "The Act of Faith, a Personal Commitment." LV 5:2-3, pp. 251-55.

Latourelle, René. "Faith: Personal Encounter with God." TD 10:4, pp. 233-38.

Wood, Geoffry. "Man's Response to God's Word." BT, pp. 573-79.

Faith: Its Growth and Development

Babin, Pierre. "Rethinking the Life of Faith, as a First Step towards Stabilization." LV 15:2, pp. 233-46.

Braun, F. "Our Faith and the Faith of the Apostles." TD 4:3, pp. 151-54.

Poelman, Roger. "Faith, an Inward Growth." LV 11:4, pp. 583-94.

3 Transmitting God's Message

Goals

Burkhardt, Edward. "Characteristics of High School Religion." W 37:9, pp. 605-11.

Van Caster, Marcel. "The Spirit of the Religious Course." LV 6:3, pp. 431-38.

Stages

Nebreda, Alphonse. "East Asian Study Week on Mission Catechetics." LV 17:4, pp. 717-30.

Stone, Theodore. "The Bankok Study Week." W 37:3, pp. 184-90.

Mentalities and Milieus

Besnard, Albert. "Is Our Technical Civilization Open to the Gospel?" LV 13:4, pp. 600-620.

Brien, André. "The Problem of God and Intellectual Unbelievers." LV 7:3, pp. 367-72.

────── "Technical Mentality and the Teaching of Religion." LV 13:4, pp. 631-49.

Dondeyne, Albert. "Religious Education in the Modern World." LV 12:1, pp. 33-40.

Godin, André. "Transference in Pastoral Counseling." TD 9:2, pp. 78-83.

────── "Trends and Groups in Positive Religious Psychology." LV 16:2, pp. 187-96.

Gruber, Alois. "Differences in Religious Evolution of Adolescent Boys and Girls." LV 7:2, pp. 301-12.

Hofinger, Johannes. "Adaptation in Missionary Catechesis." LV 7:3, pp. 425-31.

Houtart, François. "Religious Sociology." TD 4:2, pp. 116-19.

Luykx, Boniface. "Liturgical Adaptations in the Missions." TD 10:2, pp. 113-18.

Ratzinger, Joseph. "The Changeable and Unchangeable in Theology." TD 10:2, pp. 71-76.

Thivollier, Pierre. "God and the Man in the Street." LV 7:3, pp. 377-87.

Structure and Methods

Bless, William. "Role of the School in Religious Formation of Youth." LV 12:1, pp. 99-112.

Carol Frances, Sister Mary. "A New Pentecost." W 37:6, pp. 353-60.

De Bretagne, Guy. "History of the Text-Book." LV 5:4, pp. 470-76.

De Peretti, Louis. "Complete Catechesis: Essential Mission of the Parish." LV 14:4, pp. 631-49.

Dubuc, Jean-Guy. "Apostolic Collaboration of Priests and Laity in the Early Days of Christianity." LV 17:3, pp. 391-406.

Hofinger, Johannes. "The Catechism Yesterday and Today." LV 11:3, pp. 479-86.

────── "How to Further Our Lay Catechists." LV 14:4, pp. 413-22.

Jungmann, Joseph-André. "The New German Catechism. A Model Presentation of the Message of Salvation." LV 10:4, pp. 573-86.

Lawrence, Emeric. "New Directions for Religious Education." W 37:5, pp. 300-306.

Lebacqz, George. "Church Music and Religious Education." LV 6:3, pp. 480-89.

Pesch, Christian. "The Use of Pictures in Catechesis: Present Situation and Lasting Problems." LV 17:1, pp. 163-74.

Ryan, Mary Perkins. "The Focus of Catechetics." W 37:4, pp. 233-40.

Sloyan, Gerard. "Catechetical Renewal." W 37:2, pp. 96-102.

Sullivan, Mother Kathryn. "Some Paperbacks for the Study of the Bible." BT, pp. 535-40.